THE TRIPS WAIVER NEGOTIATIONS AT THE WORLD TRADE ORGANIZATION

(October 20. ___ 2022)

A REPORTAGE FROM GENEVA HEALTH FILES

By Priti Patnaik

© 2022 Priti Patnaik, Geneva Health Files, Geneva, Switzerland.

First Edition: September 2022

Imprint: Geneva Health Files

ISBN: 978-2-9701627-0-4

ISBN FOR E-BOOK: 978-2-9701627-1-1

Permission to use this content must be obtained from the copyright owner. More information can be found at: https://genevahealthfiles.substack.com/ genevahealthfiles@gmail.com

Printed in Germany

*My first book is for my son,
Kabir who has just started going to school.*

My heart-felt thanks to numerous trade negotiators, activists and scholars who have educated me on this journey.

Countless health workers, officials, and experts who have worked tirelessly during the pandemic of COVID-19, have inspired this process.

PREFACE

This book is a compilation of news reports and analyses on the TRIPS Waiver discussions at the World Trade Organization between October 2020 and June 2022 as published in Geneva Health Files. This is a weekly investigative newsletter that tracks power and politics in global health in Geneva.

The compilation is being produced at the request of some trade negotiators with the expectation that it may serve as a handy reference to review these discussions at the WTO over the last two years. I hope that this volume may in some way informs on-going negotiations on extending the WTO ministerial decision of June 2022 for therapeutics and diagnostics.

An updated version of this book will be published when the discussions on medicines and tests are expected to conclude in December 2022.

All the stories published in this volume can be accessed online by subscribers to the newsletter at genevahealthfiles.substack. com.

Priti Patnaik
Founding Editor
Geneva Health Files
September 2022

FOREWORD

About two and half years ago, on 23 January 2020, Wuhan, a city of fourteen million inhabitants, was put into quarantine due to a 'novel coronavirus epidemy'. Fang Fang, a well-known writer from Wuhan, documented this period marked by profound uncertainty and death in Wuhan Diary. To me, Priti Patnaik's reporting for Geneva Health Files were 'Geneva Diaries': dispatches from the negotiations at the WTO and WHO that described to us twice weekly in minute detail the goings-on in Geneva, before, during and after the TRIPS waiver negotiations, for the past two years.

These dispatches took us through many twists and turns, drafts, counter-proposals, procedural minefields, diplomats' comments, experts' insights, hopes and frustrations. Sometimes the Geneva Health Files newsletter contained real-time insights from just-finished meetings. As soon as the Tuesday and Friday Deep Dive emails arrived in the Inbox, this reader clicked on the message to find up-to-the minute granular reporting on pandemic politics at Geneva institutions, but always together with deep knowledge and background in global health issues. It is this combination of hot-off-the press reporting with interdisciplinary insights that made Geneva Health Files essential reading for international pandemic politics, especially on the TRIPS waiver. It quickly became a must-read for concerned academics and journalists who were trying to get a sense of Geneva institutions' responses to the pandemic.

It is especially Geneva Health Files' deep and detailed coverage of the TRIPS waiver proposal and the long process of negotiation that made it into an indispensable news source and source of documentation from the viewpoint of global intellectual property (IP) politics and law. IP law is often regarded as too 'legal technical' by journalists, which makes it perhaps not easily coverable by broadsheet, generalist news outlets. During the intensive phase of the TRIPS waiver politics, when the US Trade Representative signalled a limited support for the waiver in May 2021, global IP law may have briefly featured in the front of the news pages, but soon after, as the process dragged on over the summer following a cancelled WTO Ministerial Conference in 2021, public attention waned. It is thanks to only a handful of devoted journalists, such as Priti Patnaik, that this global issue received continuous coverage and stayed in the public eye.

South Africa's and India's TRIPS waiver proposal of October 2020 appeared radical, at first; but then again, the pandemic was unprecedented in living memory. The feeling of uncertainty and agonising worry for our loved ones was not so long ago: the first year of awaiting efficacious vaccines, then witnessing their limited production and unfair distribution by discriminating against countries and/or nationalities. We were all affected by the same virus, but depending on where we lived, we were not equitably treated in terms of priority.

IP law is intricately implicated in the supply, price and circulation – and therefore access and distribution - of health technologies, such as vaccines. The TRIPS waiver proposal put IP law into the public spotlight as directly affecting life and death decisions for the world's population. South Africa's and India's TRIPS waiver proposal and the ensuing negotiations made current IP law and its transnational constitution under TRIPS a global public issue by raising questions, such as: who does this legal structure serve? Does it serve the global public good? How should the gaps between the TRIPS treaty text (law on the books), rhetoric ("global solidarity") and reality (differential economic and geo-/political power plays) be best addressed?

Over the last two years, the public perspective has shifted from status-quo – private monopoly for medicines – to a broader realisation that it was the TRIPS Agreement itself, an international trade treaty with transnational force, that did not work equitably and fairly for all WTO member states. A small minority of rich member states continued to oppose and hinder the majority's initiative even during a global, highly lethal pandemic. July 2022 brought the ups and downs of TRIPS waiver negotiations to a deflating close for many waiver advocates. The outcome of the negotiation has become commonly known as a "non-waiver".

It is August 2022 now. Fang Fang wrote in the last Le Monde Diplomatique about Wuhan: "What the epidemic has changed is the people. Those who lived there and who it made suffer so much". In relation to the TRIPS waiver negotiations and IP law, what seems to have changed in the aftermath of the last two years of negotiations is not so much IP law and TRIPS itself. The IP legal status-quo has pushed back hard to remain largely still. Rather what the pandemic and waiver negotiations have changed are the people and nations who have suffered so much under the unfair effects of vaccine nationalism, inequitable access to health technologies and the greed of IP-owning vaccine manufacturers and the countries in which they are based. They know that the development aims of the TRIPS, especially through technology transfers, are empty promises, and that the TRIPS status-quo will be prioritised even in times of a deadly global pandemic.

It is the value of independent reporting, such as Geneva Health Files, that allowed us a close to real time glimpse into the different and divergent motivations of the Geneva actors. The highly politicised and multi-institutional issue of the TRIPS waiver proposal, different national and international actors' opposing interests, and disagreements even amongst access to health advocates on strategy, must have been very tricky to navigate. Geneva Health Files has provided a global public service by guiding us and documenting the legally and historically significant TRIPS waiver negotiations over the last two years. This compilation containing all of the waiver reporting in one place will be a unique and indispensable resource for legal scholars, international actors and negotiators, and students of multilateral institutional politics.

Hyo Yoon Kang
Reader in Law
Warwick Law School, University of Warwick
23 August 2022

CONTENTS

INTRODUCTION

This volume comprises a compilation of nearly 50 stories reported and published by *Geneva Health Files* during the discussions towards a waiver of certain provisions of the Agreement on Trade Related Aspects of Intellectual Property Rights at the WTO, in response to the COVID-19 pandemic.

The TRIPS waiver proposal first brought to the WTO by South Africa and India in October 2020, has been seen as a bold move that temporarily sought to suspend certain provisions that protect intellectual property, to swiftly respond to the pandemic. The proponents had hoped that the waiver of such provisions would boost the manufacturing of medical products needed to fight the pandemic, by addressing patent monopolies at the time of the worst public health emergency in a century.

The proposal won the support of more than 100 countries, but ultimately failed after 20 months of stalling efforts by a few countries, opaque consultations and negotiations during this period. Finally at the 12th ministerial conference in June 2022, WTO members approved a limited legal mechanism that has essentially been a clarification of existing rules in the TRIPS Agreement.

This book contains eight parts: the emergence of the TRIPS waiver proposal at the WTO, the stalling efforts against text-based negotiations, a counter-proposal made by the EU, the anticlimax that resulted in the postponement of the ministerial conference in December 2021, the establishment of the Quad group, the role of the WTO DG is putting forward a compromise text and the final lap that led to the adoption of a limited set of clarifications. Finally, the book concludes on the cusp of the next round of discussions, that are set to take place in the fall of 2022, namely extending the mechanism to therapeutics and diagnostics.

PART I

THE EMERGENCE OF THE TRIPS WAIVER PROPOSAL AT THE WTO (AUGUST – OCTOBER 2020)

This chapter contains reporting that charted what led to the introduction of the TRIPS waiver proposal, how it was brought to the WTO, the way it was received by countries and the wider reaction globally.

1.
THE RE-EMERGENCE OF THE WTO AS A KEY FORUM FOR GLOBAL HEALTH (AUGUST 6, 2020)

ANALYSIS OF THE TRIPS COUNCIL MEETING JULY 30, 2020

The coronavirus pandemic is slowly, but surely casting the World Trade Organization as a significant platform that could witness systematic efforts at the multilateral level to ensure better access to health products. This could be in the form of more formal deliberations amongst members to find ways to neutralise barriers to intellectual property, and not just patents, but other types of constraints that have affected access to diagnostics and health technologies. This pandemic has already brought into sharp focus, the inability to quickly provide essential diagnostics and medical products because of inadequate local manufacturing capacities and the dependence on global value chains.

A recent meeting of The Council for Trade-Related Aspects of Intellectual Property Rights (TRIPS) at WTO (July 30,2020), saw wide-ranging discussions on the kinds of barriers faced by countries while responding to the pandemic. It also examined questions on the existing flexibilities in international trade and in domestic laws to improve the access to health products.

Specifically, a significant proposal tabled by South Africa was the basis of these discussions.

This story tries to examine whether discussions at the WTO including at the TRIPS Council, can help shape how countries might address the big, urgent questions on the access to health products in the context of the accelerating pandemic of COVID-19.

Experts believe that the WTO is the only organisation that has the framework to ensure that the rights of all stakeholders are protected, even as "it recognises the legitimacy of government actions to achieve the required balance between private and public goods." (See below: Q&A with South African delegate, Mustaqeem De Gama on a significant proposal discussed at the meeting, that essentially broadens the scope in understanding the various barriers to effectively addressing the pandemic.)

ISSUES DISCUSSED AT THE TRIPS COUNCIL MEETING
It was under the aegis of this recent meeting that countries discussed the important role the WTO – and the TRIPS Council in particular – play to combat the COVID-19 pandemic.

At the meeting, WTO members discussed the "merit of the multilateral intellectual property (IP) system in incentivizing innovation in medical technologies and research and in enhancing the response of the global community to the COVID-19", according to an official source.

It seems that countries were somewhat divided on the successes and limitations of the prevailing IP system in addressing the pandemic.

Developing and least-developed country members highlighted the challenge COVID-19 had represented in terms of access to medicines, vaccines and associated technologies. They called for TRIPS to be applied with a focus on the rights to protect public health and promote access to medicines for all. These delegations said that the TRIPS Council must ensure that vaccines and new medical technologies are made accessible and available regardless the level of economic development, and that intellectual property rights (IPRs) are not a barrier, a source said.

These countries believe that the COVID-19 crisis allows for the utilization of TRIPS flexibilities contained in the Doha declaration on TRIPS and Public Health and calls for the removal of complexities in the TRIPS Agreement to improve effectiveness and ensure benefits to members without pharma manufacturing capacity.

According to a source at the TRIPS Council meeting, "Several developing countries joined South Africa in explaining the legal, technical and institutional challenges they face in using TRIPS flexibilities and the lack of domestic manufacturing capacity that makes them dependent on imports to meet their medical needs, particularly in time of crises." It was pointed out that key goods including protective equipment such as masks, face shields, and hand sanitizers, remain in critical shortage in many countries.

Developed country members are reported to have said that the IP system had demonstrated its value in boosting science and international cooperation against the pandemic, and in promoting and incentivizing medical technologies innovation and research. Developed countries are of the view that the production of high-quality COVID-19 medicines and treatments has been possible based on a system that promotes collaboration and voluntary knowledge-sharing and licensing, while ensuring intellectual property rights (IPRs) are respected, a source present at the meeting said.

It is understood that developed countries urged other members "to exercise caution and careful deliberation on issues related to compulsory licensing, as they have significant implications that could negatively affect investment, research and development of future treatments and restrict investment into new markets, including investment in new manufacturing facilities," a source told Geneva Health Files.

One of the members pointed out that IP was not a barrier to access COVID-19 technologies. South Africa cited the example of Gilead that has entered into 9 licensing agreements with generic manufacturers from 3 countries for the supply of Remdesivir to 127 countries. "These limited, non-transparent exclusive licenses seem to be an attempt to contain competition by creating an oligopoly. Generic manufacturers globally that can contribute to expanding global supply have been excluded. The lack of transparency, and accountability in the present dire times is extremely worrying and dangerous. It is an indicator of the IP and access challenges ahead of us, that the WTO Members need to address effectively and swiftly," South Africa said.

While members agreed on the relevance of the TRIPS Council as a forum at the multilateral level, for exchanging information, and coordinating strategies around the pandemic, members agreed on the relevance of the TRIPS Council as a forum at the multilateral there was no agreement in including the issue of the COVID-19 response as a standing item in the agenda of future TRIPS Council meetings. Some members expressed their preference to include it on an "ad-hoc" basis in the light of further developments, sources told Geneva Health Files. (Members also discussed IP-measures implemented because of the pandemic. See an earlier post on the same here.)

Other issues considered at the meeting included a new proposal by the LDC Group for a new template for annual reporting on the technology transfer to LDCs under Article 66.2 of the TRIPS Agreement. The article states: "Developed country

Members shall provide incentives to enterprises and institutions in their territories for the purpose of promoting and encouraging technology transfer to least-developed country Members in order to enable them to create a sound and viable technological base."

In addition, South Africa called for efforts "to reinvigorate the 1998 Work Programme on Electronic Commerce" in line with the General Council Decision of December 2019. It suggested that this should be a standing item on the agenda of the TRIPS Council.

THE SOUTH AFRICAN PROPOSAL – IP & PUBLIC INTEREST

A paper titled "Intellectual Property and Public Interest: Beyond Access to Medicines and Medical Technologies Towards A More Holistic Approach To Trips Flexibilities", tabled by South Africa was discussed at the meeting.

In its proposal, South Africa has essentially tried to broaden the scope in understanding the barriers in effectively addressing the pandemic.

"The use of TRIPS flexibilities to address a public health concern is usually seen as a matter concerning patents. However, the COVID-19 pandemic requires a more integrated approach to TRIPS flexibilities that include other various types of intellectual property (IP) rights including copyrights, industrial designs and trade secrets. The use of TRIPS flexibilities in other areas of intellectual property, beyond patents, is less understood at the national level. In fact, in other fields of IP, national IP laws may not even provide for sufficient flexibilities to address issues of access. A variety of IP rights are relevant in the fight against COVID-19.": South Africa's proposal at TRIPS Council, WTO

The proposal notes that the pandemic "created the need to produce essential equipment and medical supplies, there is a growing need to be able to manufacture essential medical devices such as masks, ventilators and other personal protective equipment."

Given the difficulties around finding a vaccine quickly to fight the pandemic, the proposal emphasizes the need for other "non-medical" approaches to fight the pandemic. "In the absence of prophylaxis through a vaccine and more effective treatments, non-medical measures have been an important priority in dealing with the devastating impacts of COVID-19,"

"Other goods and services that are needed to tackle the epidemic include protective equipment such as masks, face shields, and hand sanitizers. Such equipment and material remain in critical shortage in many countries around the world. Many WTO Members lack domestic manufacturing capacity and would be dependent on imports to meet their medical needs," the proposal noted. (Read more about the state of play on the trade in medical products in a recent post)

In its proposal, South Africa also highlights the limitation of Article 31bis – a provision in the TRIPS Agreement (because of an amendment). Although the provision enables a country to use a compulsory license, to export – one of the flexibilities in the TRIPS Agreement – South Africa notes that "the implementation of the Article 31bis mechanism at a national level is very limited and may not achieve its intended objectives." In addition, many developing country Members may also face legal, technical and institutional challenges in using TRIPS flexibilities, especially those countries that have never utilized flexibilities such as compulsory licenses, the proposal said. (This mechanism, in principle, sought to make it easier for poorer countries unable to manufacture medicines, to import cheaper generics made under compulsory licensing. It was a result of a decision

[30 August 2003] that later translated into an amendment of the TRIPS Agreement as Article 31bis. The mechanism waived the condition in Article 31(f) that a compulsory license should be predominantly for the supply of the domestic market.)

In the proposal, South Africa cites some examples from the current crises that show how trade barriers are affecting the access to health products crucial to fight the pandemic.

Implications for IP on Big Data outside of the health system:

"Smartphones, mobile data, artificial intelligence, databases and algorithms have been used in the COVID-19 pandemic to leverage the detection and control and control of the virus. Different types of IP rights are relevant to protect AI algorithms, some may be protected by copyright and trade secrets while other technology is protected by patents while database rights and trade secrets may also be relevant."

The proposal cautions, "While these approaches help with efforts to contain the spread of the virus, they can raise issues about the right to privacy and personal freedoms. National security concerns may also arise in the context of Article 73 of the TRIPS Agreement."

3D printing technology
South Africa cited an example of an IP dispute on ventilator valves in an Italian hospital during the pandemic. An existing valve was scanned and 3D printed replacement valves saved lives. The original manufacturer reportedly refused to share blueprints of the device. Despite demand for 3D printed valves, legal and medical constraints prevent such distribution. The proposal also discusses a warning from a law firm highlighting "complex intellectual property issues" surrounding such practices.

The proposal concludes "This case clearly demonstrates the interface between IP and new technologies such as 3D printing and may require a better understand of how a balance may be achieved between rights holders and third parties. More collaborative approaches have been achieved through various pooling mechanisms for access to medicines, this is also true for more generic IP pledges that covers a broad range of equipment, software, network and device applications useful in healthcare, containment, tracking, diagnostics, emergency response and social distancing. Such approaches nonetheless are limited and may require action on the side of national authorities to ensure access to such technologies where pledges or voluntary licenses cannot be secured on commercially reasonable terms."

Trade Secrets

Discussing trade secrets as another example in the context of the pandemic, South Africa cites experts and suggests that during the current public health crises calls such protections might be a critical barrier to accessing technologies.

"Trade secrets encompass vast quantities of information needed to discover, test, create, and manufacture diagnostics, treatments, and vaccines. Potential trade secrets include manufacturing processes, test data, medical formulas, and more. For vaccines and other biologic medicines, cell lines, genomic information, and other biological material can also be held as trade secrets. Data about the effectiveness of medicines and vaccines are trade secrets. Even so-called negative information — information about what does not work — can be a trade secret."

The proposal points out that "Article 39.2 of TRIPS Agreement requires Members to protect undisclosed information, which is secret, has commercial value and has been subject to reasonable steps to be kept secret. Both voluntary and compulsory licenses, though common in other forms of IP are unusual in trade secrets."

Finally, South Africa had suggested a few questions to guide the discussions at the meeting including:

1. *To what extent are TRIPS flexibilities embedded in areas outside patent protection well understood? If so, how are Members implementing such understandings in their national and regional laws?*

2. *What are the likely difficulties that Members may face in dealing with a changing technology landscape where embedded IP rights may affect the dichotomy between IP rights as private rights and the public interest dimensions recognised in the TRIPS Agreement?*

3. *What are the benefits and limitations of initiatives such as voluntary licenses and pledges to access much needed technology to deal with the COVID-19 pandemic?*

4. *Are there circumstances where trade secrets can be shared more broadly? If so, what are those circumstances? Would national or international health pandemics fall within this category?*

ON WHO'S COVID-19 TECHNOLOGY ACCESS POOL

While highlighting WHO's recent initiative – the COVID-19 Technology Access Pool – a platform which seeks to enable voluntary sharing of information on health products, South Africa is of the view that this will be insufficient to address the needs of the current pandemic.

In a statement at the meeting, South Africa said, "Several voluntary initiatives have emerged since the outbreak of COVID-19 including pledges and voluntary licenses. Some of these are commendable, but these are ad hoc initiatives, simply inadequate to address IP barriers systematically and comprehensively. IP holders of essential technologies may also decide not to participate in such initiatives."

WHO has called for intellectual property holders to voluntarily license such rights on a "non-exclusive and global basis to the UNITAID-established and supported Medicines Patent Pool and/or through other public health research and development mechanisms, consortia or initiatives that facilitate global and transparent access; and/or voluntary non-enforcement of intellectual property rights, as appropriate, during the COVID-19 pandemic, to facilitate the widescale production, distribution, sale and use of such health technologies throughout the world".

Soon after it was launched after the World Health Assembly, 40 countries expressed interest. More countries are now expressing interest – including an encouraging number of pharma producing countries, WHO said in an email response to queries.

In its proposal, South Africa notes that "to date no company has committed to doing so. Instead limited, exclusive and often non-transparent voluntary licensing is the preferred approach of pharmaceutical companies, which will be insufficient to address the needs of the current COVID-19 pandemic."

In response to a question by Geneva Health Files, on the status of C-TAP, a WHO spokesperson said that WHO has been working with key stakeholders to design an operational plan. These include industry and intellectual property experts. This plan is expected to be launched soon.

"Important to note that C-TAP is not a quick fix. It's a mid-term long-term approach to making a significant improvement in the way we do technology transfer. It's complementary to other COVID initiatives, e.g. ACT-Accelerator. And builds on Existing initiatives like the Medicines Patent Pool," a WHO spokesperson told Geneva Health Files.

WHAT NEXT
Sources working closely with developing countries in Geneva, on trade matters, told Geneva Health Files that South Africa is

"testing waters" to see the response to its proposal at WTO. The discussion generated at the TRIPS Council meeting because of the proposal can serve as the basis of further discussion on overall IP barriers in the context of the pandemic, one source familiar with the developments said. When countries share their experiences and perspectives on the barriers they face, it can be put together as evidence to inform future discussions at WTO, possibly for a more concrete proposal, the source added. The next meeting of the TRIPS Council is scheduled for 15-16 October 2020.

These efforts at WTO, such as those spear-headed by South Africa are in line with the priorities at WHO.

Recall from the COVID-19 Response Resolution, adopted earlier in the year, by the World Health Assembly:

OP9.8 Rapidly, and noting OP2 of RES/74/274 and in consultation with Member States, and with inputs from relevant international organizations civil society, and the private sector, as and regional economic integration organizations as appropriate, identify and provide options that respect the provisions of relevant international treaties, including the provisions of the TRIPS agreement and the flexibilities as confirmed by the Doha Declaration on the TRIPS Agreement and Public Health to be used in scaling up development, manufacturing and distribution capacities needed for transparent equitable and timely access to quality, safe, affordable and efficacious diagnostics, therapeutics, medicines, and vaccines for the COVID-19 response taking into account existing mechanisms, tools, and initiatives, such as the Access to COVID-19 Tools (ACT) accelerator, and relevant pledging appeals, such as "The Coronavirus Global Response" pledging campaign, for the consideration of the Governing Bodies

Q&A: MUSTAQEEM DE GAMA, SOUTH AFRICAN PERMANENT MISSION

(August 6, 2020)

Geneva Health Files spoke to Mustaqeem De Gama, Counsellor, South African Permanent Mission, to understand the context and objectives of the proposal considered at the TRIPS Council.

1. **What according to you, is the most promising outcome of the recent TRIPS Council meeting?**

The discussion at the meeting last week has certainly created a ripple. I believe that this TRIPS Council was different since it was the first time that we discussed in any detail a collective interpretation of flexibilities that goes beyond mere access to medicine and medical technology. Even these flexibilities are not well implemented in developing countries for a variety of reasons. In short, flexibilities beyond patent based IPRs have not really been discussed much, in the areas of industrial designs, trade secrets and exceptions and limitations with regard copyright. Placing the matter on the table was an important first step, a recognition that other IPRs are important not only in our fight against COVID-19 but also in the context of development and public interest as we are starting to confront the post-COVID economic realities. We all recognise that IPRs are important and must be protected, however these rights are not absolute and are subject to limitation, Article 7 and 8 of the TRIPS agreement reminds us of the balance inherent in IP as private rights that serve an overarching public purpose. Public interest in the fair and honest operation of the system requires that governments take the necessary steps to ensure that they align the recognition and enforcement of IPRs with the protection of public health and socio-economic rights and technological interests.

Issues discussed in TRIPS Council are reflective of broader issues within the WTO that cut across many different agreements. Part of the WTO reform debate, especially for developing countries has been how policy space can be used for countries to industrialize and develop to achieve the SDG 2030 goals.

We believe that there should be a systematic framework to enable issues such as localisation, for example, that have been brought to the fore because of the pandemic. It is not that only developed countries that will seek to reduce their reliance on suppliers overseas, but all developing countries must seek to reassess their domestic production capacities. The current crises have shown over-reliance on foreign suppliers are fraught with logistical and supply chain difficulties.

Global value chains have not benefited developing countries the same way as developed countries. The former is on the lowest rung of value chains, often only involved in the assembly component of such production processes. COVID-19 presents us with an opportunity to reassess how to address the challenges we face in a more resilient and inclusive way.

2. **How was the response from other member states to South Africa's proposal on examining flexibilities, beyond just patents, to address the pandemic?**

The reaction was overwhelmingly positive, on both sides. Most developing countries echoed much of what is in the proposal and our statement. The idea was really to open a discussion on those IPRs that are not often spoken about, but which could have a significant influence on how we understand the role and function of IPRs in society at large. We observed over the last few years that most developed economies enhanced their trade secrecy laws, much of the movement in recent years has been in the direction of invoking trade secrets as part of a strategy that may not rely so much on patent protection. In this respect, even developed countries agreed that there must be some sort of balance but emphasised the importance of protection and enforcement of IPRs. Whereas our submission does not discount the importance of the recognition and enforcement of IPRs, we do ask whether an appropriate balance has been struck in circumstances where IPRs may become barriers to matters critical to public interest and wellbeing.

While the protection and enforcement of IP rights are important, they are not ends in themselves but means to different ends. There is a need to balance the rights of holders with broader public interest imperatives. Access to and the diffusion of technology is essential to foster development.

3. **Why do you think that the WTO may be a more pertinent forum, as opposed to WHO, to push through some of these proposals?**

By its very design the WHO is not an organisation that can easily enforce legal rights related to IPRs, this is not the function of the WHO. At best it may propose actions and protocols and work with stakeholders to achieve voluntary mechanisms that are solely at the discretion of participants. In a perfect world, everything is efficient and participants in a system are enlightened to ensure optimal outcomes for all users. However, we do not live in a perfect world! Since IPRs are based on monopoly rights given to inventors and other right holders, the necessary disclosure is required and the guarantee of compensation is such that it reasonably compensate rights holders for their labour and effort. At every stage of this bargain, it is understood that mutual benefit exists only in so far as private rights are not abused or do not become obstacles to legitimate public interest imperatives. We know what happened with HIV/AIDS and what was required bring better alignment between these two dimensions. The WTO is the only organisation that has the framework to ensure that the rights of all stakeholders are protected, it also recognises the legitimacy of government actions to achieve the required balance between IPRs and the public interest.

4. **What are South Africa's plans on taking this proposal forward?**

Going forward under the rubric of IP and the Public interest, we intend to broaden the discussion by going into all instances where flexibilities exist and how they have been dealt with through several cases or within the domestic law practices of WTO members. Our interest is to ensure that especially developing country members are aware of these flexibilities and are in a position through IP reform strengthen and incorporate such explicit flexibilities where they do not already exist.

We wish to deepen discussions on several issues in the TRIPS Council and the work on e-commerce. As our proposal on IP and e-commerce illustrates, the is further scope to discuss the implication of IPRs for digital technologies not only in the context of the pandemic but well beyond it.

While there may not be appetite within the WTO yet towards more open discussions on certain issues, politically it appears that many countries may be interested in such a dialogue on these issues. Any discussion in this context must preserve the multilateral consensus, respect ministerial mandates while avoiding unilateral actions.

2.
THE TRIPS WAIVER PROPOSAL – AN IDEA WHOSE TIME HAS COME? (OCTOBER 15, 2020)

Picture this, more than half a year into the pandemic of COVID-19, upwards of 38 million infections, a million and more lives lost; vaccine nationalism embraced by politicians of all stripes; hedged bets on numerous bilateral deals; short-termism planning for vaccines for a pandemic that might last years; economies in dire straits; limited manufacturing capacities; inadequate supply of all medical products; all this on the back of rising infections and mortality, with millions still susceptible.

We are here.

And now consider this, a new legal measure which in one stroke liberalises manufacturing capacities world over for medical products to fight the pandemic, results in technology transfer, sparks collaborations across regions, redraws power dynamics between countries and companies. As a result, billions of people get access to medical products, sooner than later, at affordable prices because the causes for artificial scarcity, to an extent have been addressed. All of this can take shape in an expanded policy space for countries with reduced political and commercial pressures. We potentially can get here if countries wish so.

This in essence is what countries will discuss this week and in the coming months at WTO's TRIPS Council and beyond.

South Africa and India, with the increasing support of several other countries, have suggested that all countries should temporarily be waived of their obligations under TRIPS agreement to fight the pandemic comprehensively. The proposal essentially seeks to allow all countries to not grant or enforce intellectual property protection for the duration of the pandemic, until widespread vaccination has been achieved.

The proposal requests the TRIPS Council to recommend to the General Council a waiver for all WTO members so that they do not have to implement, apply and enforce certain provisions of the TRIPS Agreement, while responding to the COVID-19 pandemic. The proposal seeks to waive certain obligations enshrined under Section 1 (on copyrights and related rights), 4 (industrial designs), 5 (patents) and 7 (protection of undisclosed information) of Part II of the TRIPS Agreement. It also seeks to protect countries from the application of dispute settlement rules to such actions in relation to the pandemic response.

Such an internationally applicable rule will immediately free up policy space for countries to take bold measures to address the pandemic including by regional collaboration, technology transfer. It is also expected to take the edge of political pressures that decisions such as compulsory licensing of drugs, for example, typically attract.

This is a discussion that is long overdue, some experts believe, and the pandemic proves to be an inflection point to bring these deliberations into a rule-making institution, such as the WTO. The inevitable comparison will be with WHO's voluntary mechanism to share technology, the COVID-19 Technology Access Pool that has had few takers. (As Geneva Health Files has reported before, WTO is increasingly becoming crucial for global health related matters.)

THE TRIPS WAIVER PROPOSAL AND ITS IMPORTANCE

The proposal, *Waiver From Certain Provisions Of The Trips Agreement For The Prevention, Containment And Treatment Of Covid-19* was submitted to the TRIPS Council at the WTO earlier this month. Sources close to the process said that this was preceded by discussions on the proposal for nearly two months before it was tabled for the consideration of the TRIPS Council.

The following are some excerpts from the proposal, already widely reported:

> *"...Given this present context of global emergency, it is important for WTO Members to work together to ensure that intellectual property rights such as patents, industrial designs, copyright and protection of undisclosed information do not create barriers to the timely access to affordable medical products including vaccines and medicines or to scaling-up of research, development, manufacturing and supply of medical products essential to combat COVID-19....*

It notes the acute shortages in many countries on account of swift global demand for medical products. (See our *earlier story on this.*)

> *"...As new diagnostics, therapeutics and vaccines for COVID-19 are developed, there are significant concerns, how these will be made available promptly, in sufficient quantities and at affordable price to meet global demand. Critical shortages in medical products have also put at grave risk patients suffering from other communicable and non-communicable diseases..."*

"The rapid scaling up of manufacturing globally is an obvious crucial solution to address the timely availability and affordability of medical products to all countries in need."

It notes that:

Beyond patents, other intellectual property rights may also pose a barrier, with limited options to overcome those barriers. In addition, many countries especially developing countries may face institutional and legal difficulties when using flexibilities available in the Agreement on Trade-Related Aspects of Intellectual Property Rights (TRIPS Agreement). A particular concern for countries with insufficient or no manufacturing capacity are the requirements of Article 31bis and consequently the cumbersome and lengthy process for the import and export of pharmaceutical products.

The proposal is ambitious in its scope, essentially asking WTO to allow countries the choice to not grant any patent for medical products in the context of this pandemic. And yet, it is also defining in its objective, limited only to the duration of the pandemic.

Sangeeta Shashikant, Legal Advisor to Third World Network told Geneva Health Files, "We are in a global pandemic, and yet there is no global sharing of knowledge, technology and related IP. Instead, we see supply constraints and high prices due to IP. This waiver, if accepted, will be in force internationally and will give countries legal freedom to operate. This is a credible way to address IP barriers related to COVID-19 medical products."

Intellectual property has been a significant barrier during the pandemic so far. It has led to the blocking of sharing of technology. Not only patents, but also industrial designs, trade secrets, for example, she added.

IS INTELLECTUAL PROPERTY A BARRIER? MORE EVIDENCE

Notwithstanding statements by pharmaceutical industry bosses and even top officials of other multilateral institutions, experts suggest that intellectual property has indeed been a barrier to improving accessibility of COVID-19 medical products.

In a briefing document, *MSF points out that "In the last few months, treatment providers and governments have faced IP barriers over drugs, masks, ventilator valves and reagents for testing kits."*

A letter supporting the TRIPS waiver proposal, undersigned by more than 350 civil society organizations globally, activists pointed out the example of access to Remdesivir:

> *"Gilead Sciences' secret licensing agreements for remdesivir, a medicine that was developed with substantial public funding, are restricted to a few manufacturers of its choosing, thereby preventing low-cost supply to nearly half of the world's population. Unsurprisingly, there have been global shortages of the medicine, with many developing countries yet to see even a single vial of the treatment exported to them. Given the medicine's limited effectiveness, we are deeply concerned that such an approach for a safe and effective therapy will exclude even more people from treatment access." (CSO letter)*

MSF has said that, "The primary patent on the base compound of remdesivir has been granted to Gilead in more than

70 countries, which means that when countries are not covered by a voluntary license or do not use other measures to overcome the patents, they may be blocked from getting access to generic alternatives until 2031."

For vaccines development, patents have been found to be barrier not only in the current pandemic, but also in the past. It has been pointed out that "a family" of patents (more than 100) have been filed for the mRNA technology that Moderna is using to develop a vaccine. MSF has shown that patents interfered with the access to affordable versions of newer vaccines like pneumococcal conjugate vaccines (PCV) and human papillomavirus (HPV) vaccines.

To be sure, there have already been more than a few patent disputes in the context of COVID-19 medical products.

Another example of IP being a barrier for therapeutics for COVID-19, is the use of monoclonal antibodies, some of them repurposed, and others new antivirals, both of which are in clinical trials for potential treatment in response to SARS-Cov-2. WHO officials have admitted in the past, that IP issues resulting in high prices for biologic candidates including monoclonal antibodies can interfere with access to these drugs going forward in this pandemic. These candidates are protected under patents in several countries. If efficacy is proven, authorities will then have to scramble to ramp up manufacturing in the light of these barriers.

Similar dynamics prevail for diagnostics, according to experts. According to MSF, "major diagnostics companies hold a considerable number of patents, often bundled into thickets for various instrumentation, assays, methods and software, related to different aspects of the technologies, methodologies and devices. This proliferation of patents may contribute to discouraging the development of open platforms for interoperable diagnostics."

There is enough evidence to consider the effects of stringent intellectual property protection on the access to medical products. It is for WTO members to consider these impacts collectively to work on an expansive solution to address these at multiple levels. To be sure, a range of countries including high-income ones, have taken a number of legal measures since the onset of the pandemic to prepare for circumstances, as highlighted by this proposal.

WAIVER VS A DECLARATION?

Countries might have learned their lessons from 2001 in terms of pursuing some of these contentious matters such as IP protection in forums such as the WTO, sources suggested. Although the Doha ministerial Declaration , opened up policy space for public health measures that countries could take (by making room for the issue of compulsory licensing), it is viewed primarily as an influential political document which did not have as much effect as it should have over the years because of a number of caveats, some observers say. WTO members had to work to fix some of the shortcomings in terms of easing rules on exports of generic medicines, for example.

Members had to work on ways to find a solution for what was called Paragraph 6 of the Doha Declaration on TRIPS and Public Health, that recognised the inability of some countries to make use of compulsory licensing mechanisms for lack of manufacturing capacity. This resulted in the August 2003 decision of the General Council of the WTO, waiving requirements of Article 31 (f) of the TRIPS Agreement, thus enabling a country to export medicines manufactured under a compulsory license to another importing country. The Canada-Rwanda case in 2007 illustrated the problems in using this waiver effectively.

(Even following the amendment, experts point out the territorial and procedural restrictions in making use of these provisions cumbersome.)

Members decided in 2005, to make this waiver a permanent amendment in the TRIPS Agreement. This amendment (Article 31bis) took effect in 2017. (Some high income countries had decided to opt-out of this amendment, meaning that they unilaterally committed that they would not make use of the system as importers, according to a post in Medicines Law and Policy, earlier this year. These countries have been urged to reconsider this considering the pandemic.)

This circuitous path on improving access to medicines, suggests that the COVID-19 crisis requires a more straight-forward solution to meet its multi-dimensional challenges immediately, and this waiver proposal seems to aspire for such a solution, a diplomatic source who did not wish to be named explained to Geneva Health Files.

MSF has argued that a waiver "offers an expedited, open and automatic global solution that allows for uninterrupted collaboration in development and scale up of production and supply."

"The Doha Declaration has been a useful political instrument for signalling purposes. As a result, many countries stepped up and issued compulsory licenses. But political pressures continue to operate on any country considering such measures. However, a waiver from certain provisions of the TRIPS Agreement, will give countries the moral authority. To an extent such pressures will reduce on countries looking to address the pandemic," K M Gopakumar, Legal Advisor to Third World Network said.

THE MECHANICS OF A POSSIBLE WAIVER

This proposal has obviously set fire to speculations and conversations, on all sides of the small but influential community working on access to medicines. Some pointed out that a waiver is not necessary given recognised and established flexibilities in the TRIPS agreement. For one, technical capacities are uneven in countries even today to make use of TRIPS Flexibilities. The COVID-19 response resolution adopted by World Health Assembly earlier in the year, essentially seeks ways for countries to make use of these flexibilities, during this health crises.

Besides, countries, already stretched in this pandemic, are aware of the time and effort needed to use these flexibilities, given that will need work through product by product, company by company, in their pursuit for greater access to medical products, in the midst of rising infections and mortality as a result of the pandemic.

"When countries lack immediate manufacturing capacity for any of the essential parts for a product, including raw materials, components or packaging materials, removing IP barriers on one product in one country alone will not be sufficient," MSF said in its briefing on the proposal.

Others have flagged a security exception in the Agreement (article 73), that countries can make use of, instead of resorting to a waiver. The TRIPS agreement allows for exceptions including "emergency in international relations" – circumstances where there could be legal basis for overriding intellectual property rights.

Experts such as Frederick Abbott, Edward Ball Eminent Scholar Prof. of International Law, Florida State University College of Law have argued that "the pandemic constitutes an emergency in international relations within the meaning of Article 73(b)(iii) and that this provision allows governments to take actions necessary to protect their essential security interests."

A diplomatic source explained that the security exception will not protect countries from potential disputes with respect to the measures they take to address the pandemic. However, a waiver as proposed, will include the non-applicability of provisions under the Dispute Settlement Understanding.

"If a dispute is filed against a measure taken by a country even under the security exception of the TRIPS Agreement, the panel will still have to review the use of security exception in that particular case," the source said.

The proposal's suggested text on the draft decision suggests this:

Members shall not challenge any measures taken in conformity with the provision of the waivers contained in this Decision under subparagraphs 1(b) and 1(c) of Article XXIII of GATT 1994, or through the WTO's Dispute Settlement Mechanism."

So, under what provisions can this waiver take shape?

The proposal points to provisions in the Marrakesh Agreement Establishing the WTO [Article IX, (3) and (4)], that empowers the Ministerial Conference to waive obligations in exceptional circumstances based on a justification.

While the actual duration of the waiver will have to be negotiated, WTO rules require waivers to be time-bound. Supporters of the proposal suggested that the period cannot be short, given prolonged nature of this pandemic, and the time needed to collaborate and build manufacturing capacities for medical products in different parts of the world.

To be sure there have been waivers in the WTO system, in the past. And they do now.

In fact, the TRIPS Council will also consider a new proposal from Least Developed Countries: *Extension Of The Transition Period Under Trips Article 66.1 For Least Developed Country Members,* requesting that all LDCs, including graduating LDCs, would need a further extension of the transition period with maximum flexibility in light of the current pandemic. This provision waives certain obligations under the TRIPS agreement for a defined period for LDCs.

> The proposal by LDCs says, "Developing a viable technological base is a long-term process. LDCs need a continuing exemption from the Agreement on Trade-Related Aspects of Intellectual Property Rights ("TRIPS Agreement") to be able to grow economically viable industrial and technological sectors, to consolidate capacity, and to work their way up the technological value chain. To overcome the difficulties confronting LDCs, magnified manifold by the COVID-19 crisis, LDCs need maximum policy space inter alia to access various technologies, educational resources, and other tools necessary for development and to curb the spread of COVID-19 pandemic. Most intellectual property (IP)-protected commodities are simply priced beyond the purchasing power of least developed countries."

THE PROCESS AND WHAT NEXT

According to WTO rules, the TRIPS Council has 90 days to consider this proposal and a report is then submitted for consideration by the General Council and the Ministerial Conference (June 2021). The decision on the proposal must be made by consensus at the conference, as per procedure. (If consensus cannot be reached, the decision can be made by voting. A three-fourths majority is needed for a decision to be made through voting.)

Diplomatic sources close to the process suggested that at least three other countries have indicated their interest in co-sponsoring the proposal. Some of the countries that have expressed interest in the proposal include Eswatini, Indonesia, Sri Lanka, Venezuela, Pakistan, Rwanda among others, according to sources close to the process. When this story went to print, it is understood that a resolution was adopted in Chile asking its government to support this proposal at WTO.

Countries will be careful before dismissing the proposal, a diplomatic source was of the view. "The pandemic has different trajectories in different countries," so countries will approach this proposal with consideration and caution before they evaluate this. It is still a very new proposal, the source suggested.

"They are likely to raise questions formally, and will not simply close down the process," the source added. There might eventually be a ground swell of support for this, the source said.

If approved, the waiver will operate internationally, and depending on national circumstances, action may need to be taken at the national level to operationalise. However, it does provide opportunity to suspend various IP protections that may impact access. (In some countries international law applies directly, and in some countries executive action may be sufficient and in other countries, more may be required, depending on other national legislations exist.)

THE MIXED RESPONSE TO THE PROPOSAL
Both DNDi and Unitaid, among significant Geneva-based global health actors working on access issues, have come in support of the proposal.

South Africa and India may also find non-traditional allies. (FT curiously called it the awkward squad).

Given the systemic nature of this pandemic, and the overwhelming lack of infrastructure to fight health emergency the world over, and toxic co-morbidities, overlain with global health security concerns and interests, could push countries in a common direction, the diplomatic source summed up.

Existing mechanisms to fight the pandemic, crucially fall short of the kind of response the world needs, experts said.

> *Gavi's COVAX Facility is limiting in its scope and ambition. "For the moment, COVAX aims at providing vaccines only over the next two years. What happens after that? Why not bring in more players? This waiver seeks to do that, breaking this notion of donor countries "giving" vaccines to poorer ones," a source who did not wish to be identified said.*

Also, given industry's admittedly steadfast position on voluntary licensing approaches during this pandemic, a waiver of this scale, might be the only way to push for faster, more transparent production of COVID-19 medical products.

Others are of the view of that voluntary approaches might work better, pointing to WHO's Covid-19 Technology Access Pool. (By WHO's admission, the C-TAP is a more medium to long-term solution.)

In an opinion piece, Ellen 't Hoen, Director, Medicines Law & Policy, former head of the Medicines Patent Pool, said,

"...It is therefore understandable that developing countries are also looking at non-voluntary measures such as the proposal for a temporary waiver from certain provisions of the TRIPS Agreement for the prevention, containment and treatment of COVID-19. No doubt this will be met with opposition from wealthy countries and drug companies. But those countries and companies who refuse to make the WHO C-TAP a success while telling developing countries they are not entitled to take measures to protect public health in the midst of a global health crisis are not credible..."

Given the threat of such a waiver, it may well be that some companies and countries might drag their feet and join the C-TAP club.

This is a highly dynamic environment in which both governments and companies are finding ways to rise to this public health challenge including by tinkering with contracts and access policies.

Discussions in the European Union are a good indicator on which way such policy discussions may evolve. From joining the Covax Facility, to signing bilateral deals, from taking a keener role at WHO, the EU is a key player.

To be sure there has been interest in this proposal including from some members of the European Parliament [MEPs].

Some MEPs raised the question:

As representative of the European Union in the TRIPS Council, does the Commission intend to support the Waiver requested by India and South Africa?

How does the EU accommodate the proposed waiver in its global pandemic response, to ensure that global access and access in the EU to covid19 medical tools are complementary?

The support has come from different quarters, including from Progressive International - a group that brings together academics and activists, urging the WTO to "play an instrumental role in moving the world away from monopoly medicine and vaccine nationalism by adopting a suspension of intellectual property exclusivities."

It appears that this proposal is not only a mere waiver of some legal obligations. It could potentially change power equations between countries and companies, in the public interest.

"This waiver can potentially change this dynamic of manufacturers calling the shots. It is not an ideological

opposition to the TRIPS Agreement, but it is very defined and applies only to COVID-19. Low supply, and high prices of diagnostics, vaccines, and therapeutics will leave many countries without enough access to medical products during the pandemic. This waiver seeks to address this," Shashikant of TWN said.

3.

UPDATE: TRIPS COUNCIL INFORMAL MEETING ON TRIPS WAIVER PROPOSAL (DECEMBER 3, 2020)

An informal meeting was convened at the TRIPS Council today (December 3) to discuss the TRIPS waiver proposal.

Discussions on the TRIPS waiver proposal is expected to continue in the TRIPS Council in 2021. We will come back with a fuller report on this next week, here are some details which emerged from today's meeting.

It is understood that the African Group may decide to co-sponsor the proposal after consultations with the capitals. Kenya, Sri Lanka, Jamaica and Argentina are understood to have expressed their support to the waiver proposal at the informal meeting today.

South Africa and India have been joined by Kenya, Eswatini, Mozambique and Pakistan, as sponsors of the proposal. South Africa introduced a paper giving an overview of the preliminary patent landscape of selected priority COVID-19 candidate therapeutics.

Sources said that Australia, Canada, Chile and Mexico submitted a communication seeking further reflection and consideration, to identify specific IP-related challenges in the context of COVID-19. The European Union, Japan, the United States reiterated their opposition to the waiver.

A source familiar with the proceedings said that "members will have time now until 7 December to finalize the wording of the communication that will have to be ratified in the formal TRIPS Council meeting of 10 December in order to be included in the agenda of the General Council."

Today's meeting follows a bilateral discussions earlier this week, between some EU countries and the proponents of the proposal. One delegate present at this bilateral discussion, termed it "tensed".

See our comprehensive story from last week on the evolving dynamics on the discussions on the TRIPS waiver proposal.

4.

TRIPS WAIVER: THE NEEDLE HAS MOVED, BUT THE FIGHT IS ON (OCTOBER 26, 2020)

EU bloc and others, push for TRIPS flexibilities, a defining departure from the past

Countries are making slow but sure progress in discussing a proposal to temporarily waive certain obligations under the TRIPS agreement at the WTO. After an informal meeting of the TRIPS Council last week, countries are now having bilateral discussions seeking clarifications from co-sponsors of the proposal including South Africa and India.

The waiver proposal seeks to allow all countries to not grant or enforce intellectual property protection for the duration of the pandemic, until widespread vaccination has been achieved. The proposal recognizes intellectual property, trade secrets, industrial designs, as barriers to sharing technology.

While the co-sponsors of the proposal are optimistic about the extent of support the proposal has been gaining steadily, battle-hardened activists and observers who have weathered these tricky discussions on intellectual property and access to medicines for decades, do not see any let up by the few but powerful, key, rich countries opposing this proposal.

Irrespective of the outcome of this proposal, whether it will be ultimately backed by consensus (or a vote) from WTO member states, experts feel that "needle has already moved" as far as discussions on intellectual property as a barrier to access to medicines is concerned. Despite the prevailing uncertainties in the institution itself, WTO has emerged as a forum where these discussions are taking place. As we have pointed out before, this is significant, given that issues on IP and health do not often find adequate space for debate at WHO – even during this pandemic.

This story tries to capture prevailing dynamics shaping the discussions on this proposal, it also reviews key statements from certain countries and presents the possible course the proposal could run in the coming weeks.

THE TRIPS COUNCIL INFORMAL MEETING – November 20, 2020

As per a previously adopted procedure, the discussion of this item had been suspended (during the meeting on 15-16 October) to give members more time to consider the proposal. The informal meeting was meant to facilitate discussions and to find out if countries could move towards a consensus. Informal meetings do not allow for formal decisions to be taken, and yet are important since these discussions take place at a multilateral level where countries can debate and seek clarifications.

While nearly 30 countries took the floor to air their concerns and seek more details on the proposals, the co-sponsors were of the view that sufficient time was not given to conclude the discussions. (It is hard to understand why it was not possible to enable continuing the discussions on one of the most significant policy decisions this year)

The Chair of the meeting, Ambassador Xolelwa Mlumbi-Peter of South Africa, said that discussions will continue on bilateral basis.

The proposal is now being co-sponsored by South Africa, India, Kenya, Eswatini, Mozambique and Pakistan. Nigeria has expressed interest in becoming a co-sponsor of the proposal.

The co-sponsors are now working to convert interest shown by some WTO members into firmer support. "There is a silent majority who have not spoken up. But we believe that they are in favour of the proposal", a diplomatic source briefed this reporter.

It has not been possible to verify the extent of this support. Last week MSF had indicated that the proposal had support from nearly 100 countries.

India, Sri Lanka, Tunisia, Egypt, Cuba, Tanzania (on behalf of the African Group), Venezuela, Nigeria, Bangladesh and Jamaica expressed support for the proposal at the meeting.

It appeared that certain countries in Latin America were still undecided on their position with respect to the proposal including Colombia. Argentina had expressed support for the proposal in the previous TRIPS Council meeting.

While consensus is very much the tradition in WTO, co-sponsors do not rule out a vote completely. "If a country has reservations about the proposal, they might abstain during a vote. Even abstention in the event of a vote, will help us", a diplomatic source told Geneva Health Files.

There was a perception that although opponents to the proposal remained steadfastly unassuaged, the tone from some of these countries was more constructive and "less attacking", several people who followed the meeting said. Brazil, United States, the European Union, Japan, Canada, UK, and Switzerland have opposed the proposal.

SOME EXCERPTS FROM KEY STATEMENTS MADE BY COUNTRIES

We present some excerpts from the statements made by countries, in no particular order. It is instructive to see country positions on this matter.

Eswatini

"...countries that are of the view that they will not benefit from the waiver, or do not meet the waiver should not deny other countries, this policy option and curtail the tools available to them to contain the pandemic."

India

"The waiver is more than just a legal mechanism. It is a statement of intent, by all countries that they accord highest value to protecting human lives, rather than protecting private profits.

...We believe it would be naive for any country to think that it can win over a virus which knows no boundaries, by simply vaccinating their own population."

South Africa:

"...Ad hoc, non-transparent and unaccountable bilateral deals that artificially limit supply and competition cannot reliably deliver access during a global pandemic. These bilateral deals do not demonstrate global collaboration but rather reinforces "nationalism", enlarging chasms of inequity."

China

"We think in the trade toolkits waivers could be a useful tool to reduce uncertainty. There is no single answer to this proposal in terms of yes or no. It is necessary to have detailed and constructive analysis and to continue discussing."

Sri Lanka

"...temporary waiver provides a critical policy space for WTO members to take measures to enable competition through multiple producers and ensure adequate supply at affordable rates."

Mexico

"...We believe that the TRIPS agreement together with a Doha Declaration on the TRIPS agreement and public health are sufficient to address current challenges.

In addition, we should note that in virtue of the TRIPS Council agreement of November 2015, LDCs are already exempted until 2033 of these specific obligations under the TRIPS agreement regarding pharmaceuticals..."

Brazil

"...Regarding scope, we would like to request the proponents to further elaborate the rationale for including industrial designs in the proposal. Several doubts have also arisen with regards to copyright. We would invite the proponents to further specify the cases in which wavering copyrights could be pertinent for preventing containing or treating COVID-19.

We would like to request the proponents to elaborate on how members, facing legal and institutional difficulties when using flexibilities would automatically and expeditiously overcome legislative and institutional barriers for the successful implementation of a waiver."

US

"...If the waiver were granted as requested, at least 34 separate paragraphs of the TRIPS agreement would no longer apply. This is a substantial departure from past WTO waivers.

...Regarding proportionality and problem identification could the proponents explain how the waiver is a proportionate

response to covid-19? Could the proponents provide to data that establishes that the identified trips obligations have systematically hindered or block the prevention containment or treatment of covid-19? With respect to scope that the proponents explain how members would determine whether a measure is quote is related to the prevention containment or treatment of covid-19 and this falls within the scope of the proposed waiver..."

EU

"...Domestic legal frameworks should properly reflect the flexibilities provided by the TRIPS agreement, such as the possibility of issuing a compulsory license, including for production for export to vulnerable countries that lack production capacity or including fast-track procedures that can be used in health emergencies. The EU is ready to discuss with all WTO members what can be done to facilitate the implementation of these flexibilities..."

Pakistan

"...Pakistan has found it particularly difficult to implement the compulsory licensing provisions due to various limitations of time, price quantity and regional production. The grant of compulsory license is an extremely arduous and lengthy procedure, posing legal complexities. Therefore, the flexibilities are not effective and insufficient for the scale and urgency of the current crisis.

"...As custodians of the world trading order, I believe no one would like to be known for saving fish, but not human lives."

Israel

"...However so far, we have not identified how IP has acted as a barrier to accessing vaccines, treatment or technologies in the global response to covid-19. Israel would like to encourage active dialogue between governments to explore how best to

work together to prevent contain and protect covid-19 includ-
ing using TRIPS compliant license models..."

Singapore

"...the nexus between IP and access is complex and multifac-
eted. Empirically IP has been an enabler rather than an obsta-
cle to Innovation and Global change. Hence all members must
be ready to engage constructively to understand each other's
concerns regarding IP in the fight against Covid-19."

Canada

"...Canada does not see these concerns as suggestive of is-
sues with the trips such as that would necessitate the waiver.
Canada remains the only member to have used this special
compulsory licensing system under article 31bis and can thus
observe based on concrete experience that this system has
worked as intended. Article 31bis only used once does not
suggest that the system is inadequate rather Canada believes
that this suggests that the overall trips regime works as part of
the broader international framework that provides members
with sufficient latitude and flexibility such as there has been
limited or no need to issue compulsory licenses under article
31bis."

United Kingdom

"We would like to stress that and it's hard the intellectual prop-
erty system has never been about locking up knowledge. It
has always been concerned with balancing the need to incen-
tivize Innovation and creativity with the need to allow Society
to benefit from the fruit of that Innovation. Having studied the
proposal in detail we must ask how would such a waiver even
operate; how would it be implemented into national legisla-
tion? How would this help countries like in manufacturing ca-
pacities and even if limited in time the waiver creates long-term
uncertainty and undermines the system for the future including

future pandemics. Waiving the intellectual property system, it simply moves us away from solution not towards them.

In fact, the generics industry has pointed to support for an effective and balanced intellectual property framework as a key factor to enable research and development accelerate manufacturing scale up and facilitate licensing..."

THE DYNAMICS

The staunchest opposition came from United States and Brazil, two countries accounting for the highest burden of COVID-19.

(In light of these discussions, experts also pointed out how the BRICS as a group have failed to come together on such issues. One diplomatic source rued about Brazil's change in position on these issues since the country had traditionally been one of the strongest supporters in actively addressing intellectual property barriers in the access to medicines.)

Some countries had concerns on the waiver addressing copyrights and industrial designs in the same proposal. Observers pointed out that potentially there could be concerns on addressing these different aspects of intellectual property under a single measure since typically these are addressed by different ministries at the national level.

Diagnostics for COVID-19 for example, illustrate how different aspects of intellectual property from copyrights to industrial designs and patents could play a role in acting as barriers to accessing these technologies, experts point out. Already there are vast disparities in the access to diagnostics.

One of the most significant changes because of these discussions around the waiver proposal has been the way the EU has pushed for the use of existing TRIPS flexibilities at WTO. Experts point out that both the EU and the US have consistently deployed pressure on countries that had attempted to, and those that have used TRIPS flexibilities in the past. These kinds of pressures have led to a chilling effect on the use of such flexibilities, experts say.

"The EU, the US and Switzerland have variously put pressure on Colombia, Thailand, Malaysia, India, whenever these countries sought to issue a compulsory license, for example. While welcome, it is also hypocritical of these countries, to now push for TRIPS flexibilities in the light of this waiver proposal", K M Gopakumar, Legal Advisor to Third World Network told Geneva Health Files.

The crux of this opposition by producer countries boils down to this: that the waiver can set a precedence, one expert suggested.

While research and development capacities exist in the global north, few developing countries have such capabilities. This difference is already hurting countries' access to technologies especially at the time of such a pandemic. Supporters of the proposal also highlight that in many countries both research and development, and manufacturing capacities are state funded. They question how this waiver proposal can affect incentive mechanisms to the private sector, given substantial investments by governments during this pandemic.

Without strong measures to break the barriers that IP poses to access to medicines, the disparities in the access to both vaccines and therapeutics will be perpetuated further, many fear.

Some believe that rich countries' opposition to the waiver, also stems from the potential repercussions such a waiver can have on "the production of knowledge" as it were, including implications for access to genetic resources now and in the future.

Diplomatic sources believe that this proposal is being seen by some countries as having ramifications beyond COVID-19.

They believe, rich countries' hesitancy towards the proposal is also contributed by what such a waiver can mean for governance of these rights in the digital space, for example.

In addition to traditional concerns on protection of intellectual property rights, implications for access to genetic resources and digital rights could also be contributing to this opposition, one source associated with the proposal said.

"We cannot the change rules of the game in the middle of a pandemic", a negotiator from a developed country reportedly said in response to the waiver proposal.

WHAT'S NEXT?

The chair Ambassador Xolelwa Mlumbi-Peter, has said a formal TRIPS Council will be convened on 10 December with the aim of adopting a report that can be submitted to the next General Council, scheduled for 16-17 December.

Countries continue to meet bilaterally to find out if a consensus can be reached on what such a report to the General Council can look like. "Meeting bilaterally bifurcates the debate. We would have liked more time to discuss this during the previous meeting with all member states. But we were not given that", a delegate from one of the co-sponsoring countries said.

It is not clear to what extent countries will be able to have substantive discussions on the proposal at a multilateral level in the coming days. (It is understood that the next formal TRIPS council will also discuss other items on the agenda, and may not be limited to discussions only on the waiver proposal)

"We put high importance to escalate the matter to the General Council due to the political importance of having the matter considered in the General Council," a diplomatic source told us.

However, a small possibility exists that this issue could be removed from the agenda of the General Council, if there is no consensus at the TRIPS Council meeting on December 10th, a source familiar with WTO processes said. (Although the TRIPS Council can also report the lack of consensus to the General Council and discussions on the proposal can continue at the General Council.)

While it remains to be seen if this proposal will succeed, discussions around the proposal have already moved the conversation on these critical issues forward, Sangeeta Shashikant, Legal Advisor to Third World Network said.

This is not only about the final decision text of a potential waiver proposal, but also about having a forum where countries can debate and discuss the barriers of IP to the access to medicines. And a forum has definitively emerged.

Meanwhile, pressure continues to build outside of WTO. Hundreds of scientists, civil society organizations and other stakeholders across the world have come out in favour of supporting the waiver proposal.

It is the kind of "solidarity" that does not make shiny headlines.

5.

COUNTRIES FAIL TO REACH CONSENSUS ON TRIPS WAIVER PROPOSAL (DECEMBER 10, 2020)

COUNTRIES FAIL TO REACH CONSENSUS ON TRIPS WAIVER PROPOSAL

Developed countries shift narrative raising questions on safety and efficacy issues around drugs

As images of the elderly in the UK receiving the first vaccine shots to protect against COVID-19 flashed across the world, the reality of the lack of access to vaccines in the poorer countries became stark.

It is in this backdrop, that countries discussed the so-called TRIPS waiver proposal, which seeks to temporarily suspend intellectual property protection to hasten the access to COVID-19 medical products.

Countries today kicked the can down the road so to speak, even as the world is losing crucial time in its fight against the pandemic with deaths from COVID-19 mounting globally. The US, Canada, and the EU, among others, reiterated their opposition to the proposal at the formal meeting today, blocking any consensus on the proposal.

The waiver proposal seeks to allow all countries to not grant or enforce intellectual property protection for the duration of the pandemic, until widespread vaccination has been achieved. The proposal recognizes intellectual property, trade secrets, industrial designs, as barriers to sharing technology.

WTO members met at a formal meeting of the TRIPS council meeting today where they failed to reach a consensus on the proposal for a temporary waiver from the obligations of certain provisions in the TRIPS Agreement.

Members have agreed to keep the waiver proposal in the agenda of future TRIPS Council meetings. The next formal meeting of the TRIPS Council is expected to be in March 2021, and possibly consultations sooner next year.

Only an oral status report from the TRIPS Council is expected to be presented at the next General Council meeting, on 16-17 December. The General Council is the highest decision-making body at the WTO. It is unclear the extent of political consideration this proposal will garner next week.

The proponents, South Africa and India, have sizeable support among WTO members, also acquiring greater depth in recent weeks with concrete backing from capitals across many countries.

However, a handful of powerful countries continue to wield the levers to block this proposal by deploying a shift in the narrative including raising questions on the efficacy and the safety of the drugs from developing countries.

It is also understood that according to a view from Brussels on this proposal, the EU distrusts India. Allegedly, the EU views this proposal as an opportunity for countries like India to "flood the market with their products", a source aware of these opinions held by the EU, told this reporter. (*We were unable to confirm this with the EU at the time of writing.*)

In this story, we take a close look at the substantial issues discussed between members, the procedures that will guide the proposal in coming days and, how these consultations can unfold.

STATE OF PLAY

Informal meetings between WTO members and bilateral consultations in recent weeks, have delved into substantive discussions on how intellectual property and other barriers continue to manifest and interfere in the access to medical products during this pandemic.

South Africa, India and others, have responded to specific questions raised including by United States, European Union, Brazil. They have also provided clarifications to countries who had sought more details on how such a waiver could work at national levels.

"Countries are getting a better understanding on how this could work. Suddenly the message has hit home," said a negotiator from a country who is one of the proponents of the proposal. At the face of it, we may not have increased the support for the proposal, but members are beginning to have a better understanding on the issues involved, the person added. "This might translate into a higher form of support," the negotiator said.

The proposal is now co-sponsored by Kenya, Eswatini, Mozambique, Pakistan and Bolivia. Kenya, Sri Lanka, Jamaica and Argentina have also expressed their support to the waiver proposal.

Outside of WTO, the proposal has pushed its way into mainstream discussions on the response to the pandemic. Over 900,000 individuals sent an online petition to the WTO, asking governments, WTO members and pharmaceutical companies for universally accessible and affordable COVID-19 vaccines.

In an opinion piece in the influential New York Times, a health activist and economists called for a suspension of intellectual property rights to make the access to vaccines faster. (Also promptly followed up by a piece by industry leader Thomas Cueni - *The Risk in Suspending Vaccine Patent Rules,* also in the NYT)

Earlier in the week, the proposal elicited a response from the industry group - International Federation of Pharmaceutical Manufacturers Associations (IFPMA), that said "calls for the dilution of intellectual property rights are counterproductive."

At the WTO, some developed countries, including the EU bloc, are raising issues of limited capacity and knowledge in developing countries, insisting that technical know-how resides with the private sector in the west. (Also see the recent, problematic WSJ editorial, suggesting a lack of ability in developing countries to manufacture complex technologies)

"This is wrong. We have both capacity and knowledge in the South, including for mRNA platforms for vaccines production. What we lack is the enabling environment, so that latent capacities can come together. Manufacturers should be able to go ahead and produce without being sued for infringing intellectual property rules," a source from a developing country who is a part of these discussions at WTO said.

This sentiment of production capacity being a barrier was also articulated this week by a pharma industry leader at the IFPMA briefing this week where the executive said that the developed world had the capacity to "distribute" vaccines in the developing world. (At one point, one of the industry leaders also said "we do not enforce IP provisions in LMICs.)

Developed countries have insisted at WTO, that the COVAX Facility and the ACT Accelerator should be given a chance to meet the demand for medical products. But only a fraction of the total demand can be met through these limited, underfunded mechanisms, proponents of the proposal argue. (It has been reported that COVAX reserved about 700 million doses while more than 90 countries included in the COVAX advance market commitment (AMC) represent over 3 billion people.)

In one of its statements, South Africa cited a recent report from the UNCTAD to underscore the difference in the access to medical products during this pandemic. UNCTAD found that the per capita imports of the medical goods essential to mitigate the COVID-19 pandemic have been about 100 times larger in high income countries in comparison to low-income countries. (Each resident of high-income countries has benefited, on average, from an additional US$10 per month of imports of COVID-19 related products. This number is much lower for middle income countries- at about US$1, and a mere US $ 0.10 for low-income countries.)

EVIDENCE PRESENTED

At a prior informal meeting last week on December 3, South Africa presented a paper with an overview of the preliminary patent landscape of selected priority COVID-19 candidate therapeutics. The paper is a snapshot of the patent filing and granting status on five selected therapeutics candidates that are under review by the WHO Access to COVID-19 Tools Accelerator (ACT-A) therapeutics pillar. (Four out of five candidates are repurposed medicines.)

South Africa cited examples of new patent filing and granting on new monoclonal antibodies and anti-viral therapies involving companies including Regeneron, Merck, Atea Pharmaceuticals, Incety Corp, Roche and others.

Opponents to the proposal, much like the pharma industry have argued that it is the IP system which has delivered medical products including vaccines in record time for COVID-19. Countries such as India and Pakistan, have said at these discussions, that it is not the IP system that has delivered but the public funding and the institutional support in terms of research contributions.

These countries also rejected the claim that voluntary licensing of technologies was already providing access to affordable medicines.

In the previous informal meeting, Australia, Canada, Chile and Mexico also submitted a paper, where they raised questions on the kinds of challenges as a result of IP that countries have faced; sought more details on specific barriers faced by local production or manufacturing for COVID-19 diagnostics, equipment, therapeutics or vaccines; on whether members were able to issue compulsory licenses.

They also sought information on copyright-related, industrial designs-related and undisclosed information-related challenges in specific instances of procurement or of seeking local manufacture or production of COVID-19 diagnostics, equipment, therapeutics or vaccines, that countries may have faced.

In an earlier meeting, Brazil had said that the proposed waiver would pose challenges in implementation and could result in legal uncertainty to the IP system.

Brazil had also raised questions on how waiver as applicable to industrial designs and copyright could be pertinent for addressing COVID-19.

Citing examples from countries including Italy, South Africa said that for medical products such as ventilators, personal protective equipment and other technologies that may be relevant to curbing the spread of Covid-19, copyright and/or industrial design can be a barrier, in addition to patents and trade secrets.

LIMITATIONS OF TRIPS FLEXIBILITIES

Several countries including Brazil and the EU, continued to emphasize existing TRIPS flexibilities. South Africa explained the limitations of existing TRIPS flexibilities. "TRIPS rules today do not facilitate a collective use of compulsory license (CL) by multiple countries on all components needed to produce a medical product. Both Art 31 and Art31bis licenses are territorial and used on a case-by-case basis raising difficulty of using them to leverage all untended capacity in different countries together. The waiver provides a practical alternative in the context of the pandemic so that countries can be better coordinated," South Africa in response to questions raised on this.

In its response South Africa had elaborated why using these provisions can be cumbersome in diversifying and scaling-up manufacturing by relying on the issuance of CLs by way of Art. 31 and Art. 31bis of the TRIPS Agreement.

As an illustration it said that country X with manufacturing capacity decides to override the patent barriers to expand supply. It then must go through a long process of issuing a compulsory license.

Then, if this country X requires to source patented ingredients from multiple jurisdictions, each of these jurisdictions will also need to issue a CL. Each of these CLs will be limited by the condition of Article 31(f) that it has to be predominantly for the supply of the domestic market. At this juncture, country X with manufacturing capacity, although able to supply, is likely to be hindered due to the number of CLs required, and the conditions imposed. Even if country X overcomes this challenge and manufactures the product under a CL, country X will not be able to export widely to supply even neighbouring countries due to the limitation in Art. 31(f) that a CL must be predominantly for the supply of the domestic market.

Instead, the manufacturing country X and every importing country will have to issue a CL if there is a patent and utilise the procedures of Article 31bis that includes among others specific notification to the WTO by importing and exporting countries specifying the quantities to be imported and exported. As more quantities are imported and exported, more notifications may be needed, in addition to other requirements such as specific labelling or marking of products; special packaging and/or special colouring/shaping of products.

It is also worth noting that whether a manufacturing takes place is very much dependent on whether economies of scale exist. Countries may have capacity to manufacture but lack economies of scale hence making manufacturing an unattractive option.

South Africa:
"With a waiver, the administrative and procedural delays and conditions linked to Article 31 and 31bis will be avoided, meaning that countries will have full freedom to collaborate, manufacture and supply the required products," it said.

"It has become clear to countries that without a waiver mechanism, it is not possible to issue clearances quickly in order to ramp up production processes at the regional level," one negotiator told Geneva Health Files.

EXCEPTIONS IN PUBLIC INTEREST
Southern negotiators, also pointed to exceptions in the US Espionage Act and the EU Trade Secrets Act in the event of emergency. "We understand that the trade secret regime in US and EU recognise disclosure to advance public interest... disclosure to public authorities or disclosure to advance a public policy goal is well permitted under the laws of the US and EU," South Africa said in one of its clarifications for countries. Specifically it cited the exceptions in the Economic Espionage Act of 1996 in the U.S. and the EU Directive on Trade Secret.

It also added that "in many countries including the US the scope of public policy exception is determined by the court considering the facts and circumstances. This is time consuming and can delay the required result in pandemic time. In the present circumstances the waiver will bring the legal clarity regarding the scope of exception to trade secret."

Speaking to this reporter, a negotiator said, "Any discussion on waiving obligations towards intellectual property, even in the face of this pandemic, is sacrosanct for these countries".

In the same vein of greater disclosure, countries also discussed article 39.3 of the TRIPS agreement. Pakistan said that the waiver would greatly contribute in ensuring transparency in Covid clinical trial data. Art. 39.3 of TRIPS states "Members shall protect such data against disclosure, except where necessary to protect the public, or unless steps are taken to ensure that the data are protected against unfair commercial use."

"While disclosure is allowed to protect the public, there is constant pressure from trading partners and the pharmaceutical industry to limit the flexibility allowed under Art. 39.3 of TRIPS," Pakistan said responding to questions raised by the UK on this matter.

MSF DECONSTRUCTS MYTHS AND REALITIES AROUND WAIVER

Pertinent to this discussion is a recent briefing by MSF deconstructing the myths and realities around this proposal. In its document, MSF points out that "some of the main platform technologies used to develop COVID-19 vaccines were used for the development of other vaccines before the pandemic and remain under patent control, such as those concerning the Oxford/AstraZeneca vaccine candidate." It also highlighted the "large portfolio of IP, such as hundreds of patents on mRNA technology – an alternative to traditional vaccine platforms – owned by different entities."

The medical humanitarian group fears that "different types of new IP might be sought on COVID-19 vaccine product, manufacturing process, method of use and related technologies, such as the cold-chain management system for vaccine storage."

In addition, it flags other kinds of non-patent IP and exclusivities related to vaccines development including manufacturing know-how, test data and cell lines – key to facilitate diversified production and supply worldwide.

"The large portfolio of background patents, emerging new patents and non-patent IP and exclusivities comprise a legal minefield for competent developers to quickly enter vaccine development, production and supply. The waiver, if granted, can provide the needed legal certainties to competent developers without solely relying on the IP holders' willingness. This is especially relevant because most multinational corporations holding COVID-19 vaccine IP have shown insufficient plans or no plans to openly license or transfer technologies to all competent vaccine developers globally," MSF has said.

WHATS NEXT:

According to WTO rules, the TRIPS Council has 90 days to consider this proposal and a report is then submitted for consideration by the General Council.

Given that this proposal was initially submitted on 2 October, the 90-day time-period expires on 31 December 2020 and the next meeting of the General Council will be the last opportunity for members to take a formal decision, sources said.

In the meeting today, members reportedly agreed on a text for an oral status report that will be submitted to the General Council for consideration next week.

An excerpt:

"...This means that the TRIPS Council has not yet completed its consideration of the waiver request and may not be able to do so within the 90 days stipulated in Article IX:3 of the Marrakesh Agreement. Therefore, the TRIPS Council will continue its consideration of the waiver request and report back to the General Council as stipulated in Article IX:3 of the Marrakesh Agreement."

The next formal meeting of the TRIPS Council is scheduled for March 2021. Chair of the TRIPS Council, Ambassador Xolelwa Mlumbi-Peter of South Africa has called for further consideration of the waiver proposal, asking members to consider meeting early in 2021 to advance discussions.

A CHANGE FOREVER?

Given the attention that this proposal has received at the highest levels including from elected representatives from Pakistan, Colombia, the Philippines and Malaysia calling for all governments to support the TRIPS waiver proposal at the WTO, all eyes are on the secretariat, in its role in facilitating these discussions.

There is a perception among developing countries, that WTO secretariat has not often been supportive of these processes. "The secretariat has long been known to adopt "green room" tactics, but this time they know that the world is watching," a source who works with developing countries in Geneva said.

[In the WTO milieu, green room is the informal name of the director-general's conference room which is often used to hold informal "deal making" meetings between a small group of select delegations to tackle intractable issues, instead of involving all 164 WTO members. Green room meetings can happen anywhere and does not need to be in the DG's fold.]

"Even if the waiver proposal does not come through, developing countries will likely be able to force change in these discussions on access to medicines," the source said.

While it remains to be seen, how long countries can let the proposal remain in the TRIPS Council, the momentum generated in these discussions is likely to decisively influence the response to this pandemic, experts believe.

6.
ROAD AHEAD FOR GREATER DELIBERATION IN 2021: TRIPS WAIVER PROPOSAL AT WTO (DECEMBER 18, 2020)

The General Council at WTO, the organization's highest level decision-making body, this week, discussed the TRIPS waiver proposal first put forward by South Africa and India in October this year. With this, the proponents successfully pushed this crucial proposal for political consideration before the world's trade policy makers. The stage is now set for further deliberation in the coming weeks early in 2021. South Africa has also requested for an extraordinary General Council meeting to take this forward.

The significance of the discussion of this proposal at the General Council, is not lost, least of all on countries straining the under the mounting casualties of COVID-19 and those without any visibility of access to vaccines. More than 30 countries took the floor to discuss the proposal, WTO officials said at a press briefing today.

Proponents of the proposal said that the discussions around the proposal had traveled further than many had anticipated. "The foundation of concrete action has been laid. There will be more meetings early in 2021. This matter will be taken to it resolution", a source close to the process said.

The waiver proposal seeks to allow all countries to not grant or enforce intellectual property protection for the duration of the pandemic, until widespread vaccination has been achieved. The proposal recognizes intellectual property, trade secrets, industrial designs, as barriers to sharing technology. The co-sponsors of the proposal include Kenya, Eswatini, Mozambique, Pakistan, and Bolivia.

This story gives a quick update on the proceedings at the General Council this week, and some of the discussions at the TRIPS formal meeting last week.

DISCUSSIONS AT THE GENERAL COUNCIL (December 16th-18th)

An oral status update on the proceedings at the TRIPS Council over the last few months, was presented at the General Council meeting this week. Although South Africa has requested for an extraordinary General Council meeting on the proposal, it is not clear if such a request will be granted.

The discussions at the General Council on the waiver proposal were described as "an important conversation", and "a conversation that was not vitriolic or acerbic", a WTO official told reporters this evening. The proposal will continue to be discussed at the TRIPS Council in the following months.

Countries that favor using existing mechanisms, want to use these discussions going forward, to identify imperfections in the TRIPS agreement that do not make it easy for members to access these flexibilities, particularly as they pertain to compulsory licensing, Keith Rockwell, Director, Information and External Relations Division and Spokesman WTO said at the briefing.

THE PREVAILING DYNAMICS

Sources told Geneva Health Files, efforts were being made to get the African, Caribbean and Pacific Group of States (ACP, a group of 79 states), on-board for stronger support for the proposal such as by becoming a co-sponsor. It is not yet clear if the ACP will eventually commit to doing so. There are 48 countries from Sub-Saharan Africa, 16 from the Caribbean and 15 from the Pacific.

It is also understood that earlier in the week, the waiver proposal was brought up at the Heads of Delegations meet at the Trade Negotiations Committee (TNC) that operates under the authority of the General Council. Such informal meetings allow delegations to discuss matters outside of the big meetings and sometimes, help in moving WTO members towards a consensus on difficult issues. "Countries discussing the proposal at such meetings in a good indication of support for the proposal," a diplomatic source close to the process said.

"There has been a shift in the positions of some countries, such as Norway, for example. There has been a change in countries' positions, but perhaps this change has come too late," the source added. In mid-December, COVID-19 cases had reached more than 63 million worldwide and had claimed upwards of 1.6 million lives globally.

"Countries have now begun to look for solutions. The debate is slowly moving away from theoretical discussions to practicalities aimed at finding solutions," the source said. There is emerging consensus, a vote may not be required, the diplomatic source added.

TRIPS COUNCIL FORMAL MEETING (December 10th)
We bring you excerpts from key statements made by some countries at the TRIPS formal meeting last week on December 10th.

From pushing opposing countries for more details on how voluntary licensing approaches may have worked; to raising questions on whether some countries would commit to refraining from putting pressure, in the future, on other countries in their use of TRIPS flexibilities; proponents pushed for specifics on why rich countries were opposing the waiver proposal.

It was pointed out that, according to WHO, nearly one-third of vaccines have fewer than four suppliers. Supporters of the proposal wanted to know how limited number of suppliers possibly could meet the vaccination needs of more than 7 billion people globally. In an intervention, Pakistan said that 14 per cent of the world's population have bought up fifty-three (53 per cent) of all the most promising vaccines so far. It cited reports which say some countries have put in place plans to acquire up to 9 doses per person, while among 70 developing or poor countries, only one out of every 10 people will be vaccinated by the end of 2021. Some countries might have to wait until 2023 or even 2024 to get vaccines. (A risk also highlighted by Gavi's risk analysts - Citigroup - this week. *See brief later in this newsletter*)

Opponents such as the U.S., reminded countries that a vast majority of older medicines are not patented, yet remain out of reach for many patients. The U.K. for example, said that it was working on exploring initiatives such as WHO's COVID-19 Technology Access Pool (C-TAP) to work within existing mechanisms.

EXCERPTS FROM STATEMENTS AND INTERVENTIONS MADE BY COUNTRIES

South Africa

"...*The patent landscape (a document* submitted by South Africa) in IP/C/W/670 is a warning shot of the existing and emerging patent barriers to access and the need for the international community to take urgent action to overcome these barriers so that supply may be diversified and scaled-up.

...Why has pressure been applied on developing countries for implementing and supporting public health safeguards in their intellectual property laws and policies under EU's annual IP enforcement report and the annual "Special 301 Report", which was released even amidst the COVID-19 pandemic!

...The EU and Switzerland both highlight the flexibilities as the key measures for members to use, does it mean the EU and Switzerland will from now on commit not to pressure developing countries when they improve their laws on compulsory license and other TRIPS flexibilities or make use of compulsory license? Would the European Commission from now on exclude compulsory license and other TRIPS flexibilities from its IP enforcement report? Would the USTR do the same to its Special 301 report?"

India

In responding to a question raised by EU: EU has sought an explanation as to how the waiver could operate about the vaccine production, including the transfer of the required technology and know-how and how it would affect the existing licensing mechanisms and Covax in general.

India said:

"...Today, EU has reiterated that transfer of technology and know-how should be encouraged through licensing. We would like to know how EU plans to persuade pharma companies to enter transparent, non-exclusive global open licenses, where all manufacturers can be engaged without any restrictions, and what steps EU is taking to ensure full transparency and accountability in the cost of R&D and in licensing agreements.

...We also note the 'Covid19 and Beyond: Trade and Health' initiative by EU, Switzerland, Canada, and few others, which talks about enhanced preparedness to fight against current and future pandemics. Madam Chair, history will not judge us

kindly if we fail to find an expeditious solution to the current pandemic while claiming to prepare for the future ones. We hope the Membership can rise to the demand of this crisis and demonstrate that WTO can deliver on timely, equitable and affordable access for all, by agreeing to the waiver. World will remember the contribution of WTO during the pandemic for generations to come."

Indonesia

"...Indonesia also experienced different case where IP become serious threat to Indonesia public health, despite Indonesia paramount contribution to the development of H5N1 vaccines.

In August 2006, Indonesia made unprecedented move by announcing that it will make genomic data on bird flu viruses accessible to anyone. Indonesia was of the view that opening global access could be the key to unlocking such vital information as to the origin of the virus, how it causes disease, how it is mutating, the sources of infection, and how to prevent or cure the virus.

Even though, following Indonesia move, developing countries have supplied H5N1 virus to WHO Collaborating Centres for analysis and preparation for vaccine production, the resulting vaccines produced by pharmaceutical companies are in fact unavailable for developing countries such as Indonesia.

The system behind this unfair practice is closely related to intellectual protection of the vaccines development extended to pharmaceuticals companies that benefitted from the openness of Indonesia and other developing countries. It was based on this situation, Indonesia wanted a material transfer agreement for each virus sample which sent to foreign labs, specifying that the sample will only be used for diagnostic purposes and not for commercial gain.

Under that proposal, any commercial use of the virus would require prior consent of the country providing it. By retaining the intellectual property rights, Indonesia believes, a country could allow access to global vaccine stockpiles at an affordable price..."

The EU

"...According to the industry sources, some 1100 potential treatments and vaccines are in development. Much of this rapid response, like for example the vaccines based on mRNA technology, builds on knowledge and research capacity developed over many years with the support of intellectual property incentives. We would not be where we are now without the years of this research.

...What is most needed now, beyond developing vaccines, is the ramping up of manufacturing of vaccines and the best way of achieving that is by disseminating the technology and know-how of those who developed the vaccines through licensing arrangements. Manufacturing cannot take place without the required technology and know-how. In addition, we need these vaccines to be produced in a manner that ensures their efficacy and safety. Intellectual property is a key factor in providing a framework that enables these arrangements. Developers of vaccines can enter into manufacturing agreements, transfer technology and expand production with their licensees. Our main concern is that suspending the relevant IP rights will not enhance such collaboration and manufacturing but, to the contrary, will slow it down or even block it, to the detriment of all."

The U.S.

"...In fact, around COVID-19 therapeutics, licensing by generics manufacturers already exists. It appears that one company has signed nonexclusive voluntary licensing agreements with generic pharmaceutical manufacturers based in Egypt, India and

Pakistan to manufacture its drug for distribution in 127 countries. The co-sponsors of the waiver proposal are amongst the 127 countries that will benefit from these arrangements.

...Other factors that are relevant to the access question include pricing and procurement policies, taxes, mark-ups and tariffs and other national policies that result in higher costs for consumers and for health systems. In fact, some countries continue to apply tariffs of up to 20% on pharmaceuticals and 10% on vaccines. South Africa's paper does not explore these critical factors. Instead, South Africa has presented here a "[p]reliminary patent landscape of selected priority COVID-19 candidate therapeutics," which it acknowledges is a "non-exhaustive snapshot."

Switzerland
"...Switzerland is of the view that such a step would indeed be counterproductive. It would result in considerable legal uncertainty, at the national and international level. it would thus put into question a key component of the basis on which stakeholders currently engage in international initiatives and partnerships to make fast and equitable global access to medical products against covid-19 a reality.

....if we were to suspend large parts of a WTO agreement during this pandemic, an agreement that embodies a collective consensus more than 25 years and of 164 countries, what signal would we sent to the outside world on the reasons of existence of the multilateral regulatory framework, on its utility and reliability?..."

WHAT TO EXPECT IN 2021 AND BEYOND
The next formal meeting of the TRIPS Council is only in March 2021. It is expected that WTO members will gather for informal discussions on the waiver proposal early in 2021.

"Opponents should move towards where we are. It will be untenable and hypocritical of members such as the EU to continue opposing the proposal, given their thinking on this, within the European Union," a source said, alluding to recent policy discussions on IP and a wider pharma strategy at the EU level.

It is also interesting to note that these very same countries opposing the proposal, some of them key donors of the WHO, are allegedly upset about WHO's support to the TRIPS waiver proposal.

The Geneva Observer reported this week:

There is a tangible dissatisfaction of donor countries with WHO's position in support of India, as well as South Africa's proposal to guarantee a waiver to patent enforcement currently being discussed at the WTO. Some countries, opposed to the waiver, consider that supporting the idea is not the WHO's decision to make but its member states'.

International health and trade interests collide and converge across multilateral institutions. The response to the TRIPS waiver proposal is illustrative of this.

Given the momentum and public support that this proposal has received, proponents feel emboldened at the possibilities of what this might mean in the future. Supporters of the proposal see these discussions evolving into a more long-term shift in such debates at the WTO.

"The waiver is not the end, it is only the beginning," said one diplomatic source. There is a need for rebooting of trade rules, the person added.

Among key factors of production, knowledge is fast becoming, the most important one to capture, the diplomatic source is of the view. This comprises questions on data, genetic sequences, among others in the digital realm, that will be contested in forums such as WTO. The pandemic has advanced discussions on questions on data ownership, and its implications for technology transfer and intellectual property.

Detractors of the proposal had long written off this path-breaking initiative, which many believe may be a game-changer in the response to the pandemic. (There was one report that said that the waiver discussions may not reach the General Council).

In a report in Bloomberg *(Vaccinating Billions Means Finding Ways Around a Patent Impasse),* a former WIPO official said:

James Pooley, former deputy director general of the World Intellectual Property Organization, reckons that even though the proposal is "unlikely to go anywhere," it may have an impact down the line.

"It's the battering ram at the door," he said. "If they keep bashing at it, a hinge may break."

Bloomberg, December 2020

As we have reported in these pages before, the needle has moved as far as these discussions on the access to medicines are concerned. Maintaining the status quo of asymmetrical power structures in such discussions may not be tenable anymore. What this will ultimately mean for millions of defenceless people, in the face of this raging pandemic will remain to be seen.

PART II:
ONE STEP FORWARD, TWO BACKWARDS: THE STALLING OF THE PROPOSAL AT THE WTO (JANUARY – MAY 2021)

•••

Once the proposal was introduced at the WTO, this period witnessed how precious time was wasted because of the repeated stalling of a few major countries. The result was that text-based negotiations on the original TRIPS waiver proposal, among the wider WTO membership never took off. But by May 2021, the United States made a surprise move by partially extending support to a patent waiver on vaccines. This changed the complexion of the debate, but only so much.

7.
WTO TRIPS COUNCIL INFORMAL MEETING: DISCUSSIONS ON THE TRIPS WAIVER PROPOSAL (JANUARY 19, 2021)

W TO members convened at a TRIPS Council informal meeting today to discuss the TRIPS waiver proposal.

The proponents of the proposal have responded to extensive questions on the proposal from United States, the European Union, Japan, Canada, Australia, Chile, and Mexico. These responses are gold running into 30 pages addressing a number of issues from TRIPS Article 31, to trade secrets among others.

Waiver From Certain Provisions Of The TRIPS Agreement For The Prevention, Containment And Treatment Of Covid-19 – Responses To Questions : January 15, 2021

(Communication From The Plurinational State Of Bolivia, Eswatini, India, Kenya, Mozambique, Mongolia, Pakistan, South Africa, The Bolivarian Republic Of Venezuela And Zimbabwe)

Waiver From Certain Provisions Of The TRIPS Agreement For The Prevention, Containment And Treatment Of Covid-19 - Questions By Proponents: 15th January 2021

(Communication From India, Mozambique, Pakistan And South Africa)

Sample this:

Question raised by Mozambique

1. *After years of discouraging WTO Members especially developing countries to take steps to improve their patent law so that compulsory licenses may be issued in the interest of public health, how does the European Union expect all WTO Members to be ready to use compulsory licenses should the need arise?*

Question from South Africa:

2. *Following on from President Ursula von der Leyen's State of the Union call for the establishment of an EU BARDA, the EU's IP action calls for the development of an "effective framework for march-in rights that should guarantee that publicly funded IP is available in case of critical shortages". Could the European Union please provide details on the design of these march-in rights?*
Also, check this out: MSF picks apart pharma industry's arguments against the TRIPS waiver proposal. A must-read - Will history repeat itself?

8.

THE TRADE & HEALTH UPDATE: WTO TRIPS TALKS (JANUARY 22, 2021)

The next few weeks will determine the fate of the TRIPS Waiver proposal as it goes through several rounds of formal and informal consultations at the TRIPS Council, before being taken up at the General Council in March. The unabated rise in COVID-19 deaths and infections worldwide, also fuelled by mutations of SARS-Cov-2, concomitant with severe vaccine shortages lend an urgency to these discussions like never before.

At the TRIPS Council informal meeting earlier this week, as many as 30 members engaged in discussions around the TRIPS Waiver proposal as we reported on twitter on the 19th. While countries largely reiterated their previously stated positions, it appears the proponents of the proposal made greater headway in reaching out groups of countries. Next informal meeting is scheduled for February 4, when positions are expected to be stated on the record, for consideration by the General Council in early March.

The waiver proposal, sponsored by South Africa and India, seeks to allow all countries to not grant or enforce intellectual property protection for the duration of the pandemic, until widespread vaccination has been achieved. The proposal recognizes intellectual property, trade secrets, industrial designs, as barriers to sharing technology. The co-sponsors of the proposal now include Kenya, Eswatini, Mozambique, Pakistan, Bolivia, Venezuela, Mongolia, Zimbabwe, Egypt and Mali.

Sources familiar with the discussions said that the group of Least Developed Countries have also shown strong interest in co-sponsoring the proposal.

At the meeting, European Union, the United States, Switzerland, the United Kingdom and Japan continued to oppose the proposal. Some of these countries believed the proposal is overly broad. And that it does not address problems of capacity or raw materials that are impeding sufficient supply. The countries continued to insist that the existing TRIPS system contains sufficient tools to address any IP-related problems. (Do note that countries including the U.S. opposed to reference to TRIPS flexibilities on a resolution on strengthening local production at WHO this week.)

A diplomatic source suggested a shift in the position of Brazil since it had not taken the floor to voice its opposition to the proposal. "This could be significant. Clearly, like other countries, they are finding it difficult to secure access to vaccines to address the pandemic," the source said.

The position of wealthy countries is incongruous, a source familiar with the discussions told Geneva Health Files. "On the one hand they want to be seen as protagonists' donating vaccines doses, on the other, they are blocking solutions to a raging pandemic," the source said. It is not clear how long these countries will be able to reconcile this inconsistent position especially faced with rising mortalities from COVID-19 and unpredictable access to vaccines even in some richer countries.

It is understood that China, Chile, Malaysia, Australia, Colombia and Canada continued to raise questions on how waiver proposal would work at national levels, according to sources.

It is also learnt that Afghanistan, Pakistan, Zimbabwe, Egypt, Mongolia, Chad, Indonesia, Nepal, Bangladesh, Sri Lanka, Cambodia and Venezuela spoke in support of the waiver proposal.

South Africa asked countries to move the discussion towards negotiating the text of the TRIPS waiver proposal in the coming weeks. It also offered to re-evaluate parts of the proposal with respect to its scope and the timeframes for its implementation, while asking other opposing countries to reconsider their positions.

Going forward, sources said that supporters of the proposal may consider adapting the waiver proposal to address the current urgency of vaccines shortages. "One suggestion could be to have a list-based approach where, for example, IP provisions will not apply to vaccines, diagnostics and therapeutics to fight COVID-19," a source said. Another could be to getting faster issuance of compulsory licenses or using the COVID-19 Technology Access Pool to spur tech transfer to boost the production of vaccines to meet demand, the source added.

It is not clear whether limiting the scope of the proposal would mean, focusing on waiving provisions on intellectual property, while setting aside other identified barriers to access to medicines, including copyrights, industrial designs and trade secrets (undisclosed information), for now.

While the proponents are keen to open discussion on re-visiting the text of certain provisions in the TRIPS agreement, it appears that ensuring access to medical products, including vaccines may have a certain immediacy and become an over-riding priority.

The use of interpretative text or a declaration to clarify certain sections of the TRIPS agreement is not ruled out in the future, the source said.

Whether proponents of the proposal get sufficient support from key groups of countries in the coming weeks, will remain to be seen. If a WTO member does not support this proposal, but reserves its opposition to it, the proponents will stand to gain, a source explained.

9.
CRACKS IN THE OPPOSITION TO THE TRIPS WAIVER? (FEBRUARY 5, 2021)

Vaccine production woes and internal EU squabbles on accessing vaccines might have opened a new frontier that could help proponents of the TRIPS waiver proposal.

Although some countries continued to oppose the proposal and refused to engage in text-based discussions, diplomatic sources in Geneva say that there has been a perceptible shift in the position of many countries. Less opposition may not mean more support, but it opens space for discussions particularly at the bilateral level.

Countries including Canada, the United Kingdom, Switzerland and Japan, continued to oppose the waiver proposal during the informal TRIPS Council meeting on February 4th. Members including the EU and the U.S. did not want to proceed towards text-based discussions, sources said.

Egypt, Nigeria, Jamaica on behalf of the ACP Group, Pakistan, Tanzania on behalf of the African Group, Zimbabwe, India, Kenya, Venezuela and Sri Lanka spoke in favour of South Africa's suggestion to discuss "text" for the waiver proposal.

Some believe that the continuing deliberations at the TRIPS Council without agreeing to discuss the proposal in concrete steps is a stalling tactic of some developed countries. However, as infections and deaths from COVID-19 continue, and variants of SARS-CoV-2 proliferate raising concerns on the efficacy of new vaccines, these countries have been forced to consider the political implications of their decisions. This might contribute to their willingness to engage in finding potential agreement in the context of the proposal, diplomatic sources in Geneva said on the condition of anonymity.

"We need to close the evidentiary loop and get down to textual negotiations that can further refine the waiver proposal that we tabled. We cannot continue to engage in endless discussions while in the real-world millions of lives are lost to the coronavirus pandemic," South Africa said in a statement.

It is understood that several countries questioned and criticised the EU on new export restrictions.

In its statement, South Africa said: (excerpts)

"...Those countries that continue to oppose the waiver most vociferously are indeed the ones that have secretly bought up the available production and continue to collude with pharmaceutical companies under the veil so secrecy. We have now seen the chicks come home to roost, where the veil of secrecy has been lifted and one Member has now taken measures to restrict exports from its territory. Yet this Member is a proponent of free trade and the non-application of export restrictions.

This very Member has posed pointed questions to the proponents yet does everything it can to undermine global solutions being sort, even since it proclaims itself to be a major donor to such global initiatives. Secrecy is at the heart of this matter, and even under these dire circumstances where the lives of millions of citizens of this Member are at risk and vaccine supplies having been reprioritised away from this Member, it still refuses to face the reality of the situation.

The EU has gone down a slippery slope, the consequence of its export authorisation scheme, which is de facto an export restriction, will have manifold implications for all of us and may launch an avalanche of further trade restrictive measures by other Members.

The EU export control regime on COVID-19 vaccine is supposed to be implemented on objective, transparent, and proportionate grounds, can the EU give assurances to that effect? Is the authorisation process rule-based or influenced by diplomatic considerations and therefore arbitrary?"

EU responded to these criticisms by laying out the scope and duration of these restriction measures. The EU reportedly acknowledged facing "significant difficulties" with respect to accessing vaccines. It said that the decision to resort to export restrictions was in response to a possible breach of contracts signed with the EU. It said that doses initially targeted for the EU may have been exported to third countries. To prevent such violation, the Commission decided that all vaccine manufacturers should declare exports to third countries. It explained that these obligations target vaccine manufacturers, and applicable until end of March 2021. The EU assured members that these measures will be proportionate and will not slow down the vaccine trade between the EU and third countries, a source said.

Production concerns might give way to some scepticism towards manufacturing capacities of developing countries. Opposing countries have long argued that complex drugs such as mRNA vaccines will need technology transfer, for example. Therefore, a waiver may not solve these challenges, some countries have said.

Proponents also furnished information highlighting manufacturing capabilities in the developing world. "Out of the 154 pre-qualified vaccines under WHO's PQ program 72 vaccines are produced by vaccine manufacturers from developing countries. These vaccines are originating from various developing country manufacturers including from India, China, Brazil, Cuba, Thailand, Senegal and Indonesia. Similarly, LMIC countries have a substantial share in prequalified finished pharmaceutical products, active pharmaceutical ingredients and vaccines", South Africa said in a statement.

"There seems to be some interest in exploring spare capacities for boosting manufacturing capacities. Some of the bilateral discussions could focus on finding immediate solutions," one diplomatic source said.

Sources also indicated that the US said it was open to "working together with members to better understand the facts" where TRIPS obligations on patents, copyright, industrial designs, or trade secrets might have led to constraints on manufacturing capacity.

This is being read as a shift in positions of some of these countries from hard-core denial on intellectual property being a barrier to a tone which is more conciliatory. Some members are beginning to explore whether there are barriers to access posed by intellectual property protection, one official said. A greater push for the use of TRIPS flexibilities by European countries is also a distinct change, a diplomatic source pointed out.

EMERGING SIGNS OF SUPPORT?
Dr Anthony S Fauci this week called for supplementing the abilities of countries to produce vaccines in a way that countries can have the productive capacities so that they could manufacture vaccines with the cooperation from pharma companies for the relaxation of patents. He drew parallels to the interventions by rich countries during the HIV crisis.

Movement In Brussels?A Geneva-based trade official confirmed that efforts were being made to meet with EU member states individually.

Nicoletta Dentico, Head of the Global Health Programme at Society for International Development (SID), told Geneva Health Files that several members of European Parliament are pushing to discuss the TRIPS waiver proposal. There are efforts being made to get a resolution so that the European Commission could consider it.

There have been efforts to get the Italian Presidency of the G20 to extend support to the TRIPS waiver proposal. Both India and South Africa, proponents of the proposal are members of the G20. Civil society groups are advocating the Italian presidency at the G20 to support the proposal, she added.

WHAT'S NEXT?

Next TRIPS Council formal meeting will be on 23rd February to work on a draft report for the General Council that meets in early March. Countries are expected to meet in smaller groups for bilateral discussions in the coming days.

The resistance to the TRIPS waiver proposal even during a pandemic continues to exist in many quarters not just at free-market media establishments. Some academics have called this a guerrilla war against IP rules.

See this excerpt from a recent Politico story:

"Behind the spat at the WTO, a larger question looms: Is this an attempt to permanently override aspects of intellectual property rights that some countries disagree with?"

"You can essentially see it as a play by two countries, India and South Africa, who never really liked the current intellectual property rights rules of the WTO," said Simon Evenett, an economics professor at St. Gallen University in Switzerland. "I see it in a broader 25-year-long context of this sort of guerilla war against these rules."

"...Almost every major pharmaceutical exporter except India has objected to this," Evenett said. "I don't see that proposal going ahead unless circumstances dramatically change.

Europe hints at patent grab from Big Pharma, Politico

It is very likely that the current discussions at the TRIPS Council on the waiver proposal will eventually seek to move towards attempts to discuss broader rules on intellectual property, sources said.

The demand for a global solution is evident during this pandemic.

In its statement, South Africa said:

"These provisions were never designed to deal with pandemics that exist at the same time in all countries in the world. In these circumstances individual actions will not be effective and would have to be complied on a case- by-case individual basis. Such individual actions may nonetheless impede global solutions such as envisage by the TRIPS waiver proposal. Further, the flexibilities as they exist need further clarification to help us to react to pandemics such as COVID-19, clarification is required across the board ranging from copyright to industrial designs, patents and undisclosed information..."

The stage is set.

10.
TRIPS WAIVER DISCUSSIONS DEADLOCKED (FEBRUARY 23, 2021)

WTO TRIPS COUNCIL FORMAL MEETING

Countries continued to remain deadlocked in their positions on the discussions on the TRIPS Waiver proposal at a formal meeting of the TRIPS Council today at the WTO.

The proposal spearheaded by South Africa and India, now has the following co-sponsors: Kenya, Eswatini, Mozambique, Pakistan, Bolivia, Venezuela, Mongolia, Zimbabwe, Egypt, the African Group and the LDC Group.

The following countries lent support to the proposal from the floor today: Jamaica on behalf of the ACP Group (62 members) Afghanistan, Argentina, Bangladesh, Cambodia, Sri Lanka, Honduras, Cuba, Nepal, Nicaragua, Nigeria, Indonesia, Tunisia, Mali and Mauritius.

In a lengthy discussion, 27 delegations to the floor, sources said. The Holy See also presented a statement supporting the waiver proposal.

Chile, China and Colombia, in addition to some developed countries stressed on the need for more evidence-based discussions in the TRIPS Council on the waiver proposal.

At the meeting South Africa said:

"We cannot put the virus back in the bottle, we just cannot go back to the old normal, said South Africa, that shared some statistics: according to available data, the US, the UK and the EU account for about 30% of over 200 million vaccines administered globally, and countries opposing the IP waiver proposal account for 60% of the globally administered COVID-19 vaccines. Reportedly, just 10 countries have administered 75% of all COVID-19 vaccines and more than 113 countries have not yet received a single dose."

USA, Canada, Switzerland, Norway, Singapore, Japan, Australia and the United Kingdom continued to oppose the proposal.

Some countries reportedly cited a recent statement by Adar Poonawalla, chief executive of the Serum Institute of India, where he told The Guardian that there is sufficient vaccine manufacture capacity in the world and that scaling up is the main issue. They used this to contest the argument that vaccine developers have withheld licensing rights to manufacturers. This shows that IP has not been a barrier so far - opposing countries reasoned, sources familiar with the discussions said.

Members agreed to present an oral status to the General Council meeting on 1-2 March to continue discussion on this issue.

The consensus language of the oral status report reads as follows:

"At the meeting of the TRIPS Council on 15-16 October 2020, India and South Africa introduced document IP/C/W/669, requesting a waiver from certain provisions of the TRIPS Agreement for the prevention, containment and treatment of COVID-19, which had been circulated on 2 October 2020 and has since been co-sponsored by the delegations of Kenya, Eswatini, Mozambique, Pakistan, Bolivia, Venezuela, Mongolia, Zimbabwe, Egypt, the African Group and the LDC Group. The

Council continued its discussions under that agenda item at informal meetings on 20 November and 3 December, as well as at its resumed meeting on 10 December 2020. Following the status report to the General Council on 16-17 December 2020, the Council continued its consideration of the waiver request at informal meetings on 19 January and 4 February 2021, and at its formal meeting on 23 February 2021.

At those meetings, delegations also exchanged views, asked questions, sought clarifications and provided replies, clarifications, and information, including through documents IP/C/W/670, IP/C/W/671, IP/C/W/672, IP/C/W/673 and IP/C/W/674, on the waiver request but could not reach consensus, including on whether it is appropriate to move to text-based negotiations. Delegations indicated a need for further discussions on the waiver request and views exchanged by delegations.

This means that the TRIPS Council has not yet completed its consideration of the waiver request. The TRIPS Council will therefore continue its consideration of the waiver request and report back to the General Council as stipulated in Article IX:3 of the Marrakesh Agreement."

11.

THE THIRD WAY: UNBLOCKING THE TRIPS WAIVER LOGJAM (FEBRUARY 26, 2021)

The Third Way suggested by Ngozi Okonjo-Iweala, WTO's new director-general who assumes office on Monday, March 1, may pave the way for negotiations on the TRIPS Waiver proposal, sources in Geneva say. In her remarks recently, Okonjo-Iweala suggested the use of TRIPS flexibilities and the voluntary licensing approach to deftly address the pandemic.

This, proponents of the TRIPS Waiver proposal, say, could be a significant moment in these discussions, which could bring to the negotiating table countries opposing the waiver. So far, opposing countries have locked the proponents of the proposal in a so-called "evidentiary loop" without moving towards text-based negotiations. For five months WTO members have discussed and debated if and whether intellectual property and other kinds of obligations under the TRIPS agreement have impeded the response to the COVID-19 pandemic.

Earlier this week, we reported that the discussions on the TRIPS Waiver proposal continued to be deadlocked at a formal meeting that took place on February 23. Read this debrief by Third World Network for statements by the WTO members on the proposal.

Although nearly two-thirds of WTO members now support the proposal, a handful of powerful, mostly wealthy nations continue to oppose it. Although discussions continue to be deadlocked, there has been material difference to the kind of opposition to the proposal, sources suggest. This reveals potential indications on how positions on the proposal might evolve in the coming months.

Based on conversations with diplomatic sources familiar with the proceedings at WTO, this story takes a closer look at the potential evolution of these discussions going forward.

The waiver proposal seeks to allow all countries to not grant or enforce intellectual property protection for the duration of the pandemic, until widespread vaccination has been achieved. The proposal recognizes intellectual property, trade secrets, industrial designs, as barriers to sharing technology.

BENEATH THE SURFACE

"There is greater sympathy in the room given the circumstances countries face. Now we must see how we translate that sympathy to some meaningful engagement to discuss the text of the proposal," a diplomatic source said.

As indicated by previous statements in the weeks in the run-up to this meeting, proponents of the proposal have been willing to discuss about the timeframe and the scope of the waiver proposal. Proponents now want to understand the specific reservations that opposing countries have on the proposal.

It appears bolstered by a raft new co-sponsors including the African Group and the LDC Group, the proponents are hoping to build on a momentum to head into discussions in the coming weeks with greater determination. The proposal first spearheaded by South Africa and India, in October 2020, now has the following co-sponsors: Kenya, Eswatini, Mozambique, Pakistan, Bolivia, Venezuela, Mongolia, Zimbabwe, Egypt, apart from the regional blocs mentioned above.

In addition, the following countries lent support to the proposal during the meeting this week: Jamaica on behalf of the

ACP Group (62 members) Afghanistan, Argentina, Bangladesh, Cambodia, Sri Lanka, Honduras, Cuba, Nepal, Nicaragua, Nigeria, Indonesia, Tunisia, Mali and Mauritius. It is understood that there are indications that the ACP group might be moving closer to becoming a co-sponsor to the proposal.

Chile, China and Colombia, in addition to some developed countries stressed on the need for more evidence-based discussions in the TRIPS Council on the waiver proposal.

USA, EU, Canada, Switzerland, Norway, Singapore, Japan, Australia and the United Kingdom continued to oppose the proposal.

(South Africa pointed out in its statement that countries opposing the TRIPs waiver proposal account for 60% of the globally administered COVID-19 vaccines.)

FACTORS SHAPING THE DISCUSSIONS
A few decisive events can shape these discussions, sources familiar with the matter with say. The rise in the number of variants of SARS-CoV-2, the virulence of these variants, the extent to which existing vaccines will be effective against these new variants, and elections in the countries opposing the waiver proposal.

And believe it or not, vaccine diplomacy could potentially spur discussions, with the increasing perception that western countries are losing out on influence, as powerful vaccine providers such as Russia and China are distributing home-grown vaccines to countries at the back of the vaccines queue.

(Also check out: Call To Prevent Export Restrictions On Covid-19 Vaccines: Communication From Colombia, Costa Rica, Ecuador, Panama And Paraguay, to be considered by the General Council, next week)

Countries supporting the waiver are closely tracking the data emerging from the epidemiological transition of the pandemic and will potentially use information and insights into their discussions and negotiations on the waiver proposal going forward, a diplomat said.

At the meeting, opposing countries continued to showcase their commitment to a multilateral response to the pandemic by illustrating support to the ACT Accelerator set up to fund the fight against the pandemic and the financial donations to the COVAX Facility, the international vaccines mechanism for COVID-19. But as has been pointed out before, billions of dollars of funding shortfall continue.

Wealthy countries opposing the waiver also talk about donations of vaccine doses. But one diplomatic source from the global south, said, "We do not want second-hand vaccines doses set to expire soon. We want our own production capacity".

THE THIRD WAY: A KEY TO UNLOCK NEGOTIATIONS?

In her address to the General Council on the eve of her appointment, Okonjo-Iweala said, "WTO Members have a further responsibility to reject vaccine nationalism and protectionism. They should rather intensify cooperation on promising new vaccines, therapeutics, and diagnostics. There should be a "third way" to broaden access through facilitating technology transfer within the framework of multilateral rules, to encourage research and innovation while at the same time allowing licensing agreements that help scale up manufacturing of medical products." She cited the example of the licensing approach of AstraZeneca.

It is not clear whether those opposing the waiver proposal will effectively work towards technology transfer needed to address production shortages of COVID-19 vaccines.

Consider Canada's statement at the meeting this week: (excerpt)

"...Madam Chair, vaccines can be produced independently depending on the technology. For certain vaccines, production and scaling up may be contingent not only upon some form of patent freedom to operate, such as through licensing, but also on close cooperation between licensees and licensors to allow full practice of the invention and of the associated art, with a view to producing consistently safe and efficacious products. Canada is thus interested in better understanding how a waiver would incentivize these requisite collaborative relationships; and, where full practice of the art is not possible without the participation of the licensor, we are interested in better understanding the safety, efficacy, and regulatory implications of the production of vaccines independently from the licensor.

In other cases, a vaccine technology may be such that production and scaling up is contingent only upon some form of patent freedom to operate. Canada would thus be interested in better understanding how, in situations where holders of patents for such COVID-19 vaccines refused requests for voluntary licences, Members attempted but were unable to apply Article 31 of the TRIPS Agreement..."

Canada

Some believe that countries can be brought together to discuss the use TRIPS flexibilities, and potential voluntary approaches in the context of the pandemic. The distance between WTO members divided on the TRIPS waiver issue, can be addressed to an extent.

Diplomatic sources affiliated with the countries that support the proposal note the transition in the extent of the opposition to the proposal.

"Initially, the proposal was simply dismissed. Now we see greater willingness to engage." Five months since the TRIPS Council first started discussing the proposal, WTO members have met through a series of informal and formal meetings at the Council. Sources point out that the number of such meetings in the TRIPS Council is unusual for WTO. The proposal was also discussed at the General Council meeting in December 2020. (See the archives of Geneva Health Files that has captured each of these meetings in detail.)

"Getting opposing countries to the table to potentially discuss ways forward is a big win, even if it is to discuss 'the third way'," one source said. While countries supporting the waiver are open to discussing the third way, it does not mean they will stop at discussing only voluntary approaches to licensing, the source said.

Trade observers in Geneva believe that the coming weeks and months could see slow but advancing discussions on the waiver proposal with each side drawing lines as the talks progress.

VACCINE DIPLOMACY AS A TRADE CATALYST

What is also interesting is that sources believe that vaccine diplomacy is shaping trade diplomacy in the context of the access to vaccines. "Western capitals are fast evaluating the implications of the increasing use of Russian and Chinese vaccines in many parts of the world." The wealthy countries are under pressure to respond. In recent months, several countries including India, China, Russia, have made quick advances in distributing or selling vaccines to neighbours and beyond.

In the absence of local manufacturing capacities and the acute lack of access to vaccines even in countries with high burden of COVID-19, has meant that vaccine diplomacy has flourished. This might decisively contribute to the waiver discussions, some officials believe.

WHATS COMING NEXT?

Members agreed to present an oral statement to the General Council meeting on 1-2 March. The next formal TRIPS Council meeting is scheduled for March 10.

In its statement this week, South Africa said, "The reason we called for a text-based discussion is because this will help us to understand direct questions that members have on our proposal. We invite delegations to raise concerns on elements they may have concerns about and suggestions as to how we can arrive at a common landing zone, including at the regular TRIPS Council meeting of 10 March 2021 and subsequent informal and informal meetings. We once again call for our deliberation to move to a text-based discussion."

Proponents of the waiver proposal are hopeful that discussions can move towards "draft modalities" by the end of March.

Discussions in the coming weeks are likely to transition into "defining" what the waiver can entail, how it may apply. "There needs to be specific discussions to negotiate and agree on for example, the kinds of products that the waiver will be applicable for, in the context of this pandemic. It will be very limited to COVID-19", one source suggested.

Proponents suggest a list-based approach, "but not a closed-list", the source said. Potentially there could be a mechanism where WTO members notify on their preferences on which the waiver can be applicable.

Countries will need to begin thinking concretely on how they would like to operationalise the waiver, the source added.

Based on bilateral consultations with groups of interested countries and others, the proponents of the proposal, have begun to get an indication on the way some countries might want to use the waiver.

"While a country from a LDC group with no manufacturing capacity may wish to import vaccines, another may wish to use trade secrets. Some have expressed reluctance on suspending copyrights protection under the waiver for example. So, countries will need to make their own assessments as to how this waiver could apply domestically," a diplomatic source explained.

"One country may need access to Active Pharmaceutical Ingredients, another may need access to know-how to produce the vaccines, some might simply need a source code for an app. The needs are different across countries," the trade official added.

The waiver will be an internationally applicable mechanism that aims to absolve countries from certain obligations under the TRIPS agreement for a particular duration to fight the pandemic. Countries have the option of implementing the waiver or not, depending on their domestic needs and the epidemiology of the disease. Countries can "selectively prioritize" in line with their needs, the source explained.

(To read in detail on the provisions of the original proposal, see this comprehensive story from October 2020.)

THE ELECTION: THE CHAIR OF THE TRIPS COUNCIL

At a time when the most path-breaking discussion on intellectual property and access to medicines in decades, comes to a stead, the TRIPS Council will elect a new chair at the General Council meeting next week. This is not insignificant and could likely have an impact on the proceedings, although such changes are routine. The TRIPS Council is currently chaired by Xolelwa Mlumbi-Peter, the South African ambassador.

A source familiar with such appointments to the TRIPS Council suggested that these appointments are political but require neutrality for the conduct of the proceedings of the TRIPS

Council. There is a "tacit understanding" that the appointments to these WTO bodies is made by rotation to ensure representation from a Least Developed Country, a developing country and a developed country. The previous chair of the TRIPS Council was from Mongolia. And therefore, it is expected that a representative from a developed country will be appointed now.

It is understood that Norway's Dagfinn Sørli may be appointed at the General Council meeting next week, sources said. (Politico reported that a proposal to push forward Afghanistan as the Chair of TRIPS Council was "rescinded"). Note that Norway is also a co-chair of the Facilitation Council of the ACT -Accelerator.

Sources told Geneva Health Files, about the absolute professionalism and neutrality shown by the South African ambassador as chair of the TRIPS Council, even as South Africa, has been one of the lead proponents of the TRIPS Waiver proposal.

"In one instance, ambassador Mlumbi-Peter even reminded the South African delegate to stick to time," one official said recounting meetings from the last few months on these discussions.

Separately, Norway has also asked for a revised proposal on the TRIPS waiver from co-sponsors.

THE BREAKING OF THE DAM?

While the intractable discussions on the waiver proposal continue, WTO members have a greater recognition for the need to put in place a global mechanism that will help prepare countries for future epidemics, sources say.

Some observers do not rule out a "breaking of the dam", which may ultimately yield multilateral support for the waiver. Earlier this week, a cross-party group of more than 100 parliamentarians expressed their support for the waiver proposal asking the European Commission and EU member states not to block the proposal. (Declaration from Members of the European Parliament to urge the Commission and Member States not to block the TRIPS waiver at the WTO and to support global access to COVID-19 vaccines)

But no one is expecting miracles. "The pharma industry is too powerful for that," one source noted.

12.
COULD VACCINE NATIONALISM SPUR DISPUTES AT THE WTO (MARCH 12, 2021)

Experts believe that the solution to vaccine nationalism is not filing disputes, but negotiations. But lawyers anticipate disputes even if filed simply for political leverage.

Vaccine nationalism, a condition that has flourished during COVID-19, is loosely understood as the tendency of countries to hoard vaccines. But protectionist trade practices of hoarding medical supplies began as soon as the pandemic hit. This is now taking a serious turn with export restriction measures adopted by some countries. This could lead to a real possibility of countries taking the legal route to file disputes at the WTO, even if only for political leverage, experts say.

Geneva Health Files spoke to legal experts, lawyers and delegations of some countries for this story. Will rising protectionism to address the pandemic relate to a rash of WTO disputes? Yes and no, depending on who you speak to.

Earlier this week, Ngozi Okonjo-Iweala, WTO DG, said that 59 members and 7 observers, had some pandemic-related export restrictions or licensing requirements in place at the end of February, primarily for personal protective equipment. She pointed out that these figures were lower than the 91 countries that had brought in such measures over the past year.

EU-AUSTRALIA

When EU announced measures for export authorization earlier this year, amidst prevailing conditions of scarcity of vaccines production, it was met with near-ubiquitous criticism.

Our interest was piqued when Italy decided to block export of AstraZeneca vaccine doses to Australia. It is understood that Australia had discussed these concerns with DG Ngozi.

It was reported that Australia intended to work with other countries including Canada, Japan, Norway and New Zealand, "to pressure European officials in Brussels as a group."

We reached out to the Australian Permanent Mission to the WTO in Geneva, to find out if the country had plans to file a dispute. In response to our question on whether there has been any formal consideration at this stage to file a WTO dispute against the EU, a spokesperson of the mission answered in the negative.

"Australia intends to work cooperatively with like-minded states, including the EU, to deliver vaccines as a global good. Our view is that vaccines should not be subject to restrictive trade measures," the spokesperson told Geneva Health Files.

We were also told that Australia's Minister for Trade, Dan Tehan had spoken to the EU Trade Commissioner Valdis Dombrovkis on Australia's approach. The spokesperson also confirmed that the minister had spoken to the WTO DG on the matter.

Does this mean we will witness no disputes because of protectionist measures during the pandemic, will countries opt for negotiation over a litigious route to address vaccine shortages?

WILL DISPUTES ARISE?

One Geneva-based trade source on the condition of anonymity said, "The way the EU was excoriated at the [WTO] General Council meeting (earlier this month), in response to its trade restriction measures, shows that this issue will not go away anytime soon. There is a real possibility of members filing disputes." (One diplomatic source called discussions at the General Council meeting last week as "a slaughterhouse")

The view on whether members will rush into filing disputes is divided – not the least because of what it means to go through the dispute settlement process at the WTO amid a pandemic.

For one, there is the issue of time constraints. Disputes at the WTO can take long. This is apart from the current crisis facing the international trade court – WTO's Appellate Body which is not currently functional.

Disputes around the pandemic will need to be resolved quickly to have any impact. It could take up to 18 months to get a panel report in the WTO disputes settlement system. So, experts feel that WTO disputes system may not be suitable for these kinds of urgent challenges.

While it is too soon to dismiss the possibility of trade disputes, experts believe that the way to address competition for medical products during the pandemic will be through negotiation.

Experts point to the 2001 dispute brought by the U.S. against Brazil, during the AIDS crisis, which ended up as mutually agreed solution. (See *DS199: Brazil — Measures Affecting Patent Protection*). The dispute involved Brazil's local working requirements in its industrial property law.

Joost Pauwelyn, Professor of International Law, who also heads the department at The Graduate Institute in Geneva, believes that the focus is and should be on finding solutions, practical ways to address concerns, not litigation. Last year, Pauwelyn analysed the legal framework of export restrictions at the EU and WTO level. (See *Export Restrictions in Times of Pandemic: Options and Limits under International Trade Agreements*)

"There is no GATT/WTO ruling that addresses the issue (of the use of export restrictions in the health area) directly. The IP-related disputes that arose during the AIDS crisis were negotiated. It was dealt with at the political level (TRIPS council, General Council etc.) and ultimately via a waiver and TRIPS treaty amendment, not in the dispute settlement system," Pauwelyn says.

Asked whether the crisis in the Appellate Body will dissuade countries from filing disputes, Pauwelyn says, "WTO dispute settlement is currently broken given the option to block panel outcomes to a non-existent Appellate Body. In addition, the process takes about 4-5 years, but under this status quo, it means that by the time the case is settled, the world may already be facing the next pandemic so to speak. So, in practical terms, filing a dispute could be a non-starter."

Pauwelyn is also one of the WTO Appeals Arbitrators, nominated by the EU for the Multi-party interim appeal arbitration arrangement (MPIA). The MPIA is a temporary solution till the Appellate Body is functional again. It allows participant WTO members to have access to a 2-step dispute settlement system in the WTO, including the availability of an independent and impartial appeal stage.

WTO EXPORT RULES TOO BROAD?
Remember that EU has said that its measures are consistent with WTO rules. But that does not mean it cannot be challenged. It is widely acknowledged that these rules are too broad in their framing, giving WTO members ample leeway to take measures during emergencies and in the context of public health concerns.

Two provisions in The General Agreement on Tariffs and Trade 1994 come up in this discussion: (we cite this from the legal text)

THE GENERAL AGREEMENT ON TARIFFS AND TRADE 1994

Text of Article XI

General Elimination of Quantitative Restrictions

1. *No prohibitions or restrictions other than duties, taxes or other charges, whether made effective through quotas, import or export licences or other measures, shall be instituted or maintained by any contracting party on the importation of any product of the territory of any other contracting party or on the exportation or sale for export of any product destined for the territory of any other contracting party.*

2. *The provisions of paragraph 1 of this Article shall not extend to the following:*

a. *Export prohibitions or restrictions temporarily applied to prevent or relieve critical shortages of foodstuffs or other products essential to the exporting contracting party;*

Article XX: General Exceptions

Subject to the requirement that such measures are not applied in a manner which would constitute a means of arbitrary or unjustifiable discrimination between countries where the same conditions prevail, or a disguised restriction on international trade, nothing in this Agreement shall be construed to prevent the adoption or enforcement by any contracting party of measures:

b. *necessary to protect public morals;*

c. *necessary to protect human, animal or plant life or health;*
Experts say that EU or any other country bringing in export restriction measures can demonstrate that measures have been taken "temporarily" to prevent or relieve critical shortages of

"essential" products. Vaccines, raw materials for vaccines, and other medical products can be deemed essential. [See Art XI 1 above.]

Lawyers believe that members will most likely cite the Article XX. The provision enables countries to take measures on account of public health concerns. [See Article XX (b)]

"In general, as far as export restrictions are concerned, WTO law is fairly relaxed. It allows members to do quite a bit," a trade expert said.

However, as production shortages of vaccines hit both rich and poor countries, manufacturers are concerned about export restrictive measures. (See this report from the summit earlier in the week: *Towards Vaccinating The World Landscape of Current COVID-19 Supply Chain and Manufacturing Capacity, Potential Challenges, Initial Responses, and Possible "Solution Space"*)

DG Ngozi has acknowledged the supply chain problems linked to export restrictions and prohibitions. "Because vaccine production relies on sourcing components and ingredients from multiple countries, she said, trade restrictions would slow down production, and make it more expensive," according to a WTO press release this week on her comments at the vaccines summit with manufacturers.

Serum Institute of India's Adar Poonawallah, for example, has raised concerns on the Biden administration decision to invoke the Defense Production Act to prevent exports of certain materials needed to manufacture vaccines. The SII is India's vaccine powerhouse meeting the demand for both bilateral and multilateral vaccine deals.

To protect domestic manufacturers and constituencies, countries may resort to filing disputes, if only to send a signal to other members, experts believe. To be sure, this is not only about vaccines. Going forward, export restrictions on raw materials can have implications for therapeutics as well. So, the threat of a dispute may be a tool to deal with competition for scarce medial products during the pandemic, experts say.

Although trade restrictive measures are short-sighted and not a preferred policy option, governments see them as powerful instruments to meet political goals, to send a message to domestic stakeholders, sources said.

"My hunch is that all countries are sort of sitting on both sides of the fence. On the one hand, governments would like to maintain the discretion and the ability to impose export restrictions if they need to or if they think they need to. Whether that is medical products or personal protective equipment. On the other hand, everybody dislikes it when other countries impose export restrictions. So, I think there is enough of an incentive for countries to sit down and negotiate," one legal expert noted.

Sources also pointed to political declarations last year where WTO members came together and said that they would not impose restrictive trade measures. "In order to be constructive, countries decided that they were going to signal to members that will not introduce exports restrictive measures even though it may be expedient to do so," one trade expert said. The way out, some feel, is to find solution to placing limits on export restrictions.

WHY DISPUTES ARE A REAL POSSIBILITY

It is not just trade restrictive measures that could result in trade disputes. The heated political discussions on the TRIPS waiver at WTO is also aggravating the potential for disputes, according to experts involved in litigations in international trade in Geneva. Therefore, these ostensibly independent processes, can catalyse disputes.

"The waiver discussion is very heated, and it is aggravating the discussion on the EU's export restrictions. If the waiver succeeds, then the opposing members cannot do anything about it. So they will be looking at other ways to beat up on behaviour they do not like on the COVID-19 front," one trade law expert said. Do not rule out disputes against supporters of the TRIPS waiver proposal, in case the waiver is adopted, the source added.

In their statement at the WTO General Council meeting last week, the EU said, "In order to ensure that vaccines and their ingredients are not directed to export destinations in unjustified volumes, the European Union had no choice but to introduce a transparency mechanism on Covid-19 vaccine export transactions." The EU has said that the measures are WTO-consistent.

It added "Since the entry into force of the scheme on the 1 February, we have received 150 requests for export authorisation. All of them have been accepted. I repeat, all of them." This week, the European Commission extended transparency and authorisation mechanism for exports of COVID-19 vaccines.

The EU is also a part of the Ottawa Group proposal on Trade and Health that also spells out commitments towards export restrictions. (See also *E.U. Exports Millions of Covid Vaccine Doses Despite Supply Crunch at Home*)

"Members bring disputes all the time, even when they know that it's going to take a long time to get a result and often, they bring a dispute as leverage for negotiations. Filing a dispute does not mean they are looking for a solution. It does not mean the dispute will be litigated all the way to the end," a trade lawyer said.

It could also result in a negotiated arrangement, like it was in 2001 in the U.S.-Brazil case. "Why did the U.S. bring a case against Brazil? It gave them leverage in negotiations, and to satisfy domestic stakeholders," the lawyer added.

The impasse at the Appellate Body may not be a deterrent for countries to dissuade countries from bringing a dispute, some believe.

"The Appellate Body not being functional is not a problem. Countries have recourse to Article 25 under the Dispute Settlement Understanding (DSU) that provides for 'expeditious arbitration as an alternate means to dispute settlement'," a source involved in the WTO litigation process said. (The EU, for example, is a signatory to the Multi-party interim appeal arbitration arrangement, MPIA.)

While disputes may take up precious energy and resources of members already stretched in fighting to address the pandemic, it may likely be a strategy to address trade protectionism. Not all agree.

"I think the law is not really an answer here, I hate to say that because I'm a lawyer. But I really don't think the law is an answer because the law is so generically drafted right that and it's politically so sensitive. Which WTO panel will tell a member that restricting vaccine is not legitimate? It will ultimately harm the legitimacy of the trading system," the person added.

13.

WHO & WTO CONVERGE ON BILATERAL TECH TRANSFER: WHAT THIS MEANS FOR THE TRIPS WAIVER (APRIL 16, 2021)

The WTO vaccine equity event showed potential for spare manufacturing capacity and the willingness to finance it. But will this be followed up voluntary technology transfer to address production shortages, or will this be left to the discretion of bilateral deals decided by manufacturers? And was this event meant to draw attention away from the TRIPS waiver talks now reaching a critical stage?

There are emerging convergences between the WTO and WHO, on the approaches towards bilateral technology transfer to spur the production of vaccines. This will inevitably have repercussions for the TRIPS waiver proposal.

While it is not clear yet which way discussions on the TRIPS waiver will go, there is an emerging shift within the support base of the proposal even as opponents gather to buy time to stall any meaningful progress towards negotiating on the text of the proposal.

This story looks at what the vaccine equity event at WTO might mean for the wider efforts to address the pandemic including the dynamics shaping the discussions on the TRIPS waiver proposal.

The WTO convened its vaccine equity event on April 14, spearheaded by DG Ngozi Okonjo-Iweala. The event saw 50 speakers including a statement by WHO.

As we noted earlier this week, WHO has now fallen behind the idea of the COVAX manufacturing taskforce, somewhat choicelessly. In his speech at WTO, this week, WHO DG Tedros Adhanom Ghebreyesus, though, continued to push for the TRIPS waiver and the COVID-19 technology access pool, even as he batted for the COVAX manufacturing task force. Excerpts from his speech:

"To address this challenge, WHO and our partners have established a COVAX manufacturing task force, to increase supply in the short term, but also to build a platform for sustainable vaccine manufacturing to support regional health security.

We need to go beyond the traditional modus operandi to provide sustainable and effective solutions to address this extraordinary crisis.

Some manufacturers have begun sharing the know-how and technologies to produce more vaccines, but only under restrictive conditions, on a very limited basis.

The current company-controlled production sharing agreements are not coming close to meeting the overwhelming public health and socio-economic needs for effective, affordable, and equitable access to vaccines, as well as therapeutics and other critical health technologies.

We must leave no stone unturned. We must explore every option for increasing production, including voluntary licenses, technology pools, the use of TRIPS flexibilities and the waiver of certain intellectual property provisions."

In his remarks he called on companies to share know-how, intellectual property and data with other qualified vaccine manufacturers, including in low-and middle-income countries. And he said that WHO is calling for expressions of interest to estab-lish technology transfer hubs to assist countries acquire vac-cine technology and know-how as rapidly as possible. To en-able technology transfer, he offered that WHO would provide support for national regulatory authorities to become WHO list-ed authorities and to enable market entry of health products. He also urged countries to invest in local manufacturing.

THE VACCINE EQUITY "EVENT"

The vaccine equity event was conducted over two days. The first day saw the participation of international organizations, some WTO members, the pharmaceutical industry and some members of the civil society organizations. This was followed by bilateral meetings with blocs of countries the next day, sources said. The meeting has been generally perceived as an important one to have provided a framework for these discussions.

One of the key messages emerging is that there is available manufacturing capacity in the developing world, according to sources who attended the meeting. In her short video mes-sage, following the first day, DG Okonjo-Iweala acknowledges that there is indeed spare capacity for manufacturing. (Sources present at the meeting, also indicated the Coalition of Epidemic Preparedness and Innovation has an updated list with mapped capacity for manufacturing of vaccines.)

It also emerged from the meeting that multilateral develop-ment banks were keen on financing investments in low- and middle-income countries to boost manufacturing capacities.

"The outcomes of the meeting were obvious. There is ca-pacity and there is interest in financing manufacturing capacity. The missing part of this puzzle is for the pharma industry to step up and enable technology transfer to boost production," according to a source who attended the meeting on the first day.

The WTO hopes that the meeting "would serve as the basis for continued dialogue aimed at delivering results in terms of increased vaccine production volumes in the short-term as well as longer-term investments in vaccine production and enhancing the trading system›s contribution to pandemic preparedness."

The need for "open cross-border trade for access to vaccine raw materials and inputs" was also discussed at the meeting. In recent weeks, DG Okonjo-Iweala raised the question on export restrictions with WTO members including the EU. (Recent weeks also saw India place export restrictions on vaccines produced by the Serum Institute of India. And the US placing restrictions on access to raw materials needed to produce vaccines.)

Sources also pointed out that the meeting saw the need for transparency in vaccine contracts to enable better pricing and distribution which can directly impact access and equity.

In her remarks at the meeting, DG Okonjo-Iweala said, "I hope that part of what we get from today is not only concrete action to increase [vaccine production] capacity, but also the elements of a framework on trade and health that we can pull together at the WTO and put before ministers at the 12th Ministerial Conference in December," she said. "I would look to such a framework to provide for trade-related preparedness to handle this pandemic, and the next one."

She also emphasised that "I agree with the view that the WTO is a logical forum for finding a way forward on these issues, and I hope that the ideas raised here will contribute to convergence in the TRIPS Council on meaningful results that can contribute to the goals that we have."

What was also perceived as significant by some quarters, was the statement made by United States Trade Representative Katherine Tai, where she stated, "The desperate needs that our people face in the current pandemic provide these companies with an opportunity to be the heroes they claim to be – and can be. As governments and leaders of international institutions, the highest standards of courage and sacrifice are demanded of us in times of crisis. The same needs to be demanded of industry."

However, some developing country members pointed out that irrespective of the statements made, the action on the ground by the US continues to effectively impede access to vaccines, which include policies that impose export restrictions on raw materials for the manufacture of vaccines.

"The statements may be positive, but we see this as buying time and stalling discussions on the waiver proposal," a developing country source said.

ON THE ROLE OF THE WTO DG

One of the speakers at the event said that the attitude of the DG was genuine and that the meeting could lead to something more positive. "It will depend upon where Ngozi Okonjo-Iweala wants to take things," the person said.

Another person who attended the meeting, agreed and said that the DG seemed to be committed to solve the problem on vaccine shortages. "At least she is trying to do something. But some members, and even within the WTO secretariat do not like this approach. They do not know how to deal with this new culture," the source said.

Not surprisingly, some developed and developing countries are not happy with the DG's active role. But if she is upsetting both sides, Okonjo-Iweala is probably doing something right. (Those who challenge existing ways of doing things are to be welcomed, whether they also go on to challenge status quo, is a different matter.)

"The DG is exercising trade diplomacy and deploying the convening power in bringing parties together and seeking solutions. The view will always be divided on the role of the DG, some will say the DG should be 'the owner of silences', and should not go public with her intentions," a Geneva-based trade official said citing a proverb.

Last week, a former WTO official even raised questions on how many members believe that the DG is an "honest broker" and asked her to take a leaf out of past director-general's. (To be sure, the previous DG Roberto Azevêdo was criticised for not speaking out enough as many have pointed out.)

As far as vaccine talks at WTO are concerned, these have implications not only on the way WTO is run, but more significantly on possibly who lives and who dies by determining how vaccines will be made available globally.

THE VACCINE EQUITY EVENT AND THE TRIPS WAIVER PROPOSAL

So, what does all this mean for the TRIPS waiver proposal? Sources familiar with discussions say that this is a critical period that could determine the future of the proposal.

There are two meetings of the TRIPS Council this month, an informal one on April 22nd and a formal meeting on April 30th. In these meetings, countries will agree on a report to be submitted at the General Council meeting on May 5th and 6th that will discuss status of the waiver proposal. (Members have met eight times to have these discussions and numerous bilateral consultations.)

WTO member continue to have bilateral discussions on the proposal, some of which have been convened by the TRIPS Council Chair Ambassador Dagfinn Sørli.

Some diplomatic sources are not sure if these bilateral consultations convened by the Chair are being conducted in "good faith". There is a perception that these consultations are not being held in a transparent and an impartial manner. There are increasing concerns about the way the Chair may shape these crucial discussions in the coming days and the impact this could have on the TRIPS waiver talks, some trade officials told Geneva Health Files on the condition of anonymity.

One Geneva-based trade official said that by holding select bilateral consultations, the Chair can identify landing zones that could give him a picture before informal and formal meetings of the TRIPS Council this month.

It is understood that discussions on the proposal may proceed to a potential revised text to explore how such a waiver proposal can apply specifically to therapeutics, diagnostics and vaccines that could help address the fight against COVID-19.

The proposal has had 58 co-sponsors and an additional support of more than 60 countries who have called for text-based discussions on the proposal. There have been no new co-sponsors recently.

There are fears that the stalling tactics adopted by opposing countries (the U.S., UK, the EU, Norway, Switzerland, Canada among others) are inducing "waiver-fatigue", a source said. In addition, bilateral meetings organized in wake of the vaccine equity meeting, between blocks of countries and vaccine manufacturers, may tempt some countries to rely on bilateral and voluntary licensing deals to secure vaccine production lines. These considerations might affect their support to the waiver proposal, a source mentioned.

'The Third Way', mostly understood as relying on TRIPS flexibilities and voluntary licensing approaches from manufacturers, proposed by DG Okonjo-Iweala might lead to severely undermining the waiver proposal, some developing countries fear. While some were optimistic in the past about using the third way, to bring opposing countries to the negotiating table, this has so far not proved successful.

So while Okonjo-Iweala indicated that she was cautiously optimistic about the outcomes of the TRIPS waiver proposal, many do not share her optimism.

Finally there is a clear dynamic emerging within the support base of the waiver proposal, including in some civil society organizations who have increasingly articulated on the limitations of the waiver alone in addressing the pandemic and pushing for more a "realistic" appraisal of such a legal solution that entails an international suspension of rules on intellectual property, copyright and trade secrets among others.

"Some people are of the view that the waiver discussion has already achieved its task of bringing these crucial issues on access to medicines centrestage," one source familiar with these changes told us. Others have dismissed the talks around the waiver as merely "political discussions", despite the sheer legal force such an internationally applicable rule can have that would relieve countries from commercial and political pressure on using TRIPS flexibilities, for example.

There is no doubt the political momentum generated by this proposal. Experts point out the political significance of such a proposal from the global south striking at the heart of entrenched intellectual property rules setting at the WTO amid the worst pandemic the world has seen.

"The waiver proposal challenges the status quo. It has garnered so much support because it has resonated with people that it is not acceptable that a handful of companies determine global access during a pandemic. Notwithstanding the legal merits of the proposal, it interrogates the monopoly system at the political level," Dimitri Eynikel Advocacy Advisor, Médecins Sans Frontières, told us.

While it is unclear whether the waiver proposal will result in a waiver of some of the obligations under the TRIPS agreement as intended by the proponents, or it will result in a political declaration, that could then lead to a discussion on a change in rules governing these matters, remains to be seen.

Whatever the outcome, it appears the time has come and some would say likely passed. More than three million deaths on account of COVID-19 have failed to bring countries together. While a TRIPS waiver will suspend intellectual property and re-lated rights that could help access to technologies, a voluntary pooling mechanism such as envisioned by the COVID-19 tech-nology access pool seeks to disseminate know-how through sharing. Bilateral technology transfer deals, on the other hand, will continue to keep the world vulnerable to the discretion of manufacturers. For now, most of the policy capital seems to be invested in this final option that has not met expectations.

In a deeply divided world, deaths are mounting on either side. And this may well be the beginning for many countries.

"Globally, the number of new cases per week has nearly dou-bled over the past two months. This is approaching the highest rate of infection that we have seen so far during the pandemic," WHO said today.

14.
Q&A: HYO YOON KANG ON THE FINANCIALIZATION OF INTELLECTUAL PROPERTY & COVID-19 (APRIL 20, 2022)

At Geneva Health Files, we make a concerted effort to use inter-disciplinary reporting approaches given the very nature of global health which straddles so many disciplines.

It is, therefore, with great pleasure that we bring you this pertinent interview with intellectual property law expert, Hyo Yoon Kang, a reader in law at Kent Law School, University of Kent. Kang, who has cross-disciplinary training, has worked at the intersection of law, history of sciences, and science and technology studies. In this enlightening interview she examines the embedded politics in the very foundations of intellectual property law and picks apart the arguments against the TRIPS waiver.

> *Geneva Health Files [GHF]: You have argued that IP law must serve a global public, not a national one. "There is no logical reason why patent law's grant of monopoly power cannot be curtailed, if its public purpose is not fulfilled." Can you elaborate?*

Hyo Yoon Kang [HYK]: With my statement, I was transferring the commonly held justification for patent law at the level of national jurisdictions to the global level. Much of modern patent law's legitimacy rests on the belief that the public will be better served by granting a limited monopoly right in an invention than allowing market competition. This is commonly known as the 'patent bargain': private risk is rewarded and incentivised in return for a limited private monopoly right, which in turn is supposed to benefit the public at large in a trickle-down or trickle-across effect. Yet the scale of such a bargain has arguably not been in an equilibrium for some time, as pharmaceutical companies' ever-greening practices and price hikes have shown. Also, not all inventions have the same importance for the public. It is not sensible that medicines are treated in the same way as hair dryers in patent law.

In the current Covid-19 pandemic, the scale of the 'patent bargain' has become even more skewed against the public interest because monopoly rights are being claimed for inventions that have been effectively de-risked and funded with public taxpayers' money, not to mention the decade long public support for basic research that has led to these products, such as the NIH funding of the mRNA technology. These arguments have been made and published many times. (See *"Who funded the research behind the Oxford-AstraZeneca COVID-19 vaccine?* or *Challenges in ensuring global access to COVID-19 vaccines: production, affordability, allocation, and deployment)* While there is no need to repeat what has already been said, it bears pointing out that - a year into the pandemic - governments have created a de-facto oligopolistic market dominated by a handful companies that have been subsidised by governments and intellectual property protection, such as patents and trade secrets.

How does such a skewed patent bargain play out on the global scale? At least since the 1995 TRIPS agreement, what counts as 'public' and 'private' in the context of IP can no longer be national categories. Yet the understandings of what is 'public' and 'private' in much of IP law discourse have remained rooted at the national level. The result is a dissonance of legitimacy between a transnationally enforceable IP legal structure and its justification based on 19th century concepts of sovereignty, colonisation and industrialisation.

The history of TRIPS, including the de-facto impracticability of Art. 31 bis, has shown that its institutional design has not exactly been a level playing field from the start, favouring certain multinational corporations over others. We can currently observe the unequal effects of such a legal institutional design in the pharmaceutical industry's resistance to any compulsory licensing, to the C-TAP and the TRIPS IP waiver proposal. They clearly illustrate that, private interests hosted by a minority of nation-states are pitted against the global majority public health interest.

Therefore, we ought to go back to the initial motivation that legitimised patent monopolies in the first place and conceive the notion of a public clearly as a global public, and not a national one. If TRIPS is the legal architecture that underpins the ability to extract monopoly rent on a global scale, then by the same token, transnational patent law needs to serve a global public's interest.

Lastly, the public interest in rewarding 'inventions' is often erroneously conflated with 'innovation' as a desirable good. For example, the term "technological innovation" has been included as TRIPS' objective in Article 7 of the TRIPS Agreement, albeit with a caveat that it should be of mutual benefit to producers and users of "technological knowledge". Although much of intellectual property offices', media and pharmaceutical industry's PR communications assume that they are interchangeable notions, inventions, patents and innovations are not the same. The belief in 'patents equal inventions equal innovation' is rather a myth, as economic historical research has been inconclusive as to the benefits of patents until to date.

[GHF] You have also spoken about how "the entanglement of governments with university science-entrepreneurs, venture capitalists and preferred industrial champions, further complicates the notion of what is 'public'." Can you elaborate on this?

[HYK] The notion of 'public' is used by a variety of actors with different interests without asking: who does the 'public' include, who does it exclude? Are governments acting in the best interest of their citizens?

Sciences are implicated in the erosion of the notion of 'public' since at least the Bayh-Dole Act 1980, but the relationship between sciences and various industries stretches back to the 19th century [Historians of science, such as Ilana Löwy and Jean-Paul Gaudillière, have written about this, as have historians of chemistry, such as Ernst Homburg and Carsten Reinhardt]. Publicly funded universities and public research organisations are avid users of the intellectual property system, as recent European Patent Office analysis of pharmaceutical patent applications has shown. As much of their interests are monetary in nature now, university sciences, both fundamental and applied, cannot be necessarily understood as pure or public without qualifications: the high profile CRISPR patent dispute involved scientists, universities or public research institutions, and their spin-offs.

In my *Critical Legal Thinking* piece, I also explained the patent interests of Oxford University and their scientists. These existed prior to Gates' push for an exclusive contract with AstraZeneca, and it is not entirely accurate to portray the university scientists as the innocent victims of commercial influence. There are, of course, some exceptions to this by now unfortunately normalised figure of the 'scientist-entrepreneur,' as Steven Shapin has called this persona in his 2008 book, "The Scientific Life". I am thinking about Katalin Karikó who has been instrumental in inventing the mRNA technology. The pressure exerted on scientists by the university administration to apply for patents is also not negligible, and the problem of private profit motives pervading underfunded public universities is a complex one.

In relation to a government's public duties, the pandemic has laid bare how particular, private and corporate interests have permeated what ought to be essentially public processes and decision-making power beyond an advisory capacity. For example, in the UK, the Johnson government has favoured certain private actors under the guise of having no time for public procurement processes during a pandemic. Some journalists have argued that it was such 'VC thinking' that has led to the UK's vaccine success. The UK 'vaccine tsar', Kate Bingham, is a venture capitalist who has expressed that her vaccine procurement responsibility was 'outside' of politics ("Politics is separate"). In a recent FT interview, she claimed such VC thinking entailed that government could not afford to be "penny pinching," even if it was public money that she was spending. What is interesting is that the government, or the civil service, is regarded to have no capacity to direct and shape the process of vaccine manufacturing and distribution, whilst being expected to give a carte blanche. In other words, it is asked to pay and shush.

Some US patent academics had, moreover, argued on social media that more financial incentives should be given to pharmaceuticals by the government to scale-up vaccine production. Yet the COO of BioNTech stated on German TV that it was not the lack of financial incentive that made the scaling up of vaccine production difficult at the moment.

What this pandemic has demonstrated very clearly, is that we need to strengthen public sector capacity after years of austerity rather than diminishing it. This will reduce the present dependency on corporate actors. Also, governments and their officials need to negotiate harder on the public's behalf instead of accepting without question financial sector mentality in which maximising profit margin is the rational thing to do. Such a mentality forgets that it is the taxpayers' money, not their own, that they play with. The public underwrites all risk whilst the financial gain is all private and distributed among a small number of shareholders or corporate owners.

Without wishing to diminish the exceptional advances in vaccine development that we have seen in the past year, it is equally important to remember the extraordinary mobilisation of public funding into medical research and supplies which has been unprecedented in our lifetime.

It seems therefore odd and disproportionate to me that there doesn't seem to be a single contract in the UK or US, in which a government has taken co-ownership of a vaccine patent or receives future royalty, precisely because the vaccine development efforts were headed by a venture capitalist or a former pharmaceutical executive who would normally demand such returns on their investments. Beyond this incongruence, there is the fundamental political question if the government should act like a venture capitalist, at all (for example, the UK government runs the biggest venture capital fund in Europe which has received little scrutiny and is also reported to have taken a stake in Vaccitech, the Oxford University spin-off behind the Oxford/AstraZeneca vaccine.) Alternative ways to balance public and private interests could be through IP restrictions on certain subject matters, national compulsory license legislation, and the enforcement of price ceilings on publicly funded inventions, but it will also be interesting to think about higher taxation on IP rent income.

[GHF] Some believe that IP is not a barrier for medicines during the pandemic. Particularly with respect to vaccines. It has been suggested that the TRIPS waiver will not sufficiently address access barriers to vaccines or wider medical products. (Since the waiver itself will not force technology transfer.)

[**HYK**] The TRIPS waiver proposal does not only comprise patents, but also copyright, industrial design and important-ly, undisclosed information, such as trade secrets, in relation to the fight against Covid-19. Trade secrets are also part of IP. They are especially relevant in relation to Pfizer because it has decided to keep its vaccine manufacturing know-how secret.

Some argue that waiving patents is not sufficient because the knowledge-transfer and sharing of know-how are needed. This is certainly true, and because of the low standard of the disclosure requirements in different national patent laws: the disclosed inventive information in patent documents is often woefully insufficient to be used as a "recipe" or for reverse en-gineering. That is also why analogising patents with recipes and copies is not accurate.

Yet I find the arguments advanced against the waiver pro-posal claiming that as "patents are not the problem" disin-genuous because, even if know-how was shared, tech was transferred, and a vaccine was developed, it would be illegal to produce it without a license, if the substance, its parts, or its process of manufacture, remains under patent protection. The patent holder would continue to hold the power to block vaccine production, regardless of existing or shared expertise and capacity. This is not a good way of clearing all barriers for scaling-up vaccine production in a global pandemic. The IP waiver is therefore necessary as an integral part of a con-certed effort to share know-how and scale up production. We need the waiver to end the pandemic instead of prolonging it through artificial scarcity. Both IP waiver and tech transfer need to go hand in hand.

For example, the pharmaceutical lobby and the Gates Foundation have argued that it is not IP that stands in the way of scaling-up vaccine production. Turning their argument on its head, we may ask why they are defending IP so much if it does not matter so much. If they are not the problem right now, then why not waive the IP rights temporarily? It seems to me that they are fighting so vehemently against the IP waiver because patents enable monopoly power and accompany a future profit pipeline of a huge global market desperate for the vaccine.

From a purely financial perspective, it is not in the vaccine makers' and their shareholders' interest to end the pandemic as soon as possible. Even though policy makers and governments are reluctant to push the pharmaceutical players too hard, the pharmaceutical industry, universities and their technology transfer offices will not self-regulate and voluntarily open license their patents through C-TAP or share their know-how in the latest announced WHO Technology Transfer pool, precisely because it is contrary to their rational commercial self-interest to do so. In my view, there must be both a carrot and stick approach towards the vaccine makers to change their present course. This could include the introduction and implementation of national compulsory license measures.

[GHF] You have said: "An analysis of vaccine nationalism also ought to take into account the history of international capitalisation of knowledge via intellectual property." How do you see this "capitalisation of knowledge" play out in the future with respect to say biological resources and digital health?

[HYK] I don't think I can answer the question about biological resources and digital health accurately without looking more into detail into the main issues and players in these fields, but in relation to the latter we will see an increasing overlap of copyright and patent law issues because the key value driving digital health will be access to datasets for pattern recognition and correlation tracing. The current debates about privacy, social media and regulation of AI are instructive for digital health. Like internet companies, the valuation of digital health companies will be data and computing-capacity driven.

The role of IP law in the capitalisation of knowledge is that it creates a link between knowledge and speculative value through a legal monopoly right.

In a way, this is nothing new. Intellectual property rights have always acted as currencies of international trade (chemical patents in the 19th century, for example), and have been hence nationalistic instruments of trade policy. For example, it is interesting to read patent statistics against the background of different trade dynamics at a given point of time. When you examine patent office rhetoric and self-presentation, you will notice how often they invoke nationalist rhetoric of economic greatness or competitiveness.

It is also nothing new that academic or university sciences have been implicated in industrial policy since the 19th century, which in turn shaped the foundations of modern patent law in particular. Historians of science, science studies scholars, and myself from the patent law side, have studied the different phases and modalities of co-option of science into industry.

What has been novel since roughly the mid-1990s is the pursuit of IP as not only monopoly for extracting monopoly rent in a commodity market, so via monetisation, (this is the case presently in the Covid-19 vaccine oligopoly),but using IP as a financial tool: either to raise more equity or as technique of financial arbitrage. I have analysed the financialization of patents as assets. The financial forward-looking, speculative function of IP is reflected in the total reversal in the proportion between physical and intangible asset value in the S&P 500 index between 1975 and 2017. The last forty years have been characterised by increasing financialization of knowledge-making and uses via IP, both through copyright and patent laws. Nowadays inventions, IP and innovation are routinely misleadingly conflated, and this is in part driven the patent offices' rhetoric itself which equates more IP with more innovation. Patents are seen as a key asset in the so-called "knowledge economy" of disruptive innovations. In turn, knowledge enclosures create new forms of colonial dependencies, as we observe now in this current pandemic.

As much of the current financialised economy rests upon monopolies that are enabled through intellectual property law, unless health data and knowledge about them are safeguarded through privacy or other right-based measures, they will become as monetised and financialised as any other data. If they concern matters of global public health, IP rights will again stand in way of health equity. I can only hope that we will learn the lessons of this pandemic.

15.
LIKELY GREEN SHOOTS EMERGE AMID STALLED TALKS ON THE TRIPS WAIVER PROPOSAL (APRIL 22, 2021)

TRIPS COUNCIL INFORMAL MEETING: APRIL 22

Even as the on-going deadlock among countries, seemed to effectively stall any progress on the TRIPS waiver discussions among WTO members at an informal meeting of the TRIPS Council meeting on April 22, there is a possibility that coming weeks could see a push towards an "outcome" that could concretely address the pandemic using elements suggested in the proposal.

Sources familiar with the discussions told Geneva Health Files that there are potential "green shoots" emerging in the context of the TRIPS Waiver talks towards "an outcome". A diplomatic source noted the softening position of the United States during the discussions in recent weeks and at the meeting.

"If the United States eventually agrees to text-based discussions, the opposition to the waiver might implode and could possibly lead to an inevitable compromise," a source said on the condition of anonymity.

It is understood that United States and Australia, were open to further discussions and are examining the relationship between the obligations of the TRIPS Agreement and the limitations of vaccine production and delivery. Sources said that these members are willing to find ways to facilitate the transfer of manufacturing know-how and capacity necessary to produce vaccines.

To be sure, the meeting saw WTO members differing on the fundamental question of whether, and to what extent, intellectual property protection represents a barrier to the access for medical products for the pandemic. [See submission by the co-sponsors in response to questions and concerns raised by delegations: (IP/C/W/674) and previous submissions (IP/C/W/672 and IP/C/W/673)]

The proponents of the waiver proposal are now working on a revised draft that focuses on a list-based approach, that enumerates on several products essential to address the pandemic including vaccines, diagnostics and therapeutics. If and when the proposal progresses to text-based talks, this list will be negotiated between WTO members.

It is also understood that based on consultations with other WTO members, the potential time during which a potential waiver can be in force could be of a minimum duration of at least five years. This can be reviewed by the General Council, sources said. The time will be a function of the prevalence of the pandemic across the world as determined by technical agencies including WHO.

Sources also do not rule out a political declaration to clarify some of the rules on the applicability of the provisions of the TRIPS agreement in the coming weeks and months. WTO members are likely to consider any such declaration to be taken up at the Ministerial Conference later this year.

Bilateral consultations are expected to continue heading into the formal TRIPS Council meeting on 30th April. It is also understood that TRIPS Council Chair Ambassador Dagfinn Sørli of Norway acknowledged the urgency of the situation and recognized the need for an "urgent outcome".

Despite ostensible unflinching positions of certain countries opposing the waiver, aided by media, the proposal continues to gather political support. Sources suggested potentially more WTO members becoming co-sponsors in the coming weeks. (Maldives and Fiji have now also become co-sponsors).

Sources also said that while showing readiness for engagement in further discussions, the European Union, the UK and Switzerland reiterated that "undermining or upending intellectual property rights is a no-go as they represent a major contribution to expanding production of COVID-19 vaccines."

Members will now discuss a text circulated by the Chair on a draft oral status report to the General Council. This will be formally adopted at the TRIPS Council meeting on April 30th, and to be submitted to the General Council at its meeting on May 5th-6th.

16.

THE WTO BECOMES THE NERVE CENTER FOR PANDEMIC RESPONSE (MAY 7, 2021)

In the late evening of the 5th May, here in Geneva, the international trade community was jolted from its end-of-the-day fatigue with the news of the US support to the waiver of intellectual property protection for COVID-19 vaccines. While the news was cheered among the global health community that has long faced the spectre of vaccine shortages and rising deaths from COVID-19, it perplexed the trade lawyers. After all, in one stroke, the US had upended its long-entrenched position on the primacy of the protection of intellectual property, in the 25 plus years of the existence of the TRIPS Agreement.

Irrespective of the outcome and the intent of the move by the USTR, this is quite clearly a watershed moment, going beyond mere political symbolism.

"That the US has opened the door to even discuss a proposal that seeks a blanket waiver on intellectual property protection, is unprecedented. This opens possibilities to negotiate," a trade official said.

Clearly, the disruption caused by COVID-19 is evident, not only in the crematoria and even streets in India aglow with the incessant funeral pyres, but it has also surely disrupted diplomacy in both trade and health circles. Trade sources familiar with the discussions at WTO told Geneva Health Files that they learned of the announcement from the USTR, "like the rest of you", said one official.

The 'twitterati' in global health that comprises experts, academics, activists and journalists dispersed globally, were abuzz with excitement, microblogging their thoughts on the development late into the night, here in Europe.

AN EARLY WIN FOR NGOZI OKONJO-IWEALA?

The way this announcement was made reveals a new way of back-room diplomacy at WTO that caught even insiders off-guard, and it possibly underscores a win for the new DG Ngozi Okonjo-Iweala.

"It is hard to imagine that the WTO DG did not know well in advance that this announcement was coming," one official said on the condition of anonymity.

In hindsight the meeting last month, convened by DG Okonjo-Iweala on April 14th, that saw manufacturers and some WTO members engage in discussions on ways to address vaccine shortages, seemed to have spurred more engagement and might have pushed members to find solutions. For one, it certainly revealed the existence of spare manufacturing capacity that could be exploited to meet production shortages highlighted by the DG and others in recent weeks.

At the time, this "activist" role of the DG to play a deliberate role in bringing members and the industry together was criticised by some. But now, the convening powers of the WTO DG, some would say, has already yielded results. "The DG can rightfully claim that she pushed the discussions towards finding a solution, including getting members around the table for text-based negotiations on the TRIPS waiver. It is becoming clear that some members look up to her," one Geneva-based trade official said.

While many of us might have been caught off-guard by this unexpected change of stance from the US government on the waiver proposal, others argue that the signs were there to see.

The statement by USTR on April 14th, on the eve of the meeting with manufacturers, where Ambassador Katherine Tai referred to "market failure" of the industry was a distinct signal, some say. In addition, the discernible change in position was noticed as the discussions on the waiver progressed across informal and formal meetings of the TRIPS council over seven months. From outright opposition, the tone gradually transitioned into a more accommodating one indicating a willingness to engage in discussions, sources present in these consultations told Geneva Health Files.

Sources also said that the DG had been pushing for members to come together for text-based negotiations for the TRIPS waiver proposal first submitted in October 2020 by South Africa and India (IP/C/W/669). She believes that the only way these divergences between members will be resolved is through sitting down for text-based negotiations, official said. "It is very likely she knew about the US position, without which she would not have pushed for text-based negotiations," one source said.

A day before the USTR announcement, DG Okonjo-Iweala told WTO members at the General Council meeting, "I am firmly convinced that once we can sit down with an actual text in front of us, we shall find a pragmatic way forward, acceptable to all sides that allow the kinds of answers that our developing country members are looking at with respect to vaccines, whilst at the same time looking at research and innovation and how to protect them."

In a briefing at WHO earlier this week, where Gordon Brown, former Prime Minister of the UK, spoke on financing issues to address the pandemic, he clearly emphasized the change in position on the waiver in many countries.

THE BREAKING OF THE DAM: WHAT NEXT?

The US move itself is being seen as a culmination of a variety of forces coming together from high level political support from former leaders, Nobel laureates, to entire regiments of civil society activists the world over, pushing for a dialogue on ways to lift barriers due to protections on intellectual property, and on trade secrets, copyrights and others, that have been found to impinge on faster and equitable access to medical products needed to quell the pandemic.

It is also important to note the significant counter-offensive launched by lobby groups on either side of the Atlantic and elsewhere, to fight the TRIPS waiver proposal in Washington DC, Brussels and Geneva. (See The Commission's pharma echo chamber: from Corporate Europe Observatory)

Despite the wave of optimism that this change of position of the U.S. has generated, there is recognition on the uphill battle that is to follow in bringing on board other WTO members including the European Union, the UK, Canada, Switzerland, Japan and others opposed to the proposal. Further, the actual process of negotiations, redefining the scope of the original proposal in a way that attracts consensus of all members will be a long-drawn negotiation, experts say.

In recent days, WTO officials emphasised the importance of consensus-driven decision-making at WTO and the difficulty in launching negotiations among its members at the rule-making organization.

(Some experts believe that this could be problematic. Writing in Politico, on the USTR announcement, Germán Velásquez, Special Adviser, Policy and Health at the South Centre said. "Another troubling element is the reference to the "consensus-based nature of the institution. "This is a clear message to those countries dared to hope the decision would be decided by a vote, at the WHO or elsewhere. This is not the first time that the U.S. has used the concept of "consensus" to basically give itself a veto...")

A number of countries hitherto, opposed or uncommitted to support the proposal have since articulated a perceptible change in position including Norway, China, New Zealand and others, based on public statements in their reaction to the announcement by the U.S., and those made at the General Council meeting in WTO this week.

Even as pressure is building up within the European Union and on the European Commission, it will be important to see how the biggest European countries, including Germany which has voiced its disagreement with the Biden administration on the waiver proposal, will coalesce around a common position at the WTO.

Even before the US announcement, WTO officials had noted the shared objective among WTO members to ramp up production of vaccines. In a briefing this week, they had articulated that a proposed revision of the waiver suggested by South Africa and India, had generated optimism and that it was likely to have even broader support. The waiver proposal already has 60 co-sponsors and increasing willingness and support from other members.

"Many members believe that addressing the pandemic is one of the most important challenges facing WTO today," a WTO official told journalists. As many as 42 delegations took the floor on the waiver proposal at the General Council meeting this week.

The co-sponsors of the proposal will share a revised text this month. The next TRIPS Council meeting is scheduled for June

8th-9th. The co-sponsors hope that the text-based negotiations will be undertaken in good faith.

While many actors in global health quickly applauded the US support for negotiations on the proposal, some clearly also demanded that the waiver must be accompanied by agreements on technology transfer to ensure production of vaccines.

"An important component, alongside the waiver of intellectual property rights, will be the transfer of technology, so that manufacturers can receive the know-how to scale up production quickly. This equally applies to therapeutic products such as monoclonal antibodies, which could be an important tool in the COVID-19 response," Unitaid said in a statement this week.

WHO AND THE TRIPS WAIVER
With the US support to the negotiations on the TRIPS Waiver, the World Trade Organization will become the nerve centre of the international response to the pandemic over the coming weeks and months.

As the leader in responding to this international health emergency, WHO stands vindicated with the US position on the waiver. DG Tedros has peppered his weekly briefings and numerous public statements unflinchingly calling for the need for the IP waiver.

What is important to note, the Gates Foundation, one of the traditional donors of WHO, has hitherto stood, in direct opposition to the idea of sharing technology to boost vaccine production. The donor is also a part of the technology transfer hub that is underpinned by the model of bilateral arrangements to address production shortages. Following the USTR announcement, the Gates Foundation reversed its stance on the issue. (In an interview, less than two weeks ago, Bill Gates had said, that vaccine recipes should not be shared.)

This dissonance in one of WHO's most important donors, of course, has not stopped DG Tedros from supporting the waiver, even as the expense of taking a stand against those WHO member states who oppose the waiver proposal at the WTO.

On other trade measures for addressing the pandemic:

Calling vaccine policy as economic policy, DG Okonjo-Iweala suggested that members must share vaccines through the COVAX facility or other mechanisms. She added that "Those who have raw materials should allow these to flow through supply chains so that all who can manufacture can take advantage of this."

On exports restrictions and supply chains she said, "When we listened to manufacturers at the 14 April event that many members have referred to, it was clear that we need to be mindful to the issue of allowing supply chains to work. Otherwise, no matter what capacity we have we will still not be able to manufacture what is needed."

On working with manufacturers to mobilize existing capacity, she said, "We heard from countries like Pakistan, Bangladesh, India, South Africa, and so on, Indonesia, Senegal, that there is some existing capacity that can be turned around in some months to be able to allow us to manufacture the kinds of doses we may need to go from the 5 billion doses produced in the world today to the 10.8 billion being forecast for this year to 15 billion, in particular if we need booster doses."

"Countries like Russia, China, Brazil, Cuba, who have vaccines under development or who are already sharing their vaccines with others, should look at ways to boost supplies so we can increase the volume of vaccines in the world. Those who need to get Emergency Use Authorization from the WHO to enable access to their vaccines should do so", Okonjo-Iweala said.

TAIL PIECE [circa 2003]:

We asked WTO officials on the significance of this moment in the context of the new support from the US towards negotiations on the waiver proposal, especially in comparison with 2003, which was the last time a waiver was introduced in WTO.

("In August 2003, WTO members agreed to remove an important obstacle to affordable drug imports: they waived the limitation in the TRIPS Agreement to predominantly supply the local market when generic medicines are produced under compulsory licence," WTO explains. Subsequently in 2005, it was agreed that this decision would be permanently incorporated into the TRIPS agreement, an amendment which finally took effect in 2017)

This week, Keith Rockwell, director information and external relations at WTO shed light on the events surrounding the 2003 waiver decision in comparison to discussions today:

"...The provision from 2003 [was for] in cases where there is no domestic production capacity, [the question was] can developing countries import certain drugs. They were specifically named to be for malaria tuberculosis and HIV AIDS.

At that time, the United States was the only country that was objecting and as you know, [the WTO] it's a consensus-based system. So, they were holding it up. There was quite a lot of pressure on the US. It was the summer before the Cancun ministerial meeting and there was a meeting, a Saturday meeting of the General Council when the US joined the consensus. I remember it very well... The situation then was also different in that the drugs that were being considered for generic production had been under production for some time and there was capacity in place. It was a question mostly of ensuring that there was confidence on the part of developing countries that they could partner with someone else elsewhere if they lack the capacity themselves. So that's what that was all about.

What what's happening today is different because it is a waiver of the TRIPS agreement beyond patents, it deals with trade secrets, it deals with trademarks deals, with the production of ventilators and other diagnostics, and therapeutics... anything that can be used to combat the pandemic.

What we have seen today is and I would characterize the mood as being very different. I think I said yesterday that the discussions were quite constructive clearly, there is change in the atmosphere. It does not guarantee that there's going to be agreement but without this kind of change, an agreement would not be possible. We don't tend to come up with agreements by magic. These agreements tend to arise when we have when we have a text from which to negotiate.

You are seeing very clearly in fishery subsidies... a much better atmosphere, and much more traction in the talks, because of the text coming out last summer. So that's an example.

[On TRIPS waiver] So there has been a text, it was not accepted, it wasn't just the US. That's an important thing to say it other countries.... Brazil, Switzerland, Norway, Singapore and others. So that's a big difference right there.

What would happen next is...depends very much on what happens with the revised text. That [revised] text from South Africa and India not clear when it's coming up...there have been calls for there to be an informal meeting of the trips Council in the latter part of this month at which, perhaps this new text could be unveiled and discussed.

And then you have pledges from the United States, an obviously important player in the WTO context who says they will sit down and negotiate and New Zealand said that too. So, once you sit down and start negotiating, there's all manner of possibilities that could emerge. But it's a very different, very different dynamic to what we had at that time [2003].

PART III:
A COUNTER-PROPOSAL TO THE TRIPS WAIVER – THE EU'S IDEA ON TWEAKING COMPULSORY LICENSING (JUNE- OCTOBER 2021)

When you can't beat them. Join them. And that's what the EU did. In a bid to stop the original TRIPS waiver proposal in its tracks, the EU brought a smaller, less ambitious proposal to tweak the existing system on compulsory licensing. While this was laughed off by activists and proponents of the proposal, ultimately the EU had the last laugh, 20 months down the line. What was essentially adopted in June 2022, drew its roots to the EU proposal was pitched as an alternative to the TRIPS waiver proposal, which it was not.

17.

TRIPS TALKS: WTO MEMBERS INCHING TOWARDS NEGOTIATIONS ON THE WAIVER (JUNE 11, 2021)

After months of pushing for a blanket, time-bound, waiver on intellectual property protections to effectively address the pandemic, South Africa and India joined by more than 60 co-sponsors of the TRIPS Waiver proposal, finally managed to get the WTO membership to agree to talk text.

Members will convene at an informal meeting on 17 June to assess how they can move forward ahead of General Council meeting in July.

Notably, UK, Switzerland, EU, Korea, remain opposed to the waiver proposal.

As many as 48 delegations took the floor this week, during the TRIPS Council formal meeting.

Members are expected to consider both competing proposals going forward – the revised text proposed by South Africa and India, and the one filed by the EU on June 4, 2021.

During the meeting, the Chair of TRIPS Council, Norwegian Ambassador Dagfinn Sørli reportedly said, "While diverging views persist, I have not heard any objections to take our deliberations to another level by engaging in a text-based process." He added that intense negotiations are expected over the coming six weeks.

He has suggested that the goal will be to agree on a report in time for the next General Council meeting scheduled for 21-22 July.

Members have been asked to engage directly with each other in addition to multilateral meetings - under the responsibility of TRIPS Council Chair, sources said. "Quasi-daily" meetings were also suggested.

Tanzania for the African Group, Chad for the LDC Group, Mongolia, Malaysia, Fiji, Egypt, Pakistan, Sri Lanka, Indonesia, Bangladesh, Bolivia, Venezuela, Paraguay, Maldives, Argentina, Nepal, Jordan, Vanuatu, Mozambique, Angola, Philippines, Jamaica, Peru, Vietnam, expressed support for the waiver proposal.

The United States, Australia, Canada, New Zealand, Ukraine, Brazil, Norway, China and Chinese Taipei – endorsed the move towards text- based discussions.

In addition, Turkey, Chile, Singapore, Russia, El Salvador, Hong Kong and Mexico said they were ready to engage but asked for further clarifications on the proposal.

On its part, EU said it will discuss its own proposal and "announced its intention to follow up with a more elaborated text". The EU is also expected to continue discussing the waiver proposal.

Diplomatic sources affiliated with the co-sponsors of the proposal, said that the EU proposal was not comprehensive enough. They pointed out that the EU must formally submit the proposal to the membership of the WTO.

Sources said the South Africa and India have substantial support from WTO members. "This support cannot be wished away" the source said.

"It will be important to conclude the negotiations before the end of the summer, given the urgency. Failing that, it will be important make good progress before the General Council meeting in July," a senior trade source in Geneva said.

In its communication to the WTO General Council, the EU suggested a draft declaration in addition to its alternate proposal focusing on compulsory licensing.

However, the co-sponsors of the Waiver proposal are clear that they are pushing for a draft decision on the TRIPS waiver. A declaration on the overall response to the pandemic from the WTO, is separate and will be necessary, trade diplomats believe.

"We must see how far the EU wants to go with this. We cannot talk about the trade element without addressing the fundamental supply issues for vaccines, therapeutics and diagnostics," a developing country diplomat told us.

"Because of political pressure, unfortunately countries will continue to import export restrictions. Trade restrictions will continue as long as supply-side challenges are not dealt with. If you're serious about solving the situation you must address the supply issues otherwise will only be dealing with the symptoms and not the problem itself," the source added.

Meanwhile the European Union and the United States are planning on working on a manufacturing and supply-chain task force to address the pandemic. (Not clear how this fits in with a similar initiative at COVAX)

"The United States has not addressed the question of treatments for the pandemic in its statements. It will be interesting to see how United States and others will address the question of treatments given that their own domestic policies have taken a holistic view of addressing the pandemic."

Co-sponsors acknowledge the impetus generated by the US support for text-based negotiations. "We would not be here without the U.S. So, we will have to find a way to agree on text," a developing country official said.

No one expects these coming weeks and months to be straight-forward. Red lines will emerge as members divulge their true positions and interests during these up-coming negotiations. Some observers even expect the EU's alternate proposal to effectively undermine the TRIPS waiver proposal. However, there is a strength in numbers, which might make it difficult to reverse discussions on the waiver proposal. (After all, the European Parliament has also lent its support for negotiations on the waiver.)

Not only will the coming weeks be decisive in addressing the pandemic, but it is also a significant moment in the history of the WTO. No matter the outcome, these developments have inevitably opened the door for looking at the TRIPS Agreement afresh, experts believe.

18.

THE EU'S PUSH FOR A DECLARATION AT THE WTO (JUNE 22, 2021)

raft General Council Declaration on The Trips Agreement and Public Health in The Circumstances of A Pandemic Communication from The European Union to The Council For TRIPS

Follows up from EU's earlier submission. The crux is the focus on compulsory licensing:

"We agree that:

a. *A pandemic is 'a national emergency or other circumstances of extreme urgency' within the meaning of Article 31(b) of the TRIPS Agreement. For the purposes of issuing a compulsory licence pursuant to Articles 31 and 31bis of the TRIPS Agreement, a member may waive the requirement of making efforts to obtain authorization from the right holder, provided for in Article 31(b).*

b. *In the circumstances of a pandemic and to support manufacturers ready to produce vaccines or medicines addressing the pandemic at affordable prices for low- and middle-income countries, a Member may provide, for the purposes of determining the remuneration to be paid to the right holder pursuant to Article 31(h) and paragraph 2 of Article 31bis of the TRIPS Agreement, that the remuneration reflects the price charged by the manufacturer of the vaccine or medicine produced under the compulsory licence.*

c. *In the circumstances of a pandemic, for the purposes of Article 31bis and paragraph 2.c) of the Annex to the TRIPS Agreement, the exporting Member may provide in one single notification a list of all countries to which vaccines and medicines are to be supplied by the exporting Member directly or through indirect means, including international joint initiatives that aim to ensure equitable access to the vaccines or medicines1 covered by the compulsory licence. It shall be presumed that such joint initiatives supply those vaccines and medicines to eligible importing Members within the meaning of paragraph 1.b) of the Annex to the TRIPS Agreement."*

(It is understood that, in the circumstances of the COVID-19 pandemic, COVAX is an international joint initiative within the meaning of this paragraph.)

EU Submission on WTO General Council, June 21, 2021

See also our **earlier story** which talks about how the goals of a declaration is different from the objectives of the on-going TRIPS Waiver negotiations.

19.

WHY THE SCOPE OF THE TRIPS WAIVER IS CRUCIAL TO ADDRESS THE PANDEMIC? (JUNE 18, 2021)

Tough start to the negotiations on the TRIPS Waiver. Countries remain divided but agree to engage. The U.S. does not commit to a deadline to reach decision on TRIPS Waiver talks

In today's update on the TRIPS Waiver talks, we look at the informal meeting among WTO members on June 17 where countries agreed on a roadmap for the negotiations. We also look at the substantive elements in the revised proposal and the procedural aspects to this discussion.

For this story, we had extensive interviews with diplomatic sources to get as accurate an understanding as possible on the unfolding discussions.

UPDATE: JUNE 17 INFORMAL MEETING AT THE WTO

The process to begin negotiations on the TRIPS Waiver, got off to a difficult start this week, when WTO members met informally on June 16, but agreed on a plan to engage on text-based discussions on the proposal.

Sources familiar with the proceedings of the meeting were of the view that there is no consensus on the waiver approach to address the pandemic, among WTO members.

While countries have accepted to engage in negotiations, fundamental differences remain on how to ensure access to COVID-19 medical products.

"While members may consider engaging in text-based negotiations, they will have clear red lines they will not cross. Also, publicly they do not want to be seen as the players blocking negotiations irrespective of their real intent," a source familiar with trade diplomacy said.

Although members remain divided on fundamental questions, they agreed to a schedule of meetings over the next six weeks to discuss waiver proposal. The agreed calendar includes a combination of open-ended meetings and bilateral consultations. The open-ended meetings are scheduled for June 24, June 30, July 6, July 14, July 20. On July 20, members will meet formally to agree on a report to the General Council. The General Council meeting is on July 27-28. Sources said that there was an alleged resistance to open-ended meetings on the part of a few countries including the US and the UK.

The bilateral meetings to discuss the revised waiver proposal have started among WTO members.

Leading up to June 30, TRIPS Council Chair, Norwegian Ambassador to the WTO, Dagfinn Sørli will invite members in "smaller configurations" for substantive discussions. Sources said that countries will have time to engage with each other and consult with capitals during the course of these negotiations.

The Chair also said that additional, new proposals are expected, and asked delegations to submit them for consideration by the broader membership at WTO. He also underlined that these discussions were not without reservations and asked some members "not to fool themselves into thinking that substantial differences have evaporated". The Chair reportedly also said that his role would be to facilitate a process to get members to find common ground.

Sources told us that "As the TRIPS Council chair, he has the discretion to conduct these negotiations."

Members were asked to engage on substance. "Focusing procedure will not force consensus", the Chair reportedly cautioned.

While more than 20 delegations took the floor, South Africa suggested beginning discussions on product scope as discussed in proposal. The U.S. is, however, opposed to this approach on discussing the scope of proposal, wants to begin discussion with common objectives instead, according to trade sources in Geneva.

It is understood that members will first discuss the scope of the proposal (the kinds of TRIPS provisions and types of products) of proposed waiver by South Africa-India. The duration and implementation will be discussed at later.

The meeting also witnessed pressure from some developed countries to discuss the EU proposal alongside South Africa – India proposal. At the meeting, South Africa insisted that these two proposals should be considered separately on parallel tracks. The EU proposal, which is being adapted to a legal format, is expected to be discussed on June 24. (The EU is asking for a ministerial declaration)

Countries also see the discussion around the EU proposal as an opportunity to highlight and address the limitations of the TRIPS flexibilities including the use of compulsory licensing.

THE AMERICAN POSITION

The U.S. has said that it is not in favour of a Chair-led process and wants it to be a member-driven process instead. In its view, a Chair-led process "has shown to be a failure in every instance where it has been tried in the WTO." While emphasizing a consensus-based outcome, the U.S. said that it is not committed to any timeline. Sources said that the US has stressed "it has not accepted any end date for this or any conclusions".

Expressing its reservations on beginning the negotiations with the scope, the U.S. said, "...without a clear chair objective is a recipe to engage in circular process that does not go anywhere. For the US, it is worth spending a bit more time on what is the end goal and what is the timeline and the urgency with which members must move. Some of the current proposals could be very expensive and unfold over the course of 5-10 years and the US has a much different timeframe for what a solution would look like. That is an important factor before we jump in and get tangled up in scope," the US delegate is reported to have said.

THE SUBSTANTIVE ISSUES AT STAKE

As countries begin to map interests and chart the contours of their flexibility, some positions are already emerging, such as the US support for discussions limited to vaccines. It is not entirely clear whether, for example, they will be open to discussing all kinds of IP protection and not only patents. This has not been clarified. Whether they will be funding, or simply donating doses, or how they would facilitate tech transfer and create capacity in the rest of the world, is not clear yet.

"It is very clear that the Americans want a narrower discussion and they always emphasize this issue of finding a solution and essentially finding a zone which would attract consensus."

It certainly does seem that this support from the U.S., for these discussions, is intended to counter the vaccine diplomacy because of Chinese influence, now that India is mired in domestic response to the pandemic, a trade source said.

Similarly for the co-sponsors of the proposal, accepting a limited scope is a potential red line, diplomatic sources indicated. These include the scope of the kinds of IP rights and the types of products. Depending on how the discussions evolve, these elements will be debated and negotiated.

Vaccines, therapeutics, and diagnostics, among other products continue to remain in scarce supply. This is even as Africa battles a third wave of COVID-19. Given the scarcity, the importance of the waiver has never been starker, the source said.

THE IMPORTANCE ON THE SCOPE OF IP PROTECTIONS

In their many statements since submitting their proposal in October 2020, proponents have argued that COVID-19 medical products and technologies straddle across various kinds of IP protection, from patents, trade secrets to copyright. And therefore, collectively waiving these, could effectively address the pandemic, they have said.

Among other examples, experts suggested the example of track and trace technology, backed by a database. "Such a technology would be protected by copyright, trade secrets and patents. An algorithm underpinning such a contract tracing technology could be IP protected", an expert affiliated with the proponents of the proposal said. In their communications, co-sponsors have cited the example of text and data mining.

In many instances copyright protection interacts with, patents, undisclosed information, or trade secrets, to create barriers to access, experts say.

"Many companies are offering to not enforce patents, because, there is huge value in undisclosed information. If you really think of it as an iceberg that tip of the iceberg would be patents. The rest would be you know undisclosed information including confidential information protected by contracts or trade secrets – essentially the glue that makes the recipe work," a diplomatic source pointed out.

There has been a shift in the way companies to protect their IP, not through disclosures in patent filings, but by protecting these by way trade secrets and private contractual obligations. Therefore, limiting the scope to patents alone, will not suffice, sources familiar with the discussions say.

So, in the context of the EU proposal that seeks to limit the approach to the use of compulsory licensing, it is not clear, for example whether such licenses can be used to access trade secrets. Using compulsory licenses to get around patents itself, has been difficult, fraught with negotiating political pressures. Proponents believe that there should be greater clarity on how such TRIPS flexibilities can apply.

THE WAIVER AS A PEACE CLAUSE

Observers point out that countries could have trouble agreeing to provisions in the waiver proposal that prevent countries from bringing in disputes against WTO members in the context of implementing the waiver. Diplomatic sources suggest that the waiver could operate as a peace clause, where countries are protected from disputes for not enforcing IP laws when the waiver is in force.

"The waiver does not become mandatorily applicable when it is passed. It must be drawn into national jurisdictions. There is a lot of flexibility on how this can be used and implemented across countries," a source explained. (Therefore, countries who do not want to implement the waiver, will simply have to notify to the WTO, similar to previous waivers such as the paragraph 6 decision of 2003)

Every country will have different needs according to manufacturing capacity or lack thereof.

"It is important to look at different categories and not only concentrating on the products, but also the method, the means, the components – all aspects of the production. Countries have varying needs and roles in these supply chains, so a waiver can effectively deal with both the final product and the intermediary stages," the source clarified.

WHAT TO EXPECT

If the first meeting to kick off these negotiations are any indication, this is going to be a long-drawn-out fight. While the proponents and the TRIPS Council chair were keen to finish the bulk of the negotiations ahead of the summer break in Geneva before August, it appears, the U.S. and others might have a different schedule in mind.

"The report that will be submitted to the General Council will need to strike a political balance that may be hard to achieve, a trade official said. The aim may be to have a tangible outcome in time for the ministerial later in the year. It is important that the General Council be given a sense of progress at the July meeting now scheduled on the 27th-28th," a Geneva-based trade official told us.

It is an ambitious schedule, but if there is political will, this can be done. There is a lot of pressure on members to deliver an outcome, not only from their domestic constituencies, but also from WTO DG Ngozi Okonjo-Iweala, the source added.

20.
TWEAKS TO COMPULSORY LICENSING: EU AT THE WTO (JUNE 25, 2021)

The TRIPS Council had an informal meeting on June 24, to consider EU's proposal on an intellectual property response to the pandemic. This proposal, narrower in scope, competes with the revised TRIPS Waiver initiative, first proposed by South Africa and India.

The proposal titled "Draft General Council Declaration on the TRIPS Agreement and Public Health in the Circumstances of a Pandemic" seeks to facilitate the use of current compulsory licensing provisions in the TRIPS Agreement. We discussed this in an earlier edition this week.

The reforms EU suggests include fast-tracking procedures for the use of compulsory licensing, also for exports. It seeks to provide greater certainty on fair and transparent remuneration for rights holders, the EU said. In addition, it aims at streamlining notification procedures in the context of compulsory licensing.

Sources said that EU highlighted the merit of its proposal since "it could be adopted swiftly as it does not aim at amending but at clarifying certain provisions in TRIPS Articles 31 and 31 bis (on the use of a patent without the authorization of the right holder), and paragraph 2.c of the Annex of the TRIPS Agreement (on notification procedures)."

The EU has reportedly said that its proposal would not entail "lengthy debates or procedures" because the scope of these provisions would remain the same. In addition, potential legal uncertainties about their application would be removed, the EU said.

While "welcoming" EU's proposal, the United States, Singapore, Australia, Colombia, Chile, South Korea, Switzerland, and the United Kingdom also sought clarifications on it.

The delegations of South Africa, India, Tanzania, Indonesia, Nigeria, Bolivia, Pakistan, Namibia and Zimbabwe wanted to understand how existing provisions in the TRIPS agreement will actually result in ensuring an increase in the production of COVID-19 medical products and their access.

It appeared that countries were more willing than before to consider both the proposals - the EU and from South Africa-India, in the on-going text-based negotiations at the TRIPS Council, according to a trade official in Geneva.

21.
TRIPS TALKS: INTERVIEW WITH JOÃO AGUIAR MACHADO, EU AMBASSADOR TO THE WTO (JUNE 29, 2021)

A s WTO members continue to negotiate on ways to stream-line, adapt intellectual property rules in the response to the pandemic, we bring you this timely interview with EU's ambas-sador to the WTO, João Aguiar Machado. He discusses the different strands in the EU's overall strategy on trade and health at the WTO in the context of this health emergency. Later this week, members head to an informal TRIPS Council meeting on 30 June to discuss South Africa-India's TRIPS Waiver proposal and elements of the EU's alternate proposal.

[GHF] 1. Can you explain how the three different suggestions articulated by the EU, in its communication to the WTO General Council (June 4, 2021), will come together? These include: a WTO framework on trade and health, the draft Declaration on Trade and Health and a proposal on the approach to compulsory licensing.

We all agree that the common global objective in this pan-demic is equitable access to COVID-19 vaccines and treat-ments. It is certainly a top priority for the European Union (EU). We already see incredible progress in the total global produc-tion of COVID-19 vaccines with more than 10 billion doses due to be produced by the end of 2021. For comparison, the total global output of all vaccines before COVID-19 was only 5 billion doses. However, further ramping up the production and, most importantly, ensuring equitable distribution of COVID-19 vaccines remain very essential priorities in the fight against time in this pandemic.

Setting up and ramping up the production of vaccines is a highly complex process which requires adequate facilities, trained personnel, know-how, raw materials and other inputs. It is a complex issue that cannot be solved by one simple solution. The overall strategy is not only within the WTO. The WHO, other organisations, institutions and initiatives –such as the COVAX Facility – are working on these solutions. Members of the WTO must collectively find ways to address the current delays and shortages in vaccine production to the extent that is possible in the WTO framework.

We have essentially two strands of work in the WTO: on the one hand, the proposal from several like-minded members (Ottawa Group) for a Trade and Health Initiative. On the other hand, the specific debate on intellectual property issues related to the proposal by India, South Africa and others to waive the Agreement on Trade-Related Aspects of Intellectual Property Rights (TRIPS) and the recent EU proposal on optimising the use of licencing flexibilities provided in the TRIPS agreement. It is now time to work on all these issues with urgency for a final comprehensive solution on health.

More concretely, the co-sponsors of the Ottawa group Declaration on Trade and Health are discussing in particular trade facilitation and production expansion through collaboration. As the vaccine production scale-up is related also to a smooth functioning of the supply chain, the EU proposed that this aspect is also discussed in the context of the Declaration on Trade and Health. The intention is to revise the current draft Declaration and to incorporate elements of the EU's Communication to the WTO General Council. At the same time, the intellectual property strand is being dealt with in the TRIPS Council. Our objective is that these strands of work form a basis for a general understanding on health in the WTO General Council, at the upcoming WTO 12th Ministerial Conference.

[GHF] 2. The EU proposal to the TRIPS Council has focused a lot on compulsory licensing. What is the EU's position on other aspects of South Africa-India proposal including on copyrights and trade secrets as barriers to equitable access?

The EU proposes to the WTO a comprehensive approach addressing trade issues related to the actual bottlenecks that affect the manufacturing speed and the fair supply of vaccines and medicines in the current pandemic. The component on compulsory licensing as proposed for discussion at the TRIPS Council is thus only one element of this comprehensive approach. We consider that intellectual property plays an important role as an enabler that contributes to our overall objective of ramping up production of COVID-19 vaccines and medicines. However, it is not and should not be a barrier to achieve this objective. We have been clear that in a global emergency like this pandemic, if voluntary licensing fails, compulsory licensing is a legitimate tool to scale up production. Therefore, we propose to clarify and simplify the use of compulsory licensing in times of a pandemic.

If we examine how intellectual property can enable the production of vaccines or medicines, the focus is primarily on patents. We believe that a debate on the entire intellectual property system will only delay urgently needed action. Moreover, the intellectual property framework is already a system of checks and balances. There are relevant exceptions that could be used about every intellectual property right, be it copyright, design, or protection of undisclosed data. Moreover, we must be realistic as to what can be achieved with the proposed lifting of the Members' obligations under the TRIPS Agreement. For example, in case of trade secrets, waiving Article 39 does not grant access to companies' confidential information. It only removes certain minimum remedies against a misappropriation of that information.

[GHF] 3. The proposal by the EU recognizes the "urgent challenge" to ensure a rapid and equitable roll out of vaccines and therapeutics – but the proposal does not mention diagnostics. Can you elaborate why this is so?

The ongoing discussions concern the whole spectrum of essential medical goods, diagnostics tools being one of them, even if the EU Communication to the WTO focuses specifically on vaccines and therapeutics. The availability of safe and effective COVID-19 vaccines and therapeutics is now the main global priority that needs to be addressed urgently.

Diagnostic tools of course remain important for containing the pandemic. When we speak about "medicines" in the EU proposal to the TRIPS Council as regards the facilitation of compulsory licences, diagnostics as well as therapeutics fall under that term. We are looking forward to discussing the EU proposal with other WTO members and will certainly be open to clarifying the text as necessary.

[GHF] 4. Some critics are of the view that the EU communication at the WTO is more driven by protectionist industrial policy than motivations to safeguard public health. How would you respond to that?

On the contrary, the EU's commitment to the global efforts of equitable access to vaccines and therapeutics against

COVID-19 cannot be put in doubt. Just to recall that the EU is a leader when it comes to deliveries of effective vaccines to the rest of the world. By now, over 350 million doses have been exported out of the EU to the rest of the world. This equals around half of the production in the EU. We are also a major contributor to the COVAX Facility.

As already noted, the WTO can and must contribute to delivering equitable access to vaccines and medicines in this pandemic, but this complex issue needs to be addressed comprehensively. This is the reason for the EU communication. It seeks to be as concrete as possible and identify which actions should be taken. The EU proposal is very much driven by the need to ensure equity in the distribution of vaccines. While the production of COVID-19 vaccines has been increasing significantly, their distribution across the regions of the world remains unbalanced. The WTO can certainly act and ensure that this objective is unimpeded by trade barriers.

[GHF] 5. How will the EU reconcile its opposition to the TRIPS waiver proposal led by South Africa and India, with the support for this proposal by the European Parliament?

The Commission has carefully analysed the resolution of the European Parliament (EP). The resolution reflects a mix of positions expressed in the EP. The Commission is in full agreement with the EP that intellectual property is an enabler rather than a barrier to vaccines availability.

The Commission also shares the view of the EP that the proposal for an indefinite waiver as proposed in the WTO would pose a significant risk to innovation and research. At the same time, the EP calls on the Commission to support text-based negotiations for a temporary waiver of the TRIPS Agreement that aims to enhance global access to affordable COVID-19-related medical products.

The Commission has engaged in all strands of work and continues to be engaged in the text-based process that has been launched in the TRIPS Council. The EU proposal submitted to the TRIPS Council on 21 June 2021 is a significant step in that direction and a constructive contribution to the debate, as underlined by several other WTO Members. While the TRIPS waiver proposal and the EU proposal represent different approaches, they seek to address the same issue of the availability of COVID-19 vaccines and medicines.

[GHF] 6. How will the 1 billion dose vaccine donations announced by the G7 affect the negotiations at the WTO? Will it ease the public and civil society pressures for a sweeping waiver of IP?

Indeed, total G7 commitments since the start of the pandemic provide for a total of over 2 billion vaccine doses, with the commitments made since February 2021, including the last meeting in Carbis Bay, providing for 1 billion doses over the next year. To that, we should add the pledges of Pfizer/BioNtech, Moderna and Johnson & Johnson to provide 1.3 billion does of vaccines to low- and medium-income countries at cost or at lower prices respectively by the end of 2021. We should not forget the EU's massive financing of the COVAX Facility to help deliver vaccines where they are most needed. Finally, we have predictions of the manufacturing capacity reaching around 10 billion doses by the end of 2021. These are all causes for cautious optimism and indications that our efforts are paying off. Of course, that does not mean that we should not try to produce more – and hence our proposal to the WTO on how to increase production, ensure well-functioning supply chains, etc.

At the same time, we must also look at the future. The crisis has demonstrated the importance of diversifying and enhancing the resilience of global value chains. Therefore the

EU and its Member States – or "Team Europe" - committed to supporting the vaccine production in non-EU countries. The crisis opened a window of opportunity for Africa and Europe. During the G20 Global Health Summit in May 2021, President von der Leyen announced a Team Europe initiative on manufacturing and access to vaccines, medicines and health technologies in Africa. Through this initiative, Team Europe will help create an enabling environment for local vaccine manufacturing in Africa and tackle both supply and demand side barriers. It will serve to complement existing efforts. As a first step, the initiative will be backed by EUR 1 billion from the EU budget and European development finance institutions, such as the European Investment Bank.

[GHF] 7. What according to the EU will be corners of a compromise as far as the waiver proposal is concerned? Will it the compulsory licensing approach as suggested by the EU?

The EU is engaging in the text-based process constructively to find a way forward in this discussion on the role of intellectual property in enhancing access to affordable COVID-19 vaccines and medicines. The objective is to proceed with concrete, pragmatic short- and medium-term solutions to enhance universal access to COVID-19 vaccines and medicines at affordable prices.

We would like to emphasize again that the EU considers that only a multi-pronged approach addressing the identified bottlenecks such as limited manufacturing capacity and access to raw materials can bring about a real change. Intellectual property is only a part, and not the key part, of the solution.

The EU is ready to continue discussing the revised TRIPS waiver proposal although we are not convinced that the broad waiver as proposed is the best immediate response to the reach the objective of the widest and timely distribution of COVID-19 vaccines that the world urgently needs. Therefore the EU included in this discussion a different and more targeted approach focusing on facilitating the use of compulsory licensing, in other words how the flexibilities in TRIPS can be used to waive certain protections.

This approach can bring legal certainty to Members that are ready to produce COVID-19 vaccines and medicines based on compulsory licences and to those that would be interested to import those. WTO Members should try to progress on this approach because it can bring solutions quickly. We hope that we will be able to convince Members that our approach, including the components that will be addressed in the General Council, represents the best way for an effective and pragmatic short-term response to the crisis.

22.

COUNTRIES WRESTLE WITH REGULATORY DATA, TRADE SECRETS AND TECH TRANSFER: TRIPS WAIVER DISCUSSIONS AT THE WTO (JULY 9, 2021)

A s countries get deeper into discussions on how a potential waiver of certain obligations of the TRIPS agreement can be implemented, they are beginning to engage with the question on how the implementation of such a proposal can look like at the national level.

Even as a small group of countries including the EU, UK, Switzerland, among others continue to remain entrenched in their positions, unconvinced that a temporary suspension of intellectual property rules will help address the pandemic effectively, in general, the WTO membership continues to clarify certain questions in the on-going negotiations unfolding at the bilateral level and in wider consultations over the last few weeks.

Countries have also been addressing specific elements including the ways to improve access to regulatory data, trade secrets during these past few days. Enabling technology transfer is also emerging as a significant issue among members as they find ways to boost production to address current shortages in the production of medical products for COVID-19.

UPDATE FROM THE TRIPS COUNCIL MEETING: JULY 6

On July 6, WTO members met informally at the TRIPS Council meeting. The meeting reviewed the progress made by small group consultations among countries on July 5.

Countries have been discussing issues of duration and implementation of the waiver proposal.

Sources said that South Africa and the EU had differing perceptions of the progress made in these small group consultations. While South Africa is more upbeat about these discussions, and the EU "has no reason to be optimistic", according to trade sources in Geneva familiar with the discussions.

While South Africa believes that despite continuing divergence of views, members "finding each other", the EU is of the view that discussions confirm the great concern of a number of delegations on the TRIPS waiver. The EU has said that countries need to be "clear-eyed" and pragmatic if they want to move "fast".

UK, Switzerland, Japan, Norway and Mexico are of the view that a lack of common ground shows that there is no consensus on the TRIPS Waiver.

India was of the view that although some members have favoured the text-based negotiations, it is not clear whether some countries have the real intent in advancing these discussions.

The chair of the TRIPS Council, Ambassador Dagfinn Sørli of Norway, said WTO members discussed how the termination of a potential waiver could take effect. Countries discussed the proposed annual review of a potential waiver and how that is linked to the duration of its intended operation.

Sources also said that WTO members have questions on the implementation of the waiver. Chair Sørli indicated that these issues will need greater consideration by countries. A small group consultation convenes today on July 9, to specifically discuss implementation issues with respect to the waiver.

United States wanted to know how the existing waiver proposal fits in with the provisions articulated in the Marrakesh Agreement Article IX (4) that suggests the requirement of a termination date for a waiver.

"A decision by the Ministerial Conference granting a waiver shall state the exceptional circumstances justifying the decision, the terms and conditions governing the application of the waiver, and the date on which the waiver shall terminate. Any waiver granted for a period of more than one year shall be reviewed by the Ministerial Conference not later than one year after it is granted, and thereafter annually until the waiver terminates. In each review, the Ministerial Conference shall examine whether the exceptional circumstances justifying the waiver still exist and whether the terms and conditions attached to the waiver have been met. The Ministerial Conference, based on the annual review, may extend, modify or terminate the waiver."

Marrakesh Agreement Article IX (4)

South Africa clarified that the proposal is to look at a minimum duration of three years three years from the date of the decision. And that the waiver would not automatically terminate after three years but needs to be reviewed by the General Council factoring in prevailing circumstances. Vaccination rates and effectiveness of vaccines, among other factors, could contribute to such an extension, South Africa has argued.

The U.S. has largely been "subdued" in these discussions without revealing much, sources were of the view. One developing country diplomat told Geneva Health Files that the U.S. has been "clever" in not saying much, but the diplomatic source expected greater engagement with the U.S. at a bilateral level.

Members are also discussing in greater detail the impact of protected regulatory data and trade secrets. Countries raised questions on "how the impact of disclosure of data during the waiver period could be limited."

In addition, there is an emerging view in the context of these discussions that tech transfer is key to alleviate current production shortages. Some observers believe that it moves these discussions in a tactical way towards *the third way* suggested by WTO DG Ngozi Okonjo-Iweala. (The WTO and WHO will reportedly have a closed-door meeting with the industry on July 21.)

The EU believes that the waiver proposal works against addressing tech transfer by introducing legal uncertainty. Pakistan has asked EU to come up with a text-based proposal on technology transfer in a way that goes further than merely reiterating available provisions in the TRIPS Agreement.

Next informal TRIPS Council Meeting July 14, and formal meeting on July 20. General Council meeting on July 27-28 to take up report on the waiver proposal. Countries need to agree on the text of such a report.

TRADE SECRETS, REGULATORY DATA AND THE WAIVER DISCUSSIONS

The EU proposal that discusses ways to improve the implementation of compulsory licenses - although limited to patents - is potentially opening the door for a wider discussion on using this approach to also talk about undisclosed information, sources involved in the discussions at WTO told Geneva Health Files.

While the TRIPS agreement does not explicitly prohibit the issuance of compulsory licenses for trade secrets, there is no mechanism that governs this, a trade law expert said.

Several countries have domestic legislations to protect undisclosed information including trade secrets such as the EU's directive on the protection of trade secrets and American laws to protect trade secrets. Countries are now discussing what the suspension of the protection of trade secrets because of the waiver could mean. Prevailing laws that protect trade secrets, seek to discourage "unfair competition". However, during a pandemic, public non-commercial use trumps these concerns, experts say.

Supporters of the waiver proposal, see undisclosed information as key to enabling access to information that could speed up the production of medical products including vaccines.

Access to regulatory data, a kind of undisclosed information, has now assumed importance in these negotiations.

The TRIPS Council chair has proposed that members address regulatory data in their consultations. Proponents of the proposal have been keen to include trade secrets in the waiver proposal, to address the question of regulatory data. But countries are also keen to understand the implications on protected information such as regulatory data in the context of the duration of the waiver, and what such disclosures would entail.

"Making regulatory data available to a third party would be breaking into a new ground. It is important that exclusivity rights around such data be relaxed to enable resulting production and exports," a diplomat involved in the discussions said. The issue of the treatment of regulatory data in the context of the waiver, should be addressed in a way that allows generic producers to access this information, without having to go through lengthy processes including reverse engineering products, the source explained.

Under these conditions, governments should also exercise caution in ensuring that such undisclosed information is used responsibly and with confidentiality. Conditions for public non-commercial use, or government use are already specified in current rules. "If the requirement is for commercial use, patent holders could expect reasonable royalties typically 2%-4% of the price on generics," the source suggested.

The discussions around temporary suspension of the protection of trade secrets will be far from straight-forward. Trade secrets have become far more critical in protecting rights of producers than mere patents, legal experts believe.

In his interview, Ambassador Machado clarified, "...we must be realistic as to what can be achieved with the proposed lifting of the Members' obligations under the TRIPS Agreement. For example, in case of trade secrets, waiving Article 39 does not grant access to companies' confidential information. It only removes certain minimum remedies against a misappropriation of that information."

THE TECH TRANSFER "GAUNTLET"

It has long been acknowledged that by itself the waiver will not enable technology transfer. Countries are now discussing what measures can be taken to enable technology transfer in the context of the waiver.

The proponents are keen on having a focused discussion on technology transfer within the specific rules of the TRIPS agreement. Article 39 of the agreement sets out rules to effectively protect against unfair competition and how countries must protect undisclosed information.

See below what Article 39.3 of the TRIPS Agreement says:

Section 7 TRIPS Agreement: protection of undisclosed information

Article 39.3:

Members, when requiring, as a condition of approving the marketing of pharmaceutical or of agricultural chemical products which utilize new chemical entities, the submission of undisclosed test or other data, the origination of which involves a considerable effort, shall protect such data against unfair commercial use. In addition, Members shall protect such data against disclosure, except where necessary to protect the public, or unless steps are taken to ensure that the data are protected against unfair commercial use.

Proponents of the waiver proposal believe that legitimate public purpose that needs to be serviced is not in opposition to unfair commercial use.

It is not clear yet, how the EU sees the issue of technology transfer in the context of these discussions. The proposal by the EU centres around Article 31 of the TRIPS Agreement.

QUESTIONS ON THE IMPLEMENTATION OF THE WAIVER

Undoubtedly the question of implementation will dominate discussions as these negotiations progress. Naturally, approaches that push for continuing with existing rules in the light of perceived implementation challenges will also gain consideration.

In his interview to Geneva Health Files, the EU ambassador to the WTO, João Aguiar Machado said, "....the intellectual property framework is already a system of checks and balances. There are relevant exceptions that could be used about every intellectual property right, be it copyright, design or protection of undisclosed data...."

Critics of the waiver, for example have also questioned what they refer to as "assumed limitations" in the existing rules - that the use of TRIPS flexibilities are cumbersome. The issuance of compulsory licenses, for example, is restrictive because it needs to be done on a case-by-case basis. Some critics have questioned it.

Governments are already empowered under existing rules to issue government use orders, they point out. (Article 31 [b] of the TRIPS Agreement)

FOR, AGAINST AND THE SPACE IN BETWEEN

A Geneva-based trade expert we spoke with sought to highlight the implementation concerns that some WTO members have raised.

"It seems that one has to be in one of the two camps. Either you are for the waiver in that you believe that this is beyond business as usual. Or you are of the view that intellectual property is important for innovation and we need incentives. But there is a huge amount of territory between these points that has not been explored. Many member governments have questions on implementation. Many are not aware of the potential that exists in the current legal framework," the official added.

Using existing mechanisms that allow governments to override intellectual property considerations and then using the waiver are not mutually exclusive. One paves the way for another, the official said.

Geneva-based trade experts highlighted what they think are "misconceptions" in these discussions. One that existing rules may not be sufficient in addressing the pandemic. "This is unfortunate, because a huge amount of work has been done since the Doha Declaration," an expert said on the condition of anonymity. And second, that a waiver under the WTO agreement, will somehow remove pressure or obligations of the member governments. "A waiver by itself will not free up the transfer of technology. All that the waiver will do is give governments wider latitude than they already have under existing rules," the expert added.

"It is not as if the chair of the General Council can bring down the gavel and suddenly 164 member countries do not have to implement their contractual obligations," the expert said. The influence that the WTO and the TRIPS agreement can have, is quite modest, the expert was of the view.

It could be quite complicated to "work out things domestically" to implement the waiver, the expert cautioned. "What is more difficult: using existing rules, or suspending obligations? Politically it is not going to be easy for countries to implement the waiver," the person cautioned. The implication on investment treaties, because of the waiver will be an important consideration for countries, for example.

Supporters of the proposal are of the view that potential implementation challenges are not insurmountable given the diverse legal systems in countries and the flexibility that the proposal provides.

"Any short-term legal uncertainty will barely make a dent on the billions in profits that drug companies are making in the context of this pandemic," a source pointed out.

LDCs & THE WAIVER

Emphasizing the importance of existing rules, critics who see little use of the waiver also point out how LDCs have no obligations under the TRIPS agreement.

One expert cited the example of Bangladesh that has no obligations under the TRIPS agreement, since it is classified as a Least-Developed Country, suggesting that there are few restrictions on Bangladesh for example, to use existing rules.

However, others point out that even to produce medical products, Bangladesh would need raw materials – in this case Active Pharmaceutical Ingredients. A waiver would help countries like Bangladesh to import APIs. Without a waiver,

Bangladesh would not be able to export medical products if the said formulations are protected by patents, for example.

"The TRIPS Waiver could allow LDCs to sell their products in the markets of countries that implement the waiver. Generic therapeutics or vaccines can reach non-LDC markets that implement the waiver," an expert who advises developing countries in Geneva explained to us.

HOW TO READ THE PROGRESS ON THE NEGOTIATIONS

Proponents of the waiver believe that they have managed to change the narrative on the discussions around intellectual property, also noting the recent 301 Special Report from the United States Trade Representative (USTR).

No matter where one stands on the waiver, there is a growing recognition that countries may be able to come up with a compromise on a proposed solution. How deep the compromises will be on either side, the coming weeks will reveal.

"I do not think anyone is trying to game the system", a Geneva-based trade official said.

"If it is about taking practical action, get on with it. Do what is possible under existing rules, and if it does not work, bring the waiver," the official added.

Some countries are positive about wrapping up the bulk of the negotiations in time for the General Council meeting at the end of July.

"The wind is filling up our sails" one developing country diplomat summed up.

Despite the optimism, these discussions are now getting into "crunch-time". It may be wise to be cautiously optimistic about the distance that multilateralism in trade can travel under the existing circumstances.

23.
EXCLUSIVE: CONFIDENTIAL COMMUNICATION ON THE TRIPS WAIVER SHOWS THE EU'S UNWILLINGNESS TO NEGOTIATE (JULY 16, 2021)

When the European Commission presented a proposal in June 2021 laying out its strategy on the role of intellectual property in addressing the pandemic, critics were quick to conclude that it was an effort to undermine the TRIPS waiver. Yet, many diplomats at the WTO hoped to engage in what they call "good faith negotiations". Internal communications suggest this may not be the case.

A confidential communication sent by diplomats of a Western European Country in June 2021, has come to light that illustrates the EU's stated reluctance to negotiate the waiver proposal. Experts suggest that it also reveals the problematic ways in which the European Commission - mandated to negotiate on trade matters at the WTO - interprets a recent resolution of the European Parliament that supported text-based negotiations on the waiver proposal.

The waiver proposal submitted in October 2020 by South Africa and India, revised in May 2021, seeks a temporary suspension of IP rules under the TRIPS Agreement at the WTO. Proponents of the waiver believe that this will boost the production of COVID-19 medical products and will help in addressing what has now become "a two-track pandemic".

This story analyses this internal communication and seeks to understand what this means for the on-going TRIPS waiver negotiations. Geneva Health Files has reviewed it and confirmed its veracity from multiple sources. The text of the document was originally conveyed in a European language. The excerpts cited here is based on translation.

The EU's reluctance to negotiate the waiver is well-documented over the last few months, but to read in print about its intentions on pushing its alternate proposal and a reluctance to negotiate on the waiver, is nevertheless striking.

We also have an update on the TRIPS Council Informal meeting (July 14) that discussed the waiver proposal, where members are veering towards seeking additional time from the General Council to discuss this further.

WHAT THE CONFIDENTIAL COMMUNICATION FROM JUNE 2021 REVEALS ABOUT THE EU POSITION

Two key issues emerge from the confidential communication: one, is that it appears the EU does not want to negotiate the text of the waiver proposal; two, the interpretation of the European Parliament's resolution on the waiver discussions.

ON THE EU'S RELUCTANCE NEGOTIATE THE WAIVER

Following a meeting of the TRIPS Council on June 17, a communication sent by Western European diplomats described the EU's objective towards the waiver discussions.

[GC is WTO's General Council; EU DEL is the EU's Delegation to the WTO]

"The objective for the EU was not to negotiate the waiver, but to initiate discussions on our proposal and in this context the EU is ready to commit. According to EU DEL, the EU succeeded in this: the EU proposal is an alternative to the waiver, which the EU is willing to negotiate, but not the waiver. The EU

is not sure that India and South Africa will be willing to accept this," the communication said.

[Translated] Confidential communication sent by Western European Diplomats

It goes on to add that:

"The objective of the EU currently is that both the European proposal and the waiver are treated simultaneously to determine which approach will best increase production. However, the EU must submit a text proposal for this, which is now given the highest priority"

"...Like-minded countries welcome our proposal and are seen by a number of them as a way out of the current impasse. It is clear that the EU will have to take the lead on this."

A month later, it appears the EU has already achieved this objective. Not only is the EU proposal being discussed in the context of the TRIPS waiver, but it also has the support of countries including the US and others, who have welcomed "pragmatic" proposals. [Switzerland, Mexico, Norway, United Kingdom, Chile, Singapore, among others have tended to side with the EU in recent weeks during these discussions.]

Further, the communication notes:

"The chairman's objective is to have decisions [in time for] the GC, but that does not seem realistic to EU DEL."

It is referring to the Chair of the TRIPS Council, Norwegian Ambassador to the WTO, Dagfinn Sørli.

(See below *Trade & Health Update*: WTO members are now seeking additional time from the General Council during its meeting later this month, to discuss the waiver further)

Reflecting on the TRIPS Council meeting on June 17, the communication also notes that:

"...Putting certain provisions on paper does not automatically lead to a consensus. There are still substantial differences of opinion between the Members for the time being.

...About his role: the chairman contributes to reaching a substantive consensus through a balanced approach. Continued debate about the procedural approach does not contribute to a solid substantive consensus. An agreement must now be reached on the procedural approach to the waiver in order to reach a consensus on the content."

Confidential communication sent by a Western European Diplomat

In several consultations and meetings since June 17, the EU has consistently stated that fundamental questions on the use of a waiver approach to address IP issues in the context of the pandemic continues. Sure enough, differences among members continue. However, it is also important to note that South Africa, a key proponent of the waiver views the progress in these discussions differently. South Africa and the EU have differed in the way they perceive emerging consensus or the lack of it, in the course of these discussions on the waiver.

THE COMMISSION'S INTERPRETATION OF THE RESOLUTION OF THE EUROPEAN PARLIAMENT

A small group of experts who are aware and have seen the communication, raise a key concern described in this diplomatic text.

They express concern on the role of the European Commission - which negotiates intellectual property issues on behalf of EU member states at the WTO - in interpreting the recent resolution of the European Parliament.

The translated communication says:

"...Regarding the resolution EP, the EU delegation found that there was contradiction in the text: on the one hand it calls for text-based negotiations on the waiver, on the other hand a waiver of indefinite duration is rejected. In the Commission's view, the EP's resolution supports the Commission's position on most points. Moreover, apparently an MEP pressed the wrong button during the vote on the waiver, so that there is no majority for the waiver within the EP, according to the Commission. Commission asked Member States to support its reading of the EP resolution."

Confidential communication sent by Western European Diplomats

However, experts have challenged not only the "apparent contradiction" in the text of the resolution, but also the process of voting as discussed in this communication.

(See also: statements by João Aguiar Machado, EU Ambassador to the WTO in an interview with us, a few weeks ago on the interpretation of the EP resolution)

We spoke with Kathleen Van Brempt, Member of European Parliament, from the Group of the Progressive Alliance of Socialists and Democrats in the European Parliament. She elaborated on the voting process and the significance of the resolution.

In a comprehensive response to our queries, she told Geneva Health Files:

"The final text of the resolution was carried by a near 100 vote majority, which makes the Parliament's support for constructive and text-based negotiations for a temporary waiver unquestionable. The idea of an unlucky vote on one paragraph is, in this sense, ludicrous. It is also not in accordance with the spirit of the text, which repeatedly confirms support for a temporary waiver. In the beginning, for instance, the resolution states that the temporary waiving of IPR protection obligations for COVID-19 related medicinal products, medical devices and other health technologies is one of the important contributions to global equitable access.

The Commission's efforts to discredit an official position of the European Parliament shows how much of an issue it is for them that the executive's strategy was not supported by the EU's elected representatives. This spinning does not add to the Commission's credibility and will lead to inter-institutional friction if they are not careful. The Commission, of course, has an autonomous mandate to act on behalf of the EU, but its position should be informed by the Council and Parliament. The Council, so far, has failed to take a clear position vis-à-vis a waiver. But the Parliament gave a clear mandate, and this should weigh into the discussions now.

I also would like to say that members of the European Parliament have been voting remotely during the pandemic. It is not possible to "push the wrong button".

All the voting lists are vetted by the legal services of the European Parliament before distribution. If one amendment passes, the other amendments that are in contradiction with that text automatically fall. This ensures that contradictory votes in one text are not possible.

The waiver should be a contribution to this pandemic and be separated from discussions on intellectual property rights during normal times. That is a clear position. Personally, I believe that the discussion on the effectiveness of compulsory licensing for countries that do not have production capacity should go beyond the pandemic, but this has nothing to do with a waiver.

RESPONSES TO THE CONFIDENTIAL COMMUNICATION FROM THE EU DELEGATION TO THE WTO

To protect sources, we are unable to reveal the identity of the diplomats or the specific information which identifies this specific communication. We reached out to the EU delegation to the WTO in Geneva seeking clarifications on the said communication.

We wanted to know whether the EU delegation was indeed not in favour of negotiating the text of the waiver and if it will limit itself to its alternative proposal, as suggested by this confidential communication.

A spokesperson from the EU's delegation to the WTO told Geneva Health Files:

"The EU is not commenting on leaked documents and even less so on alleged third-party reports of what a Commission official speaking informally may or may not have said."

An official position of the European Commission on the issue of the TRIPs waiver discussions was stated as follows:

"In relation to the broad waiver proposed by several WTO members, the European Commission, while ready to discuss any option that helps end the pandemic as soon as possible, is not convinced that this would provide the best immediate response to reach the objective of the widest and timely distribution of COVID-19 vaccines that the world urgently needs. The EU's proposals to WTO (4 June) aim at achieving that objective in a swift and effective manner.

- We would need to have more information to assess the US position and how it compares to the proposal already made by India and South Africa at the World Trade Organization.

- The priority for the EU is to ramp up production of COVID vaccines to achieve global vaccination. The EU is at the forefront of deliveries of effective vaccines to the rest of the world: so far, more than 500 million doses have been exported outside the EU. As many as have been delivered to Europeans (by mid-July).

- In the short term, we maintain that it is key for all vaccine producing countries to allow export immediately and to avoid measures that disrupt the supply chains.

- Vaccine production requires complicated biological processes, involving know-how, technology, skilled personnel and infrastructure. It is not by simply waving intellectual property rights that safe and effective vaccines can be produced, but rather by collaboration between those that have the knowledge and those that have the capacity.

- If voluntary solutions fail and intellectual property becomes a barrier to treatments or vaccines against COVID-19, the necessary mechanisms are already available under the TRIPS Agreement. This is why the EU presented specific proposals on how to facilitate the use of compulsory licencing in the context of a pandemic. This is a practical response to the specific concerns related to potential difficulties for making use of this existing TRIPs flexibilities.

- The EU is engaged in a text-based process in the TRIPs Council to ensure that the IPR regime supports efforts to enhance access to COVID-19 vaccines and therapeutics.

- This is also why Europe committed EUR 1 billion to create with our African partners and our industrial partners manufacturing hubs in different regions in Africa."

THE EUROPEAN PARLIAMENT'S RESOLUTION ON THE TRIPS WAIVER

On June 10, members of European Parliament, supported discussions towards the temporary suspension of IP rules for COVID-19 medical products. The resolution won the majority of the votes. (See: *European Parliament resolution of 10 June 2021 on meeting the global COVID-19 challenge: effects of the waiver of the WTO TRIPS Agreement on COVID-19 vaccines, treatment, equipment and increasing production and manufacturing capacity in developing countries.)*

While the resolution recognized voluntary licensing as a key tool, it also cautioned against an "indefinite waiver" of IP rules that could risk innovation.

However, this comprehensive resolution acknowledges and refers to key elements in these discussions including the TRIPS waiver proposal; the Doha Declaration on the TRIPS Agreement and Public Health; the exemption given to Least Developed Countries on pharma patents under the TRIPS agreement; the statement of US Trade Representative of 5 May 2021 affirming support for a temporary TRIPS waiver; the open letter from 243 civil society organisations to the WTO Director-General on access to medical products; the COVID-19 Technology Access Pool (C-TAP) spear-headed by Costa Rica among others.

The EP resolution clearly calls for "support for proactive, constructive and text-based negotiations for a temporary waiver of the WTO TRIPS Agreement, aiming to enhance global access to affordable COVID-19-related medical products and to address global production constraints and supply shortages."

THE ROLE OF EUROPEAN COMMISSION AND WHY IT IS IMPORTANT

Experts believe that this communication also potentially brings into focus a wider question - the ability of the European Commission to inform EU member states adequately and accurately on trade policy issues.

Dimitri Eynikel, an advocate with the Access Campaign at Médecins Sans Frontières (MSF) in Brussels, told us:

It is unacceptable that the European Commission is misleading the EU member states on the position of the European Parliament on the TRIPS waiver. The resolution supporting the waiver was unquestionably supported and adopted by a broad cross-party majority.

The European Commission also reiterates the views of a few hardliners in parliament that refuse to accept the outcome of the vote. This does not represent the views of the other parties and MEPS that spent weeks informing themselves and weighing their position on the issue. From a democratic perspective it is a very problematic practice.

The resolution mentions support for the negotiations on the waiver on two occasions. The resolution may not be perfect, but it is not contradictory. It calls for the consideration of all options including the waiver. While the resolution does caution about the impact of an indefinite waiver, it is does support a temporary waiver. The WTO TRIPS waiver proposal is a proposed as a temporary measure.

I think it is time for the member states to take their own responsibility in keeping themselves informed, as this incident puts into question whether the Commission can be trusted to provide reliable information to member states. All this on a matter that is highly important and sensitive in and outside the EU.

Dimitri Eynikel, MSF to Geneva Health Files

Recent discussions suggest the MEPs are not happy with the way TRIPS Waiver discussions are going on.

WHAT DO WE EXPECT FROM THE TRIPS WAIVER NEGOTIATIONS?

In the weeks to come, while we are likely to see a continued push back from some countries including the EU, the proponents of the waiver proposal, buttressed by the support from more than 60 other co-sponsors will no doubt engage bilaterally and address concerns of the wider WTO membership. (See update below)

Although the discussions on the waiver are likely to be dragged on in the TRIPS Council in the months ahead, there is also pressure on the WTO DG, Ngozi Okonjo-Iweala and the institution itself to deliver on this matter.

MEP Van Brempt, told us, "The European Parliament asks in its resolution to establish a WTO Trade and Health Committee during Ministerial Conference [MC12] to draw lessons from the pandemic, make proposals to increase the effectiveness of the WTO response during international health crises and to prepare a trade pillar for an international pandemic treaty. The WHO is already doing such an exercise – why should the WTO stay behind?"

Notwithstanding, the wider efforts of the EU on trade and health initiatives to address the pandemic, in the context of the Ministerial Conference, its opposition to the waiver approach remains a critical stumbling block at the WTO, where decisions are mostly subject to consensus of all its members.

It is very likely that the impetus for consensus will entrench status quo.

Earlier this week, we asked Germany's health minister Jens Spahn, how Germany reconciles its leadership in global health with its opposition to the TRIPS waiver. Spahn said that the need for additional vaccines can be met by companies co-operating to produce more. "We don't need the burden of an ideological debate on intellectual property for this", he added.

24.
THE EU SEEKS TO STEER TALKS AWAY FROM THE TRIPS WAIVER PROPOSAL (JULY 30, 2021)

Calling the crucial discussions on the TRIPS Waiver as a "stalemate", the European Union this week, urged the WTO membership gathered for the General Council meeting, to consider its "pragmatic", albeit, watered down proposal on the IP response to the pandemic instead of the TRIPS waiver proposal, a far more comprehensive approach to address IP barriers in the context of COVID-19. The EU proposal mostly focuses on the use of compulsory licensing, while South Africa-India's proposal seeks a temporary suspension on rules across a range of intellectual property protections from patents, copyright, to trade secrets among others to address production shortages of personal protective equipment, vaccines and therapeutics among other classes of medical products relevant for COVID-19.

In addition, the WTO has put in place a process to comprehensively respond to the pandemic by appointing New Zealand Ambassador David Walker to spearhead a coherent approach by the international rules making body to address challenges in the wake of COVID-19.

THE GENERAL COUNCIL MEETING AND THE IP DISCUSSION [July 27-28]
The meeting of the WTO General Council saw a number of different approaches to address the pandemic, a draft declaration

on trade and health, the EU's proposal on compulsory licenses to the revised TRIPS waiver proposal and a new process under the aegis of New Zealand's Ambassador Walker.

Last month, General Council Chair Dacio Castillo of Honduras appointed Walker as "a facilitator responsible for leading WTO members in finding a multilateral and horizontal response to the COVID-19 pandemic."

THE WALKER PROCESS

When Ambassador Walker was appointed last month, WTO had said in an update that delegates felt there was a need for all pandemic related issues to be channelled "into a hori-zontal, multilateral process". Choosing a facilitator, "would not only help us streamline and organize our work but also en-sure transparency and inclusiveness" GC Chair Ambassador Castillo had said.

In a press briefing during the General Council meeting this week, WTO spokesperson Keith Rockwell told reporters, Ambassador David Walker will not be focusing on the TRIPS Waiver since it is being addressed in the TRIPS Council under Norwegian Ambassador Dagfinn Sørli who chairs the Council and is facilitating the waiver discussions.

The Walker process is expected to address trade policy is-sues and the DG's Third Way, Rockwell said. (Asked if there was a formal document on "The Third Way", Rockwell denied. "The Third Way" in the context of the IP response to the pandemic, suggested by DG Ngozi Okonjo-Iweala, is loosely understood as approaches including voluntary licensing and using TRIPS flexibilities under existing WTO rules.)

Some of the elements of what this process will yield could include aspects on export restrictions, technology transfer, regulatory coherence, among others. Elaborating on the role of Ambassador Walker, Rockwell said that Walker could work specifically with WTO members to focus on these areas in a concrete way. By putting it all together, some of these issues could be addressed across the various silos. "Without someone spearheading the work it will be difficult", Rockwell said.

Walker, he pointed out, is one of the most able and respected ambassadors in town, who had steered the membership as chair of the General Council and the Dispute Settlement Body.

It is understood that Ambassador Walker has consulted the WTO membership on what is required to effectively address the pandemic. "It is not clear yet what David's efforts will deliver. It is not determined what is to be expected and what is to be delivered," Rockwell said in response to a question on the role of the facilitator and the specific outcome for the upcoming Ministerial Conference in November.

(The WTO is yet to make public the following document: *General Council - Agenda item 7.a: WTO response to the pandemic - Report by the Facilitator - H.E. Dr. David Walker (New Zealand) - Tuesday, 27 July 2021*)

THE DRAFT DECLARATION ON TRADE AND HEALTH
In a revised document submitted in mid-July 2021, EU and nearly 25 other co-sponsors including China, have come together on the trade and health declaration first submitted in 2020.

Among other priorities such as eliminating unnecessary export restrictions, easing customs rules, on tariffs, and transparency of trade measures, the new text also has language on expanding production of COVID-19 medical products.

The revised draft also says, "We strongly support the works of the COVAX Manufacturing Task Force that can help in gathering the necessary intelligence, foster partnerships between manufacturers and developers, and respond to trade issues." (As we have reported earlier, the priorities of the COVAX

Manufacturing Task Force appear to be around bilateral and voluntary tech transfer arrangements.)

In addition, what is also important to note that this declaration is being crafted keeping future health crises in mind. The text suggests:

"At the 12th Ministerial Conference, Members will consider a decision to establish a work programme on pandemic preparedness in relation to the health-related trade policy measures above. Without prejudice to the decision of Ministers, the work programme could include, for instance, a review of lessons learnt during the COVID-19 crisis, the preparation of guidelines or codes of best practices, or potentially lead to additional commitments that could help Members to enhance their preparedness and crisis resilience."

A potential work programme on pandemic preparedness at WTO, but must and be understood in relation to on-going discussions on pandemic preparedness at WHO including the push for a pandemic treaty, notably spearheaded by the EU.

THE TRIPS WAIVER TALKS
Despite continuing disagreements on the use of "the waiver approach" to address the production shortages during this pandemic, the TRIPS waiver proposal dominated what is becoming a contested policy space within the WTO with competing proposals.

The TRIPS Council chair presented a status report on the discussions on the waiver proposal to the General Council.

WTO officials said that more than 30 delegations took the floor on the waiver discussions, Rockwell said.

When we asked if there will be a specific deliverable on the waiver discussions in time for the Ministerial Conference in November, Rockwell said:

"There is no way that they are going to stop these discussions. Everyone accepts that it is a very important issue. It is a very emotional issue...It does not have to be a binary.

The DG has said that she cannot take sides on this issue. But what she has said is TRIPS alone is not enough. If you listen to the manufacturers, what they say is the most important thing is technology transfer and know-how, equipment, technical assistance, proper regulatory environment. The DG has said that we need to have a pragmatic approach. What she has also said that it is essential that we have agreement by MC12. She has been quite clear that ministers, finance, development and health ministers will be producing outcomes between now and the end of the year. It will not be a good look, if trade ministers do not do the same.

She has not taken a position, very deliberately on the TRIPS issue, because the members are very divided. While she is very pleased that negotiations are under way, but it can get frustrating if people just read papers and talk past each other"

On the negotiations on the waiver, Rockwell said:

"According to Ambassador Sørli, where the negotiations are getting stuck is couple of different points: duration, and scope (products covered, and TRIPS provisions covered), issues of implementation of the agreement and the protection of undisclosed information among others."

Apart from opponents to the waiver including EU, Japan, Korea, "there is a healthy slice of members who want a pragmatic outcome", he added.

Geneva-based sources told us that the US did not take the floor on this item.

(See related from the FT: *US vaccine diplomat urges producers to back low-cost jab hubs abroad*)

DISSECTING THE EU STATEMENT ON THE TRIPS WAIVER:

The EU's statement at the General Council meeting was the clearest indication of its intention and the unambiguous nature of its opposition to the TRIPS waiver discussions. (See Confidential Communication on the TRIPS Waiver Shows the EU's Unwillingness to Negotiate)

The EU said that as the biggest producer of mRNA vaccines, it is "at the forefront of deliveries of vaccines to the rest of the world". According to the EU, more than 500 million doses have been exported from the region and similar amounts have been delivered to Europeans.

(Check out recent Reuters story: *EU has shipped tiny percentage of planned COVID-19 shot donations - document*)

The EU has also said that with nearly EUR 3.2 billion as donation to COVAX, the EU has been the largest donor to the vaccine's facility.

(We discuss here how donations to the COVAX facility has been instrumentalized in the discussions against the TRIPS Waiver).

At the meeting this week, the EU said, "To support short-term actions for ramping up vaccine production, the European Commission set up a vaccine task force in the EU whose objective is to match supply with demand and to lift bottlenecks. Its main tasks are to promote partnerships through matchmaking events. And this has brought tangible results: we have seen that so far; technology transfer is working well with several high-level partnerships announced recently. Fifty-three (53) EU manufacturing sites are already engaged in relation to the COVID-19 vaccines, based on voluntary partnerships."

The EU also flagged the Pfizer/BioNTech – Biovac deal to underscore the kind of voluntary licensing approaches that it is favouring. (See our recent story: The Mechanics of the Tech Transfer Narrative during COVID-19)

"To this end, the European Union and its Member States are launching an initiative to develop vaccine production in the African continent entailing investment in infrastructure and production capacities as well as skills development, supply chains management, and the necessary regulatory framework to create conditions for technology transfer. The objective is to develop several regional hubs distributed across the African continent. And we have already identified promising projects in South Africa, Senegal and Rwanda. One billion EUR has already been allocated from the EU budget and the EU finance institutions to deliver on this goal," the EU has said.

The EU is of the view that examining export restrictions, minimizing barriers to trade and ensuring trade-facilitation measures will help arrive at an effective response to the pandemic.

Limited manufacturing capacity, restricted access to raw materials and other inputs as well as complex supply chains are the main bottlenecks as regards the production and distribution of COVID-19 vaccines, the EU said. "In addition, having the required know-how is key due to the complexity of the production process of these vaccines," the EU said at the meeting.

In its opposition to the waiver, the EU said:

"Given the nature of the identified bottlenecks and the need for the sharing of know-how, the European Union does not believe that the proposed suspension of the TRIPS Agreement by the waiver proposed by South Africa, India and a number of other WTO Members, is an appropriate and effective response.

The proposed waiver will not increase production of COVID-19 vaccines and medicines, as it will not address any of the existing bottlenecks that have been identified. It rather risks having counterproductive effects on our common efforts to enhance access to such vaccines and medicines. It will undermine the ongoing collaborations, which are based on the well-established platform of intellectual property protection and will have a chilling effect on future such collaborations.

In addition, the waiver may have harmful effects going forward when it comes to fighting future pandemics and more generally on incentives for research and innovation. The European Union has provided details on these risks in the discussions in the TRIPS Council."

While emphasizing the role of IP in the context of access to COVID-19 vaccines and medicines, the EU said, "It is to this end that the European Union has put forward an alternative proposal to the proposal on the waiver – the European Union proposal focuses on the clarification and facilitation of the use of compulsory licensing system."

It added: "Given the stalemate we are experiencing in the TRIPS Council, we encourage all WTO Members to try to find convergence on the basis of the European Union proposal as the one that is pragmatic, targeted and effective in responding to the current needs while keeping intact the necessary incentives for innovation."

(Also see: *Questions and Answers: EU Communications to the WTO – EU proposes a strong multilateral trade response to the COVID-19 pandemic*)

EXCERPTS OF SOUTH AFRICA'S STATEMENT AT THE GC

At the General Council Meeting, South Africa, the chief proponent of the TRIPS Waiver, said:

"...We are disappointed that we could not reach consensus on the Waiver once again. The cost of our deliberations is measured in lives. As of 26 July 2021, 4.2 m people have died from this virus. A total of 3,6 bn vaccine doses have been administered. But so far, approximately 75% of these have gone to people in high-income and upper-middle-income countries. To put it into perspective, only 13% of the world population is fully vaccinated, with much of the vaccination focused on higher income countries."

"...Almost all the vaccines forecast to be made in 2021 have already been sold, according to data from Airfinity. This data shows that rich nations have bought up most doses long into the future, often far more than they could conceivably need. This situation must greatly worry all of us, for it shows that the current production, supply and distribution is only working for a small percentage of countries."

"...While we welcome progress from the voluntary mechanisms including the launch of the vaccine mRNA technology hub in South Africa and partnerships between SA companies and IP holders towards the production of vaccines in SA, much more needs to be done to scale up production. The urgency of passing the Waiver has not abated."

"...The co-sponsors have argued that the TRIPS waiver is a necessary, targeted, time-limited and proportionate legal measure directed at addressing intellectual property (IP) barriers in a direct, transparent and efficient fashion, which is consistent with the WTO legal framework."

"...Passing this waiver allows companies the freedom to operate and to produce covered COVID-19 health product and to use health technologies without the fear of infringing another party's IP rights and the attendant threat of litigation. Furthermore, passing a TRIPS waiver acts as an important political, moral and economic lever towards encouraging solutions aimed at global equitable access to COVID-19 health products and technologies including vaccines, therapeutics and diagnostics, which is in the wider interest of the global public.

While vaccines are important, saving lives necessitates access to diagnostics, treatments, oxygen and personal protective equipment, to prevent, treat and combat COVID-19. It is likely that millions more people will contract COVID-19 and would need treatment and care in the years to come, as the realities of vaccine production makes it difficult to replicate and ramp up production in all countries at the same time. Many products related to the prevention, containment and treatment of COVID-19 are potentially patent-protected, so a TRIPS Waiver could promote and enhanced access to better care for sick people, even if the vaccines are not imminently available."

South Africa at the GC meeting July 27-28

Alluding to the EU proposal, South Africa also clarified: "All proposals and initiative aimed at addressing barriers to production are not substitutes but contribute from different perspectives and should be welcomed with a view to find landing zones on all."

COME SEPTEMBER?

It appears that the messaging from the WTO and the EU are near identical, in terms of the importance of "pragmatic" approaches and the push for voluntary licensing arrangements.

The EU may well be the lever that could turn the entire WTO membership away from what has become the fulcrum of pandemic related trade policy - the South Africa-India TRIPS Waiver proposal. Ultimately, if WTO members do not come together to find consensus on this bold proposal, the waiver, irrespective of the critical mass it has achieved will not pass muster. That will be a failure not of the creative diplomacy and bold leadership of the proponents and the co-sponsors, but a failure on account of the lack of imagination on what is possible in the face of production challenges to meet the global demand for medical products to address the pandemic.

While it continues to be impossible to predict the outcome on the TRIPS waiver discussions, for clues, look elsewhere:

At a recent briefing, WHO DG Tedros Adhanom Ghebreyesus, suggested a narrowed down waiver proposal that caters only to vaccines and for a limited period of a year or two. This is similar to the stated US suggestion of limiting the waiver discussions to vaccines.

TAILPIECE:

For all the emphasis on technology transfer, it is not clear whether there will be a specific text on technology transfer coming from the opponents to the waiver.

The EU has announced specific investments in regional hubs to create conditions for technology transfer in three countries in Africa. But in a pandemic, with a global requirement of medical products these isolated investments pale in colour compared what is truly required. Can the 164 countries, members of the WTO, be persuaded to give up on a wider waiver proposal merely by investments in select countries by donor countries?

25.
THE GENEVA HEALTH FILES INTERVIEW: MURALI NEELAKANTAN (AUGUST 6, 2021)

ndia has played a crucial role in supporting South Africa, as a lead co-sponsor in bringing the TRIPS Waiver proposal to the WTO in October 2020. In the months since, more than 60 other WTO members have formally supported the proposal - a bold initiative that seeks to temporarily suspend a range of intellectual property protections to decisively respond to the pandemic by seeking to unblock production shortages for critical COVID-19 medical products.

As these discussions reach a critical juncture ahead of the WTO ministerial in November this year, concerns have been expressed on India's commitment to the waiver proposal. Perplexing as it may sound, it is easy to see why. Look no further than Indian government's stated policy announcements on these matters at home in the context of the pandemic, notwithstanding its leadership on the waiver proposal in Geneva.

To understand this complex, discordant position, we spoke with Murali Neelakantan, Principal Lawyer, amicus. Former Global General Counsel, Cipla, who has been familiar with the terrain of IP policy and politics in India.

Q1. [GHF] At the WTO, led by South Africa, India is a co-sponsor of the TRIPS Waiver proposal. And yet, domestically, the Indian government has made statements that are contrary

to the spirit of the waiver proposal including a reluctance to issue compulsory licenses. How do we understand this?

[MN] I think the Indian government has had a consistent position on the issue of compulsory licensing. The aberration was issuing a compulsory license for Bayer's Nexavar. But, other than that, the government has consistently discouraged compulsory licenses and dissuaded everybody from applying for compulsory licenses. So even if you went and spoke to somebody in the Department for Promotion of Industry and Internal Trade (DPIIT) or with the Patent Controllers Office they would dissuade you from even applying for it.

In 2014 there was a move to seek a compulsory license for Daclatasvir, but they were dissuaded by the government. They were quietly told by the government, "don't bother, you will not get it". But this attempt to seek a compulsory license led to Daclatasvir being included in the MPP in November 2015.

Another one was Cipla's move to get a compulsory license for Indacaterol, a product for Chronic Obstructive Pulmonary Disease (COPD) - the same thing happened.

It is therefore very clear that the government doesn't intend to issue any compulsory licenses. More recently, an affidavit was filed by the Indian government in the Supreme Court in the sou moto matter, where they said the same thing - if we exercise the statutory power of compulsory licensing, it will come in the way of what we are doing - in terms of diplomacy. It does not make any sense at all. *(See below excerpt from affidavit)*

Even where the Indian Supreme Court specifically told the Indian government in April 2021- why don't you implement Section 100 *[The Patents Act, 1970, Section 100: Power of Central Government to use inventions for purposes of Government],* they have simply responded stating that they are processing it. It shouldn't take more than an hour to draft and issue a notification under section 100 but more than three months later, we don›t see any outcome from that process.

So, I think there's been a consistency - whether this government or the previous one, they have been consistent in discouraging generics from apply for compulsory licensing.

[What the Indian government said in an affidavit in May 2021:

"Any exercise of statutory powers either under the patents act 1970 read with TRIPS agreement and Doha declaration or in any other way can only prove to be counter-productive at this stage, the central government is very actively engaging itself with global organisations at a diplomatic level to find out a solution in the best possible interest of India. It is earnestly urged that any discussion or a mention of exercise of statutory powers either for essential drugs or vaccines having patent issues would have serious, severe and unintended adverse consequences in the country's efforts being made on global platform using all its resources, good-will and good-offices though diplomatic and other channels."]

Q2. [GHF] Over the last few years, the Indian government has ostensibly moved towards a pro-IP position. But the pandemic muddies the water in the context of shortages of medical products, isn't it? Do you think there has been an apparent change in the government's position?

[MN] Whether there has been a change in position or not, we can only gather from what government is saying and doing. We have the National IPR policy, 2016 that didn›t say anything encouraging about compulsory licenses. It only spoke about encouraging more IP, and more patenting and Geographical Indicators, trademarks in traditional knowledge etc. They did not deal with compulsory licenses in any detail.

Then we have the report of the Parliamentary Standing Committee on IPR, released in July 2021. And again, look at who they have consulted. When they invite experts to give evidence to them, they didn't ask anybody from the pharma industry even though there are industry groups like Indian Pharmaceutical Association (IPA), Indian Drug Manufacturers Association (IDMA); they didn't invite any of the lawyers representing pharma clients; they did not consult Civil Society nor any of the patient rights groups. How can that report be a credible account of the state of IPR in India?

So, whether it's the Parliament or the government, they have been consistent in that they do not want to address this issue at all. Yes, they make the usual noises that this is a pandemic and we should do something about compulsory licenses.

Parliamentarians should have said: this is a pandemic, here is a chance to address it, and the government did nothing. They should have said: here is what you should have done and this is our evidence to say if you had issued licenses, this is what would have happened. They could have done that, but even the Parliamentary standing committee did a wishy-washy job of producing the long report without addressing the issue.

So, we do not see anybody whether in government or in the Parliament, anybody holding the government to account and saying - you should have done it, you didn't do it. Or explain to us, why you did not. None of that has happened. There is a consistency and it doesn't matter, which party is in power, or in opposition. Nobody has forced it upon the government to answer this question for us. Why didn't you do it? And what's stopping you from doing it? Isn't that the point of parliamentary standing committees?

[GHF] Q3. It is understood that Indian diplomats in Geneva have not had enough support from New Delhi on the waiver proposal. At the same time, we also note that the waiver proposal has been taken up with other world leaders at the highest levels in the Indian government. It appears as if

there isn't enough fleshed-out thinking about these issues even during COVID-19. With this kind of dissonance within the Indian government, it is hard to understand how India can play an effective role in pushing the waiver. The waiver aside, the Indian government does not seem to support Compulsory Licensing.

[MN] Absolutely right. I said it once before when this issue came up before the Supreme Court that this just makes us look terrible in Geneva. We are not sure where the Indian government stands. We say something once to the Supreme Court, and then a few weeks later, the government's official stand is, we don't know and then a few weeks later it is reluctant to exercise statutory powers. Then you have a stand in Geneva which is - we need the IP waiver, Doha [Declaration] is important and all of that.

The Supreme Court itself writes in an order [30th April 2021], where Justice Bhat has effectively written the book on compulsory licenses, everything from Doha, TRIPS, 31, 31bis etc. No one asked Justice [Ravindra] Bhat to write it, but he still wrote it. All the government should have done is follow that and start issuing CLs.

And yet the government's response to that is very brief. It does not even address the issue. Sadly, the response of the Supreme Court is to let it go. When the second affidavit was filed on 26 June the Supreme Court should have said, «This affidavit is inadequate. You have to answer these questions.» Instead, a judge feels pleased with himself that the court nudged the government into action.

That case before the Supreme Court has now gone to sleep. There are a few different and contradictory positions - by the health ministry, the home ministry, then the position at the WTO. Inevitably, the question that gets asked is - why doesn't the Indian government implement the TRIPS flexibilities and the Doha Declaration?

(Also see Supreme Court's May 31st order questioning Government of India's basis of pricing of vaccines)

Q4. [GHF] Indeed, these questions are being asked by the opponents to the waiver, and others. The discussions as you know, are at a critical juncture.

We also noticed that senior Indian officials from other ministries [science and technology, for example] have made a statement saying, that IP is not a problem for vaccines. This is not in line with the Indian government's position at the WTO.

But we also understand that in many countries there is a huge gap between the trade and the health ministries, since interests are different. It is nevertheless difficult to reconcile this, given India's leadership on the TRIPS waiver talks.

[MN] The government's Press Information Bureau issued a press release and it was fronted by VK Paul, and was written as a "myth buster". He says that IP is of no relevance at all for vaccines, the problem is with raw materials supplies. The problem is tech transfer. So, this is their position.

This is VK Paul talking for, I don't know which ministry now, but he speaks for the Indian government. He's talking across ministries here and this is the official position. If you then look at India's stand at the WTO, it's exactly the opposite. Paul is saying everything that Germany, Britain and others are saying which is that even if the IP waiver is approved, it's not going to be very useful. So why are you asking for it?

So, it's very difficult, I think for those of us are watching this to make sense of it. What is the game? None of us has been able to figure it out. I think we are all struggling to understand what India really wants. Do you want the waiver or not? Are you just there to hijack this South Africa proposal from the inside? What are you trying to do here?

[V K Paul, NITI Aayog, a policy think tank in the Indian government. *[See PIB statement:*

"Myth 4: Centre should invoke compulsory licensing

Fact: Compulsory Licensing is not a very attractive option since it is not a 'formula' that matters, but active partnership, training of human resources, sourcing of raw materials and highest levels of bio-safety labs which is required. Tech transfer is the key and that remains in the hands of the company that has carried out R&D. In fact, we have gone one step ahead of Compulsory Licensing and are ensuring active partnership between Bharat Biotech & 3 other entities to enhance production of Covaxin. Similar mechanism is being followed for Sputnik. Think about this: Moderna had said in October 2020 that it will not sue any company which makes its vaccines, but still not one company has done it, which shows licensing is the least of the issues. If vaccine-making was so easy, why would even the developed world be so short of vaccine doses?"]

Q5. [GHF] At this point, India is not even speaking forcefully in favour of compulsory licensing. In contrast, the EU, the prime opponent to the waiver is actually discussing compulsory licensing in its internal policies in the context of COVID-19, and some individual EU member states have actually gone ahead made changes to their rules. This is striking. It may not be too far-fetched to say that as a co-sponsor of the TRIPS Waiver proposal, India is undecided on its position, or worse is probably against the waiver in so far as its actions at home are concerned. We believe it is important to highlight this incoherence.

[MN] I hear you. But you should not punish the world because of the Indian government. I think there is a way to reconcile these two positions. So, when I criticize the way, the Indian government has behaved and yet support the waiver, I'm not undermining the waiver by criticizing the government. I have argued before that countries have to be criticized for their response to the pandemic, but that does not undermine the merits of the waiver.

Q6. [GHF] What is difficult to understand is that India was seen as a vaccine manufacturing powerhouse till a few months ago, and a pharmacy for the developing world, but the actions by the government and the industry do not meet these expectations. It shows a lack of leadership and a disservice to the developing world dependent on India.

[MN] Yes. But also, a disservice to India's own Pharma Public Sector Undertakings (PSUs). One of the big questions that the government has not answered is - why are you not using your pharma PSUs to produce drugs and vaccines. You own the rights to Covaxin so why don't you use your own facilities to manufacture it. You can make a billion doses with the facilities you have, so why don't you use those facilities. You knew all this last year. Even to this day you have not produced one vaccine out of those PSUs.

The government has spoken in very general terms that they are exploring the possibility, increasing capabilities, upgrading technology, etc but there is no specific plan that has been disclosed that says here is a vaccine that will be produced by this facility by this date in 2021.

The only institution which could have made the government answer was the Supreme Court. And now they don't seem to be keen anymore. The question was asked in the Supreme Court order and by many high courts, but the government seems to have successfully sidestepped it. So, even when the question was asked, in Parliament, there was not a clear answer to it.

The High Court of Madras has asked why the vaccine production was limited to private manufacturers and why vaccine manufacturing facilities owned by the government were not utilized. The government has refused to answer that question.

When the Supreme Court told them to do it, the Indian government could have licensed the IP widely and got many manufacturers involved in the production of Covaxin. The government would have had a very good excuse if questioned by the west: we were pushed by the Supreme Court! But the government did nothing.

Q7. [GHF] What according to you is Indian government's position on trade secrets, and other aspects of the waiver proposal? There are number of countries who are raising this in the context of the waiver discussions. The US, and the EU have more evolved legislations to protect Trade Secrets, but many countries do not.

[MN] The Patents Act, 1970 requires the transmission of knowledge to be the basis for the grant of a patent. So, one of the conditions for a grant of a patent is that they will be a transfer of knowledge. You could argue...the developed world will argue that it is only transfer to the extent of what is disclosed in the patent. But to me, that limitation is not logical. When a patent must disclose the invention, it does not need to be said that it must be full disclosure. When it specifically mentions that there must be a transfer of knowledge in technology, clearly the Patents Act expected that with the patent will come all that knowledge necessary to work the invention. There is no place for trade secrets within patented inventions. That's cheating the patent system.

I have a slightly different view to say we need a trade secrets act – maybe we do, but what we have is sufficient for what we need to do now. One of the ways in which we can force tech transfer is by saying that if a compulsory license is issued, and it requires a tech transfer and you don't provide a tech transfer, then the patent will be revoked. This is what Brazil has threatened to do. So, within our existing system, we can do it too. Whether we need a trade secret act for everything else, we will see. But we have enough in the patent legislation to make sure that if the government wanted, it could get companies to transfer trade secrets with the license.

The government's position should be - if you do not cooperate with the licensing, either voluntary or compulsory, by transferring technology to make the patent work then we revoke it because you have not disclosed the invention completely. If you want to look at it differently, you will only be granted a patent if what you have disclosed in the patent is sufficient to work it. If you are saying that the disclosure in the patent is not sufficient, because you need know-how, or tech transfer, then you are admitting that your patent application is defective for incompleteness. In which case, there is a threat of revocation. Perhaps you can be given a chance to fix by adding the "secret sauce" to that patent to avoid revocation.

This doesn't require any change in the legislation. I don't think enough people write about it in this way. We don't need new legislation. We have legislation that is adequate, but we just don't read it, don't use it.

[Section 83 - The Patents Act 1970:

83. General principles applicable to working of patented inventions.

—Without prejudice to the other provisions contained in this Act, in exercising the powers conferred by this Chapter, regard shall be had to the following general considerations, namely:

  a. *that patents are granted to encourage inventions and to secure that the inventions are worked in India on a commercial scale and to the fullest extent that is reasonably practicable without undue delay; (b) that they are not granted merely to enable patentees to enjoy a monopoly for the importation of the patented article; (c) that the protection and enforcement of patent rights contribute to the promotion of technological innovation and to the transfer and dissemination of technology, to the mutual advantage of producers and users of technological knowledge and in a manner conducive to social and economic welfare, and to a balance of rights and obligations; (d) that patents granted do not impede protection of public health and nutrition and should act as instrument to promote public interest specially in sectors of vital importance for socio-economic and technological development of India; (e) that patents granted do not in any way prohibit Central Government in taking measures to protect public health; (f) that the patent right is not abused by the patentee or person deriving title or interest on patent from the patentee, and the patentee or a person deriving title or interest on patent from the patentee does not resort to practices which unreasonably restrain trade or adversely affect the international transfer of THE PATENTS ACT, 1970 Page 65 technology; and (g) that patents are granted to make the benefit of the patented invention available at reasonably affordable prices to the public.]*

Q8. [GHF] What do you think is driving the motivations of the Indian government in these discussions?

[MN] The narrative 20 years ago, during the AIDS crisis - was that we are the pharmacy of the world. In the 20 years since, all those Indian pharmaceutical companies have cozied up to Big Pharma. We have nobody now who can lead the fight for a compulsory license, or those who led the fight against Big

Pharma in the past. You are left with perhaps NATCO and BDR Pharma, who are not comparable in size to Cipla.

Q9. [GHF] And this is also by design. It also appears there is some amount of self-censoring among developing country manufacturers. While they want tech transfer, they don't want to be too loud in asking for it. In some sense, they have been co-opted.

[MN] Completely by design. You may have read the recent remarks by Dr Hamied, the Chairman of Cipla. He is now saying the opposite of what he has been saying for 50 years. He says that, in the context of biologics, there are trade secrets and issues of tech transfer and therefore, compulsory licensing is not really an effective instrument anymore. However, in the past, while speaking about Erlotinib, he said that Cipla will make biologics on its own terms and will fight this battle against Big Pharma monopolists.

But today, he is saying the exact opposite, and exactly what big pharma is saying. It is shocking that somebody who led the fight against Big Pharma monopolies has moved over to the other side. The narrative sounds different because the players have all moved over to the other side. They have all benefited from voluntary licensing of products from Big Pharma. They are very scared that they will lose the oligopoly if compulsory licenses are issued and the voluntary licensing deals they have done will not be as profitable for them anymore.

So, almost everybody who could have potentially sought a compulsory license, has now been given little sops by Big Pharma, by offering licensing, production, or export deals.

Q10. [GHF] But the pandemic could have been a game-changer for Indian pharma servicing not only the Indian market but much of the developing world.

[MN] Yes, but it is not really a game changer. It has just accelerated the process of co-opting Indian generics into the Big Pharma world because now big pharma is saying we will "work with you" and Indian generics are happy with those crumbs.

Take TB drugs for example. Why can't we get Indian manufacturers to make any of the key TB drugs like Bedaquiline and Delamanid? Why can't you get one of them to apply for a compulsory license? We can't say there is no market for TB drugs - thousands die of TB every year in India.

But we can't get a single generic manufacturer to apply for a compulsory license. Why is that? If a compulsory license was granted and Indian pharma companies manufactured large quantities of these two drugs, we could have the same impact on TB around the world like we did for HIV/AIDS.

Q11. [GHF] Do you think this can change if a Bangladeshi or a Thai company would step in.

[MN] I think the Indian companies feel secure that they have a closed market. I sense that they think that "nobody is going to enter it, and so let's do deals that will help us in this market." So even if manufacturers from other countries get rights to export vaccines to India, Indian companies will be happy to just distribute.

Cipla had signed up with Moderna, others like Dr. Reddys too. Who amongst the leading Indian pharma companies is left? Who is left to fight any of these big deals?

Everybody has been co-opted. COVID-19 would have been a great opportunity, but unfortunately, Indian pharma has decided to take the easy way to profits.

Q12. [GHF] Even as Indian companies do not take the lead, the population continues to be under served.

[MN] Yes, but Indian pharma companies are not expecting significant quantities to be imported. It's not as if Bangladesh is going to be making vaccines or drugs at such scale that it will be able to sell it in India. Even if Bangladesh manufactures, it will come to the Indian pharma companies for distribution and they are very happy to do that. They would think that they have got the market covered by distribution, not necessarily, because of production. So even if we do not have production, we are going to distribute it and make profits.

If you look at Tocilizumab, Cipla has been distributing it for years now, without bothering to manufacture it. We have several of these examples, take raltegravir from MSD. Cipla has been distributing from MSD for years but did not manufacture it initially.

Q13 [GHF] So I'm just trying to understand where is the leadership in all of this? Either from the Indian industry or the government? You were at this cusp of a challenging moment in time where you have been asked to step up, but it has not quite happened that way.

[MN] Yes, and that I think all the activists have just been feeling so let down. I have heard many say – "When the AIDS crisis happened, you guys stepped up but those who stepped up then have been unwilling to step up now. What is happening? They are just so keen to do private deals." And that's the shocking part of it - not one of them is willing to stand up and fight for patients. And obviously, if they are not willing to stand up and fight, who's going to tell the government that compulsory licensing is a good idea? Just the activists or the judges saying that the government should do it seems insufficient to get the government to act.

Until there is enough pressure from industry to tell the government: we are here, we are going to do it if you support us. If only a few Indian drug manufacturers held a press conference and said: "We have been chasing the Indian government down for compulsory licenses. We can produce the vaccines, we can produce these drugs and we have been stonewalled." But I am not optimistic that anybody is going to do it.

Q14. [GHF] Finally, in terms of the climate in India for activists and lawyers fighting for these issues, the fact that, committed access to medicine advocates have been targeted, how does one reconcile India's push for the TRIPS waiver in the context of all this.

[MN] I think we have a crisis now in very, very different ways. I think the previous dispensation sometimes saw activists as a nuisance, but it engaged with them. Now we are all "anti-nationals". So, we don't even get any engagement with the government.

Earlier, we used to also be able to have our day in court. Now we don't even get that. All the cases that have been filed in the last eight years have had no progress at all. We really have nowhere to turn to. No one will publish activists' opinions or policy briefings in the mainstream media.

The government won't listen to us. They don't invite us to standing committee meetings, consultations, none of that stuff. Even if there is a pretence of public consultation, they won't publish all the responses and be transparent about what the consultation resulted in. So, all of what we have said goes into a bin somewhere and they declare that public consultation has been done. Then the policy comes out to be exactly as it was before. So, you don't see any outcome from the consultation.

We can't do anything with the executive, legislature, or the judiciary, and the press is ignoring us - it's just a state of muted helplessness.

We can have round tables and discuss amongst ourselves but that's probably not going to make much of a difference. We are really locked out.

(No responses were received from the Indian government to our queries sent on these issues by the time this interview was published.)

If you want to get in touch with Murali Neelakantan, write to him here: murali@amicus.net.in

PART IV:
THE RACE AND THE ANTICLIMAX - THE 12TH MINISTERIAL CONFERENCE AT THE WTO (AUGUST - NOVEMBER 2021)

The COVID-19 pandemic was at its peak in the summer of August 2021. And yet, the WTO went into hibernation for a month. When talks restarted on the TRIPS Waiver, they took the shape of bilateral consultations between key players, namely South Africa and the EU, India and the US. This led to opacity, confusion and misunderstandings. But these were last ditch efforts to reach a consensus in time for the 12th Ministerial Conference in December 2021.

SARS-CoV-2 had other plans. The emergence of the Omicron variant threw a spanner into the works, that made travel for trade negotiators impossible in the light of politically motivated travel bans and grave public health concerns. The ministerial conference was postponed less than 72 hours before it was scheduled to begin, in a late evening decision by the WTO General Council.

26.

UNDERSTANDING GERMANY'S TRENCHANT OPPOSITION TO THE TRIPS WAIVER (AUGUST 13, 2021)

By Rithika Sangameshwaran

In January 2021, Achim Kessler, member of the Left Party of Germany (known as *Die Linke*) co-submitted a motion in the *Bundestag* (Parliament). It called on the German Federal Government to support the TRIPS waiver. After months of deliberation, the motion was rejected in May 2021, with majority members voting against it. While they unanimously agreed that more needed to be done to increase global vaccine production, just like at the WTO, they differed on ways to achieve it.

"*There is a difference even within the government, between members of the Social Democratic Party (SPD) and members of the conservative party. Some members of the Social Democrats have been more open. They also rhetorically supported the TRIPS waiver. But when it came to voting, and to the final votes, they opposed it,*" Achim Kessler told Geneva Health Files.

First proposed by South Africa and India in October 2020, the TRIPS waiver proposal seeks to expand access to COVID-19 vaccines, diagnostics and related medical products by temporarily relaxing certain intellectual property rules. Almost a year later, the EU, led by Germany, remains a prominent opponent to the waiver. Notwithstanding the farrago of arguments against the waiver, it is useful to examine Germany's reasons for doing so.

This story maps German policy positions and politics on intellectual property and its implications for the TRIPS Waiver discussions.

The politics of scientific knowledge: who owns it and who gets to use it?

The belief that relaxing patents would impede innovation was one of the main reasons for rejection of the Left's motion. Responding to a question thereon, the federal government stated that it was skeptical about the need for a waiver. It added (translated from German; can be accessed here):

"The European Commission, which leads the negotiations in the TRIPS Council for the member states of the EU, has not yet been convinced by the arguments put forward, according to which intellectual property rights represent a barrier to increasing global production capacities for vaccines against Covid-19. It sees the protection of intellectual property rights as an essential stimulus for research and development of new vaccines and drugs. This position of the European Commission is shared by the German government. The current international and national legal framework for the protection of intellectual property rights already provides the basis for patent holders to grant other companies (voluntarily) licenses for the use of their pharmaceutical invention. Private companies are already making extensive use of this possibility of cooperation to expand the necessary resources and should do so even more in the current pandemic. If voluntary solutions to increase production are not sufficient, the TRIPS Agreement already enables the granting of patent compulsory licenses at national level."

Germany, and in particular, Chancellor Angela Merkel's party, the Christian Democratic Union of Germany (CDU), places great importance on intellectual property (IP) as a driver for innovation and considers it inviolable. "*I think to understand Germany's opposition to the waiver, we must look back on German beliefs on IP rights. And I think, in the German conservative party there is a strong belief that IP is key and an important incentive for creation of medical tools.*" Lara Dovifat, International Campaign Manager at Médecins Sans Frontières (MSF) told Geneva Health Files in an interview.

However, this view does not acknowledge the importance of the 'no-strings attached' public investments that allowed the speedy development of vaccines. The German government awarded $445 million to BioNTech and $298 million to CureVac. "*I think it's a longstanding tradition in Germany that the German government funds medical research and development and yet allows private companies to hold a monopoly. This is an ethical and moral failure,*" Dovifat added.

The role of IP as the primary incentive for R&D is debatable considering that some of the largest pharmaceutical companies, including Pfizer and J&J, rejected an EU proposal to develop vaccines against priority pathogens including coronaviruses in 2017. Further, ample evidence from present and past health emergencies, debunk the disingenuous claims of IP not being a barrier to lifesaving products.

While an analysis of the strengths and weaknesses of the IP system is beyond the scope of this article, it is interesting to note the concurrent emphasis on pathogens-sharing in this context. The rapid sharing of genomic data that contributed to vaccine development is desirable and even encouraged by the same countries filibustering the waiver. However, the resultant scientific knowledge and its benefits are not shared with similar fervour.

TRIPS waiver as a threat to the flourishing biotechnology industry

Although it may be difficult to establish with certainty, Germany's decision to oppose the waiver may well be due to a desire to protect its thriving biotechnology industry. Hyo Yoon Kang, a reader in law at Kent Law School, University of Kent, referred to this as a case of economic nationalism coupled with biopolitical nationalism. She explains:

"German opposition to the TRIPS waiver is a clear case of economic nationalism (like the UK in relation to Vaccitech and Oxford University Ventures). It overlaps with biopolitical nationalism by artificially restraining knowledge dissemination and training that would allow other countries to produce vaccines locally and regionally at the earliest, lessening this unequal dependency of knowledge and manufacture. Therefore, this economic nationalism leads to a scarcity which justifies the biopolitical 'my nation's health first' policy. What does the German economic nationalism entail? Germany holds some of the most valuable patents in mRNA technology. BioNTech has shared technology and know-how with Pfizer to manufacture its proprietary and patented mRNA vaccines. It knows that these patents are very valuable in the future for other therapies. Accordingly, it doesn't want to share more information than what is currently contained in the patent documents. These are (by themselves) insufficient for reproduction of vaccines or by license agreements bound by non-disclosure clauses. Undoubtedly, Germany has most to lose by the systematic waiver of IP during this pandemic. Arguably, US stands to benefit the most from such a waiver in the future without having to pay license fees to BioNTech and being technologically able to work around existing BioNTech patents, if they were waived (therefore the Pfizer opposition to TRIPS waiver strikes me as ambiguous)."

Allegedly, the first calls made by the Chancellor's Office following the US' announcement supporting the waiver were to Bill & Melinda Gates Foundation and the chief executives of BioNTech, CureVac and Pfizer, a source familiar with the waiver discussions in Germany told Geneva Health Files on the condition of anonymity.

Prior to the pandemic, Germany's biotechnology industry earned 4.87 billion euros (2019) in revenue. In contrast, BioNTech single-handedly hauled in over 5.3 billion euros between April to June 2021. BioNTech estimates annual revenues at 15.9 billion euros this year. Meanwhile, the German government has recovered its early subvention in BioNTech four times over with a whooping 1.75 billion euros in income tax up until June 30, 2021. While economic losses continue to ravage the Global South, Germany's economy is predicted to grow 4% this year, with 0.5% attributable to BioNTech alone.

This is not to make a case against economic growth or profits for vaccine manufacturers per se. Clearly, there is a need for vaccines and companies will earn their profits irrespective of the waiver. The question is about meeting market demand and making vaccines accessible at an affordable price.

As Kang puts it, "*BioNTech could also benefit by being the market leader with a proven track record of high-quality R&D. Beyond offering adequate compensation for sharing of its know-how and engaging in more tech transfer, it will benefit from its technology and market leadership, having the power to negotiate beneficial deals with license partners. BioNTech, if it wanted to, could call for better terms for itself and negotiate better supply for developing countries. Beyond IPR mechanisms, private companies engaging in publicly purposeful market activities can be rewarded in other ways such as via compensations, tax or subsidies.*"

Voluntary licensing as the pragmatic alternative

The insufficient focus on technology transfer in the waiver discussions is another recurring argument against it. German Development Minister Gerd Müller also emphasized this in an interview with the German weekly, *Zeit*. *"A patent release does not mean that we can quickly eliminate the shortage of vaccines for developing countries. Rather, we need to rapidly expand production based on licenses granted by pharmaceutical companies to qualified production facilities. This is different from uncontrolled patent release! This also ensures that vaccines are produced in the same quality,"* he said when asked the reasons for not supporting the waiver. Additionally, arguments about the quality are baseless old tropes since all regulatory processes remain the same, many critics believe.

While proponents of the waiver have repeatedly acknowledged the need for tech transfer, it is important to remember that the implications of the waiver go beyond vaccines and extend to diagnostics, treatments, and related medical products required to respond to the pandemic. Nonetheless, there remains the question of how technology transfer should be achieved.

Germany has repeatedly insisted that voluntary licensing would be sufficient to increase vaccine production. Speaking on Germany's perspective on global health cooperation, the Federal Minister of Health, Jens Spahn remarked that *"tech transfer is easier if done on a voluntary basis and enforcing cooperation is not very productive."* He emphatically stated anticipating an overcapacity of global mRNA production the following year. However, these ambitions of overcapacity remain a distant dream. As per BioNTech and Pfizer's quarterly reports, combined annual manufacturing capacity is expected to total only up to 3 billion doses by the end of 2021 and 4 billion doses by 2022. Furthermore, this is subject to continuous process improvements, expansion at current facilities, and addition of new suppliers and contract manufacturers.

It is also evident that companies which benefit most from the pandemic, have not done enough to address production shortages, a concern unaddressed by opponents of the waiver. Notably, Knowledge Ecology International (KEI)'s database estimates a timespan of 1-3 months for delivery of mRNA vaccines post technology transfer. This is comparable to BioNTech's Marburg facility, which doled out the first vaccine doses in April 2021, post the final handover by Novartis in December 2020.

Moreover, in stark contrast to BioNTech's expansion in Singapore and China, Pfizer/BioNTech's bilateral deals with Biovac in Africa focuses only on the final phase of manufacturing. Experts argue that such fill-finish agreements do not involve any technology transfer and keeps Africa reliant on Europe. Notably, although Biovac is a partner with WHO's mRNA tech-transfer hub, Pfizer/BioNTech have forged bilateral deals rather than committing to the hub. In this context, the promise of voluntary licensing and consequent technology transfer seems bleak. Lastly, if voluntary licensing was indeed the panacea Germany argues it to be, WHO's C-TAP would not be languishing since its establishment in May 2020.

Compulsory licensing as the (un)viable last resort

Germany has persistently argued that, if pharmaceutical companies fail to cooperate effectively, the option of compulsory licensing already exists under the TRIPS flexibilities and an IP waiver is therefore not needed.

Despite its belief that IP is not a barrier, Germany altered its patent laws early in the pandemic. The Epidemic Protection Act (EPA) amended Germany's patent laws by giving more powers to the Federal Ministry of Health. We asked Kang to explain how this move should be viewed considering Germany's opposition to the TRIPS waiver: *"From a legalistic point of view,* the German government's opposition to the TRIPS waiver is not necessarily inconsistent with its domestic patent law and provisions for compulsory license or "use order" under EPA 2020. The German Government's Opposition and also the EU Commission, have stressed that the TRIPS allows for compulsory license "flexibilities", which are individual governments' responsibilities to streamline and strengthen, and that these existing possibilities are sufficient in times of pandemic, obliterating the need for a more systematic waiver of IP protection in times of a pandemic."

The option of compulsory licensing to navigate the intricate web of intellectual property is a thorny one, particularly ill-suited for a world fraught with power imbalances. As Kang explains, "*My view is that the terminology of "flexibility" gives the impression that there is a ground of equal set of rules applicable to everyone and that they give enough freedom to TRIPS member states to adjust to their individual circumstances. But the word is a euphemism. What these perfectly valid legalistic terminologies and arguments ignore are political realities of power differentials: jurisdictions who are net owners of IP rights have more power to invoke (or choose not to invoke) such compulsory licenses. International rules may look equal on paper, but they cannot be applied in the same way when the IP playing field is as starkly skewed as it is now, in the case of COVID-19 vaccines. There are intra-domestic and international reasons why compulsory licenses exist on paper but have been so rarely invoked either unilaterally by a country or under existing WTO route. Powers in global trade vary enormously. Therefore, the reference to existing TRIPS compulsory license provisions downplays the reality of already existing patent thickets.*"

In essence, the rules of the game apply differently for LMICs and the rich world. Precedents exist of developing countries being discouraged from evoking compulsory licenses. The consequences of doing so, even for life-saving drugs (in the case of HIV, viral hepatitis etc.), have led to threats of trade sanctions from high income countries including the USA and the EU. Referring to history, Kang adds, *"Germany seems to have understandable horrors of expropriation, as it was shaped by its war and post-war histories, but a compulsory license is not legal expropriation and the property title remains with the IP holder who is obliged to be compensated adequately."*

See: *The TRIPS Intellectual Property Waiver Proposal: Creating the Right Incentives in Patent Law and Politics to end the COVID-19 Pandemic* to understand the reality of global trade politics and why compulsory licenses are not enough.

Aid as a proxy to solidarity

Germany assumed leadership and financed its influence in global health in the backdrop of a changing geopolitical landscape during COVID-19. With US and China moving in opposite directions, the EU propelled by Germany and France, has decisively taken the reins on the international response to the COVID-19 pandemic and what follows. Germany is currently the largest donor to WHO contributing $881.6 million. It is also a prominent donor to the COVAX Facility, having contributed about $2.58 billion so far. Additionally, Berlin will soon be housing the new WHO Hub for Pandemic and Epidemic Intelligence.

An article by the German Federal Foreign Office highlights Germany's contributions to improve global vaccine distribution:

By the end of the year, Germany will be supplying at least 30 million doses of vaccine, mainly to developing countries, around 80% of which will be through the vaccine initiative COVAX and about 20% bilateral. The first tranche of 1.3 million doses of the AstraZeneca vaccine has already been received by COVAX and will be delivered to Afghanistan, Ethiopia, Sudan, Tajikistan and Uzbekistan. The recipient countries were selected by COVAX. These are states that have a particularly urgent need and can use the vaccine immediately in their vaccination campaigns. The federal government also dispenses bilateral vaccine doses on a smaller scale. The target countries for this include the Ukraine, Namibia and the states of the Western Balkans. All in all, the EU is donating at least 200 million doses and the United States has donated around 110 million to date, while the G7 will provide a total of 870 million doses by the end of 2022."

Data shows the disparity between the share of fully vaccinated people in Germany, UK, Switzerland, Japan, Norway, Canada, compared to Afghanistan, Sudan, Tajikistan and Uzbekistan. The aggregate population of these four countries in the developing world is 123.74 million, the 1.3 million vaccine donations making up for a measly 1% of the population. Absolute numbers conveniently mask the magnitude of inequity. Note that most of the rich countries in this graph have expressed their opposition to the waiver proposal during the last few months.

The EU, under the leadership of Germany, has so far shared less than 3% of pledged doses, most of them AstraZeneca. Although praiseworthy, it cannot be denied that this results from the EU's row with AstraZeneca, which has caused significant damage to the uptake of the vaccine in LMICs.

In contrast, the EU with a population of 450 million has ordered up to 2.4 billion doses from BioNTech alone. This also includes a provision to purchase new formulations that may address potential viral variants. Thus, if the crisis intensifies, contracts may well take precedence over pledges.

What does Germany's position mean for the EU?

In a statement to the TRIPS council in February 2021, the EU remarked:

"Last year, Germany did not modify the conditions for the granting of compulsory licenses. The Patent Law was only amended to change the competence for the issuance of a government order (and again not the conditions for the issuance of a government order). Previously, a government order for the use of medicinal/pharmaceutical inventions required a decision by the Federal Cabinet (Kabinett-Beschluss). This has been changed. It is now the Ministry for Health which can issue such an order, provided that the (unchanged) requirements have been met."

When asked whether this statement obscured Germany's use of the TRIPS flexibilities, Kang explained that the statement was *"consistent with Germany's insistence that current TRIPS provisions are sufficient for introducing domestic exceptions to patent protection."* She further adds, *"It is also consistent with the window-dressing function that compulsory license provisions (both at TRIPS and domestic levels) have played thus far in the history of TRIPS that have served US and Europe well in terms of IP capital dominance to the detriment of other countries' development in science and technology."*

However, the statement is an inaccurate representation of the situation. It does not highlight the differing positions of Germany vis-à-vis other EU member states and the EU Parliament. As explained by Kang, *"(The statement) obscures the complete picture by omitting that other EU states' interests are not the same as the German government's interest. I find it odd that the French, Spanish, Dutch and Italian governments' as well as the European Parliament's support for the TRIPS waiver are being consistently silenced and ignored at the Commission level. The EU does not seem to represent its member states' interest regarding the TRIPS waiver accurately."*

A Geneva-based trade source familiar with discussions at the WTO told us that Germany is increasingly isolated, but decisively becoming the only EU country to block the TRIPS waiver. France, Netherlands, Spain, have varyingly made statements suggesting support for the waiver proposal, as individual member states. But since the EU votes as a bloc at WTO, Germany can effectively coerce others to oppose the waiver. As the largest EU economy, Germany has the latitude to do so, in addition to being dictated by domestic political priorities.

See: *Confidential Communication on the TRIPS Waiver Shows the EU's Unwillingness to Negotiate*

A test of internationalism

In its arguments, Germany and other opponents to the waiver miss a crucial point. It is well-known and conceded that companies around the world are working hard to ramp up vaccine production and that the world's vaccine needs will be met at some point in the future. However, the questions that demand an answer are: who will need to wait for the vaccines? (Hint: it will always be LMICs) And for how long? (Hint: Depends. Even in the best-case scenario, it could be 2023).

The arguments against the waiver hinge upon suppositions that depend on multiple factors; some of them beyond our control, such as new variants of SARS-Cov-2. None of the waiver's opponents can assert exactly when and how the rest of the world will be vaccinated and who is to be held accountable if this fails to happen. Based on how the pandemic has unfolded so far, here is what one can say with reasonable certainty: As new variants emerge, rich countries will hoard up vaccines; they will ensure multiple booster shots for their population; their population will have access to better quality healthcare irrespective; they will mostly not face a shortage of masks, diagnostic tests, or therapeutics. Suffice to say, if the conditions were reversed, this issue might have never warranted this long a debate.

The COVID-19 pandemic in Germany presently is unlike anywhere else in the world (except, perhaps other rich countries). As of July 2021, half of Germany is fully vaccinated and every fifth 12- 17-year-old has received the first jab. Vaccination campaigns nationally are now plateauing and vaccine hesitancy persists. Despite lack of evidence, the country intends to administer booster doses from September 2021. All this, while it deals with the 'problem' of excess vaccine doses, which it now plans to donate to other countries. Against this background, it may be worthwhile to remember Chancellor Merkel's call for the vaccine to be a global public good. Ursula von der Leyen, President of the European Commission echoed these sentiments. Yet, more than a year into the pandemic, vaccines are far from being a global common. With the Delta variant posing a new challenge, it is clear no country can booster-shot their way out of the pandemic.

As Chancellor Merkel's term ends, Germany is in a state of flux with elections scheduled for September 2021. Morality and a sense of duty require that Germany do the right thing. As Kang eloquently puts it, "*Germany ought to be informed by an obligation to internationalism rather than by its current economic nationalism that is leading to devastating effects outside Europe.*"

It remains to be seen whether, as the champion of global health, Germany will place people over profit.

Like this story? You can write to Rithika Sangameshwaran here: rithika.sk9@gmail.com

27.
THE SHRINKING SPACE FOR THE OPPONENTS TO THE TRIPS WAIVER (SEPTEMBER 17, 2021)

month is too long in geopolitics. As trade diplomats resumed discussions this month on the TRIPS waiver proposal after a month-long break in August, they returned to changing contours of these discussions.

At the face of it, not much has changed namely that the key opponents including the EU, Switzerland and the UK, have continued to dig into their heels, resisting the approach to temporarily waiving intellectual property protections for COVID-19 medical products. In the meantime, the co-sponsors were joined by more WTO members including Jordan and Malaysia. Australia and China have also said that they will support the TRIPS waiver.

As we reported out last week, just as diplomats race to conclude competing negotiations in the run up to the Ministerial Conference later this year, the pharma industry announced the possibility of reaching surplus production of COVID-19 vaccines within a few months.

However, as we saw these increased numbers in doses do not mean much in terms of concretely addressing vaccines inequities given that orders have been tied up and secured by paying countries. WHO and African leaders this week, pushed for buying doses from manufacturers and urged lifting of export restrictions on vaccines.

In what finally sounded like a significant moment for account-ability, Gavi's Seth Berkley asked fellow partners of the COVAX facility – the pharma industry: "where are these doses"? The IFPMA is part of the ACT Accelerator and the COVAX Facility is the vaccines pillar under this international mechanism set up to address the pandemic.

All of this underscores the continued importance of the TRIPS waiver discussions at the WTO.

This story charts out how the coming weeks will likely unfold. We spoke with diplomats and experts to understand the different commercial, political and epidemiological factors associated with this pandemic that could influence the outcome on these discussions.

THIS MONTH AT THE TRIPS COUNCIL
A string of formal, informal, consultations and negotiations will continue between WTO members over the coming weeks to craft a compromise on the way forward on the TRIPS Waiver proposal.

It is not clear yet what the cornerstones of such a compromise will look like, but we also know that there are parallel process-es within the WTO to work on a presentable outcome in time for the 12th Ministerial Conference later this year in Geneva. It is these institutionalized processes that might result in a more mainstream outcome that may be palatable to a diverse WTO membership.

Many diplomats are of the view, that any potential agreement of the TRIPS Waiver proposal will have to be seen in the larg-er context of the Ministerial Conference where several other issues will compete as instruments for quid pro quos between WTO members. Further, that the priorities for each WTO mem-ber will be different. While some may want to give in on the waiver, for other fisheries negotiations may be more important to win, trade diplomats told us.

THE TRIPS COUNCIL INFORMAL MEETING: 14 SEPTEMBER

Earlier this week, WTO members met on 14 September in an informal, open-ended meeting that sources said was "unusually short". Countries reiterated their previously stated positions with respect to the South Africa-India proposal that seeks a bold, temporary suspension of intellectual property protections to fight the pandemic, and the European Union proposal, a less ambitious declaration which also seeks to tweak mechanisms such as compulsory licensing. The former was brought to WTO members in October 2020, and the latter arrived in June 2021.

Sources said that TRIPS Council, currently chaired by Norwegian Ambassador Dagfinn Sørli of Norway, believed that there was "no narrowing of differences" between diverging views of members. And added that delegations will continue to meet bilaterally or in small groups to discuss matters of scope, implementation of the waiver proposal, in addition to issues such as regulatory data and technology transfer.

It is understood that questions were also raised on the relationship between these discussions at the TRIPS Council and the wider WTO response to the pandemic led by New Zealand Ambassador David Walker.

Sources said that 20 members took the floor. Cuba, Bangladesh, Bolivia, Tanzania (on behalf of the African Group), Malaysia and Indonesia took the floor in support of South Africa and India, the proponents of the TRIPS Waiver. China and Australia also spoke in favour of the proposal.

A spokesperson from Australia's Department of Foreign Affairs and Trade told us, "Australia will support a TRIPS waiver and is engaging constructively in WTO negotiations to deliver a positive, meaningful and consensus outcome. This has been Australia's longstanding approach to the TRIPS waiver negotiations."

New Zealand, Korea, and Brazil did not oppose the proposal, but reportedly stressed on the need to find a solution, according to sources familiar with the proceedings of the meeting. Brazil was in favor of using the EU proposal on compulsory licensing to find a "landing zone" among members, sources said. (Note recent changes in Brazil's approaches to address the pandemic)

Some of the members have faced recent surges of SARS-CoV-2 infections, without having adequate access to vaccines. The evolution in the epidemiology of the disease has directly contributed to the openness in engaging with these discussions.

In addition, some members have struggled to get licenses for manufacturing of vaccines leading to frustration. Irrespective of the prevailing narrative on voluntary licensing approaches, it appears some members are not happy with the pace of manufacturing of vaccines. This might explain growing support for the waiver.

Sources said that the United States took the floor to emphasize increasing vaccine manufacturing capacity domestically and in other countries around the world. While the U.S. was reticent in previous meetings, it is reported that that the U.S. has begun to take a greater role including engaging bilaterally with the co-sponsors of the proposal.

The opponents to the proposal, the EU, UK and Switzerland reinforced their views against the waiver by highlighting the risks of legal uncertainty and "undermining ongoing collaborations". The UK is also understood to have drawn attention to mRNA hubs in South Africa and Latin America, to showcase ways to voluntarily share technology. (Although there have not been any instances of sharing technology, these collaborations have been limited to putting place fill-and-finish facilities.)

Switzerland was reportedly of the view that it was export bans, bilateral deals, vaccine diplomacy, delays in regulatory approval, vaccine hesitancy, the absence of vaccination campaigns and logistical deficiencies that led to unequal access and not IP protection.

COMING UP:
While the next TRIPS Council meeting is scheduled for 4 October, members will meet in small groups on 23 September and on 29 September. The TRIPS Council will formalise a status report to be submitted in time for consideration at the next meeting of the General Council on 7-8 October, according to Chairperson Ambassador Sørll.

Sources told us that any breakthrough in these discussions will emerge in bilateral discussions with the U.S., particularly at the political level. (See more on this in the section below *On Political Factors*)

THE WIDER DISCUSSIONS AT WTO
In the two months, ahead of the Ministerial Conference, the TRIPS Waiver talks cannot be looked at in isolation to other issues discussed among members.

In late July, the WTO said, quoting the chair of the General Council, Ambassador Dacio Castillo (Honduras), "certain choices will have to be made in terms of what we can deliver by and at MC12, and what work can usefully continue post-MC12 in the way that members deem appropriate, including through work programmes." (In July, members had considered a joint proposal from 25 WTO members for a General Council declaration proposing a series of trade policy responses to the pandemic)

In June, he had appointed Ambassador David Walker (New Zealand) on the WTO response to the pandemic for a "facilitator-led multilateral process". (Significant to note that opponents to the TRIPS Waiver proposal have spoken on the "Walker process" to find pragmatic outcomes on IP issues.)

In an earlier document dated July 21, seen by Geneva Health Files, on the discussions in the Informal Sub-Group on the WTO's Response to the COVID-19 Pandemic, it appeared that there was some support for the DG's Third Way to address vaccine shortages. The Third Way is loosely understood as using voluntary licensing approaches to boost manufacturing of vaccines.

On measures related to IP rights, the document said:

"Many showed support for separating the TRIPS Council work from other issues being discussed in the subgroup and the Facilitator's process. Different views, however, were expressed on how the outcome would address the issues discussed in different processes, including the discussion in the TRIPS Council. Some indicated difficulties in envisaging an outcome on the WTO response to the pandemic without an agreement on the IP waiver.

1. Ensure that the TRIPS Agreement is applied and IP rights are managed in a manner that complements Members' response to the pandemic, including through the dissemination of technology and know-how, as well as the full use of policy options in the WTO system, while preserving the IP system's incentive function for innovation

2. *[+Results of the text-based process related to the TRIPS waiver (IP/C/W/669/Rev.1)]*

3. *[+Results of the text-based process related to clarification of TRIPS flexibilities (compulsory licensing) (IP/C/W/681)]*

4. *Welcome and support implementation of a joint WHO-WIPO-WTO platform to provide technical assistance to*

countries relating to their needs for COVID-19 medical technologies.

So, it will remain to be seen to what extent these parallel discussions will edge out or supersede the TRIPS Waiver discussions.

THE PACKAGE AROUND THE MINISTERIAL CONFERENCE

In her report dated 28 July 2021 as the chair of the trade negotiations committee, DG Ngozi Okonjo-Iweala said:

"If we are to achieve anything meaningful, we need to focus on a limited number of issues for delivery before or by MC12 – three or four at the maximum and intensify processes from 1 September as laid out by the Chairs or Facilitators. 1.12. Given where we are today – from what I have heard in the past months and last week – intensifying efforts on some areas such as Fisheries Subsidies, Agriculture, the WTO's Response to the Pandemic, WTO reform and dispute settlement – seems reasonable and could take us within the realm of what could be possible for deliver"

Restricted WTO document: JOB/GC/265

One developing country diplomat told us that countries have varied interests. "Members will have their own set of quid pro quos in the context of the outcomes for the Ministerial Conference.

"For some the TRIPS waiver may not be so important, and for others, the fisheries negotiations may be key," a developing country diplomat told Geneva Health Files. The diplomat also drew attention to processes outside of WTO, including EU investments in capacity-building for vaccines production in African countries, that could shape these negotiations at WTO.

THE POLITICAL FACTORS

Politics drives international trade and certainly in a pandemic with scarce resources and shrinking economies. Domestic politics on either side of the Atlantic will impact waiver discussions in Geneva. Both United States and Germany will play a significant role, apart from scores of co-sponsors of the TRIPS Waiver proposal.

As we noted earlier this week, the electoral results in Norway, for example, will surely have an impact on global health in Geneva. The Norwegian Ambassador to the WTO, Dagfinn Sørli, is also chair of the TRIPS Council overseeing the formal and informal consultations on the waiver. Norway is also at the helm of governance of the ACT Accelerator.

GERMANY

Observers are paying attention to domestic politics in Germany and the extent to which it can impact the waiver discussions in Geneva. German elections on 26 September could be crucial.

Germany has led the opposition to the waiver proposal, among EU members. The elections in Germany might contribute to the overall EU position on the waiver, observers say. (See also our earlier story: *Understanding Germany's Trenchant Opposition to the TRIPS Waiver*)

In a separate event this week, Sarah Matthieu, a Member of the European Parliament alluded to BioNTech as a particularly big donor of Germany's ruling Christian Democratic Union Party.

This week, in a letter addressed to candidates for a new German chancellor, more than 140 former heads of states and Nobel laureates urged them to support the waiver, to overcome vaccines monopolies and push for transfer of technology. (The People's Vaccine Alliance, a coalition of more than 70 organizations coordinated the campaign)

Excerpts from the letter:

"Dear Annalena Baerbock, Armin Laschet, and Olaf Scholz,

We, the undersigned former Heads of State and Government and Nobel Laureates, write to you in the conviction that Germany has a significant role to play in global efforts to bring the COVID-19 pandemic to an end. The impact of that would be of huge significance to people in Germany and around the world.

As candidates to be the next German Chancellor, responsibility for your country's leadership on this issue will fall on one of you.

German publicly funded science developed the world-class mRNA BioNTech-Pfizer vaccine which was a huge achievement. Yet vaccines are zero per cent effective for those who cannot access them...."

Pressure on Germany could also be building on account of the United States. US Congressman Ro Khanna said at an event, organized by civil society organizations, that Biden had shown strong leadership on the TRIPS waiver, but he now had to "convince our European allies, who are often fond of lecturing the United States about moral responsibility, to live up to theirs".

WHAT THE AMERICANS HOLD

Diplomatic sources told Geneva Health Files that if the U.S. can be brought on board with a text that will be agreeable to both sides, opponents to the proposal will "fall in line with the American position."

There is pressure on the U.S., to show moral leadership in wake of the crisis in Afghanistan, one trade diplomat told us. (President Biden will host a Global COVID-19 Summit next week, on the side-lines of the United Nations General Assembly, to urge leaders to commit to vaccinating 70% of the world population within a year).

Health Policy Watch declared this week: "Pressure is mounting on US President Joe Biden to provide global leadership to ensure equitable access to COVID-19 vaccines in the face of the European Commission's refusal to support a waiver on intellectual property rights."

In a separate event organized by Public Citizen, South African trade ministry advisor Zane Dangor hinted at the possibility of an American proposal on the waiver that could reinvigorate the talks.

THE ROLE OF CIVIL SOCIETY AND ACADEMICS
Irrespective of the outcome on these discussions, the role of civil society and certain scholars of IP has been significant in raising the profile of this proposal and in educating the world at large on the issues at stake.

In an event, earlier this week, organized by The Third World Network, MSF and Health Action International, parliamentarians and other leaders participated in the merits of the waiver proposal.

Scholars including Siva Thambisetty, Associate Professor in intellectual property law at London School of Economics, who spoke at the event, called for a 'waiver regime' that could entail plural measures and imaginative solutions such as open sourcing of manufacturing know-how, buying out know-how, compulsory license of trade secrets, among other approaches.

TAILPIECE
TIME magazine put the burden of ensuring a successful Ministerial Conference on the shoulders of WTO's charismatic and skillful boss, Ngozi Okonjo-Iweala.

In his remarks on Thursday in Geneva, Executive Vice-President Valdis Dombrovskis, said:

"...On the pandemic response, I would like to take this opportunity to thank Director-General Dr Ngozi for her unfailing efforts to promote equity in vaccine production and distribution. By connecting the relevant dots and actors, she has really moved the needle on the international debate."

Internally at WTO, trade experts are still grappling with the priorities and the direction taken by the DG, especially in the context of the pandemic.

December will tell us if Okonjo-Iweala is able to bring the WTO membership together to deliver.

28.

EXAMINING THE "SUBTLE SHIFT" IN THE TRIPS WAIVER TALKS AT WTO (OCTOBER 15, 2021)

The EU calls on South Africa to resolve impasse

Over the last two weeks, there have been indications of some behind-the-scenes movement that show WTO members' willingness to arrive at a consensus on the intellectual property response to the pandemic. Although at the face of it, there has been no structural change in the way countries have aligned on the TRIPS Waiver discussions, nevertheless there has been greater engagement among members, sources familiar with the discussions say. As we reported last week, during the General Council meeting at the WTO, officials had suggested "a subtle shift" in these discussions.

What continues to be unclear however, is whether the direction of this shift is towards the bold proposal made by South Africa and India, on temporarily suspending a range of intellectual property protections in order to unplug bottlenecks in the manufacturing of medical products, to swiftly respond to the pandemic.

The "shift" was welcomed by the EU, UK, Norway and other opponents to the waiver proposal, at a TRIPS Council formal meeting at the WTO this week, where they highlighted the emerging "points of convergence".

Soon, there were reports on a new proposal by the EU that underscores existing flexibilities in the WTO TRIPS agreement, without changing intellectual property ownership and the benefits that accrue.

The proposal appears to take forward its intention of mostly tweaking with compulsory licensing provisions (EU's earlier proposal), but having "waiver-like characteristics".

(Sources close to the discussions clarified to us, that this proposal was not clearly EU's proposal, but admitted that the said document was a technical paper used in the discussions and closely portrays prevailing EU's position on these issues.)

It is understood that the EU invited negotiators from developing countries, particularly South Africa.

Reuters reported that South Africa and the EU were in intense talks to resolve impasse. Separately, Politico also discussed a September 30 position paper that showed no change in EU's plan (Politico: *EU stands by opposition to vaccine IP waiver but touts' 'convergence')*

This story discusses this new EU proposal, considering the demands made by the proponents of the waiver. We also bring you updates from the TRIPS Council discussions this week. In addition, significant remarks made by WTO DG Ngozi Oknojo-Iweala and USTR's Katherine Tai are also featured here.

THE EU PLAN: A WAIVER WITH CONDITIONALITIES?
The leaked document, titled "Ideas on the points of convergence on the TRIPS issues for discussion" reads:

"....it is important to ensure that the intellectual property system plays an enabling role in deploying existing capacity or creating new capacity to produce COVID-19 vaccines and medicines. In that regard, ensuring that all WTO Members can make effective use of the TRIPS Agreement is crucial and consequently a waiver with respect to certain requirements related to granting compulsory licenses for the production and

export of COVID-related pharmaceutical products, allowing for their rapid supplies, could be considered."

"The objective would be to lift or simplify the key requirements related to exporting COVID-related pharmaceutical products under a compulsory license to the Members in need."

Critiquing this proposal, one IP law expert said, "It is as if they are talking about a waiver for compulsory licensing, without calling it a waiver. I doubt if the proponents will accept this".

According to the EU proposal, such a waiver can be a decision of the Ministerial Conference and can follow a prior waiver format. It refers to the "Decision of the Ministerial Conference in a waiver format, based on the precedent of a waiver adopted in the wake of the HIV/AIDS crisis in 2003, i.e. Decision of 30 August 2003 on the implementation of Paragraph 6 of the Doha Declaration on the TRIPS Agreement and Public Health (WT/L/540)."

Experts point out that most of the waivers in the WTO system, have been a decision of the General Council and not a Ministerial Conference.

On paper, the product scope in the EU proposal includes "Product Scope Pharmaceutical products, i.e., vaccines, diagnostics, therapeutics against COVID-19". This is wider than the US stand, that has so far restricted any waiver only to vaccines.

The EU proposal limits the scope of the waiver in terms of the TRIPS provisions covered mainly to Article 31 of the TRIPS Agreement. It suggests waiving the following provisions (fewer than those proposed by the proponents)

- Article 31(b) – prior negotiations with rights holders – to be waived

- Article 31(f) – requirement to supply predominantly the domestic market – to be waived.

- Article 31bis – mechanism for compulsory licenses for exports – to be waived, with conditions, e.g., on eligible importing Members, for discussion.

- Article 31(h) – remuneration – to be waived and replaced by specific rules on remuneration to support deliveries of the products at discounted prices.

The EU proposal is not in favor of waiving Article 28(1), 39 and Part III of the TRIPS Agreement, in contrast to the original waiver proposal.

According to the EU, these provisions are "outside the scope of the waiver as the inclusion of these provisions is not required for the objective described above and would not be justified or proportionate."

Finally on the duration of the waiver, EU suggests "3 years with a possibility of further extension if the General Council so decides (e.g. if the circumstances of the pandemic persist)."

Critics are of the view that necessitating an extension by the General Council is problematic given the experience of developing countries in the context of extending the transition period under TRIPS Article 66.1 for Least Developed Country members. In addition, some have argued that this might disincentivise investment.

The EU proposal further suggests notification to the WTO of the measures taken and exports made, for greater transparency. But experts say that incorporating transparency requirements such as notifications are procedurally unworkable and could make it difficult to use the waiver, citing the experience of using Article 31*bis*.

THE DEMANDS OF THE WAIVER PROPONENTS:

As per the South Africa-India proposal, the TRIPS provisions that need to be waived include Article 28.1; Articles 31(a), (b), (f) and (h), Article 31bis; Article 39 Sections 5 and 7 of Part II of the TRIPS Agreement. They also suggest waiving "Part III of the TRIPS Agreement with respect to Sections 5 and 7 of Part II of the TRIPS Agreement, shall be waived in relation to vaccines, therapeutics, diagnostics, their materials and components as well as methods and means of manufacture, for the prevention, treatment or containment of COVID-19."

Briefly, proponents have sought a waiver on these elements (to read the provisions in full find them here):

Article 28.1: on exclusive rights enjoyed by the patent holder

Article 31(a): on authorizations of Compulsory Licensing on "individual merits"

Article 31(b): prior negotiations with the right holder before issuing of a CL, except in situations of national emergency, other circumstances of extreme urgency and public non-commercial use.

(Proponents say waiving the above is especially crucial for vaccines given the complex patent landscape)

Article 31(f): CLs to be "predominantly for the supply of the domestic market"

Article 31*bis*: An amendment, based on the waiver in 2003, that was supposed to have enabled a country to export medicines manufactured under a compulsory license to another importing country. Given additional procedures and notifications, the use of this mechanism has been cumbersome, it is widely acknowledged.

Article 31(h): on the payment of adequate remuneration to the right holder when issuing a compulsory license.

Article 39.2: On the right to prevent disclosure or unauthorised acquisition and use by third parties...

Article 39.3: On undisclosed test data or other data submitted by the originator company for purposes of approving the

marketing of the pharmaceutical product against "unfair commercial use", "except where necessary to protect the public"
or "unless steps are taken to protect the data against unfair
commercial use".

*[Article 31bis background: Members had to work on ways to
find a solution for what was called* Paragraph 6 of the Doha
Declaration on TRIPS and Public Health, that recognised the
inability of some countries to make use of compulsory licensing
mechanisms for lack of manufacturing capacity. This resulted in
the August 2003 decision of the General Council of the WTO,
waiving requirements of Article 31 (f) of the TRIPS Agreement,
thus enabling a country to export medicines manufactured
under a compulsory license to another importing country. The
Canada-Rwanda case in 2007 illustrated the problems in using
this waiver effectively. Members decided in 2005, to make this
waiver a permanent amendment in the TRIPS Agreement. This
amendment (Article 31bis) took effect in 2017.]

THE RISK OF A WAIVER WITH TOO MANY CONDITIONS
Experts are of the view that the EU proposal as it stands risks
being ineffective in addressing current challenges if the use of
a waiver is linked to conditionalities.

"The EU paper presents the 2003 TRIPS waiver that became
Article 31bis as some type of precedent to follow. But the 2003
waiver is well known as a big screw up that has not worked,
and not by accident.... Any effort to limit or condition who can
import under a compulsory license is bad, and making the
WTO more involved in remuneration decisions is not a good
idea either," James Love of Knowledge Ecology International
said on Twitter.

Civil society organizations have, in the past, pushed for the
use of Article 30 of the TRIPS Agreement.

Article 30: Exceptions to Rights Conferred

Members may provide limited exceptions to the exclusive rights conferred by a patent, provided that such exceptions do not unreasonably conflict with a normal exploitation of the patent and do not unreasonably prejudice the legitimate interests of the patent owner, taking account of the legitimate interests of third parties.

In the context of the EU proposal, Medicines Law and Policy, points out:

"...Alternatively, the EU could propose an interpretation of article 30 (which details exceptions to rights conferred by a patent) that would allow export of products as a straightforward exception. In the past the EC has indeed proposed a solution based on article 30...."

THE TRIPS COUNCIL MEETING OCTOBER 13-14

At the TRIPS Council formal meeting this week, sources indicated that there were areas of convergence between members on the COVID-19 IP response at WTO.

The EU was reportedly "encouraged" by recent small group meetings where scope and implementation of the waiver was discussed. Its proposal on TRIPS flexibilities was also discussed in these meetings. In addition, the UK, Norway saw emerging areas of convergence but continued to emphasise on "pragmatic" outcomes. Switzerland's response to new developments were more "lukewarm" sources said. Swiss continue to be unclear on how waiver can be effective and expeditious to address pandemic.

Singapore urged members to "synergize" discussions at the TRIPS Council and with the Walker process. Brazil, Japan, Korea, asked members to be flexible to forge consensus.

Proponents of the waiver were said to be open to working on trade and health package. South Africa saw the possibility of aligning on a package of trade related IP aspects for MC12

"Our objective is not to win a debate, but to reach a concrete outcome". South Africa also expressed disappointment at the lack of progress on text-based process on the waiver.

India said that a "handful of members have chosen to remain unconvinced regarding the content and intent of the TRIPS waiver proposal". China is open to engaging in discussions, source said.

While the US reiterated its support for a waiver of IP protections for COVID-19 vaccines, it also emphasised "consensus" at WTO. (See below on USTR comments on the waiver this week)

Pakistan, Bangladesh, Bolivia, Cuba, Venezuela, Nigeria, Egypt, Indonesia and Namibia extended support to waiver and welcomed any initiative that address access to vaccines, medical equipment for COVID-19. Colombia suggested it is open to addressing IP issues either through a waiver for vaccines or in terms of TRIPS flexibilities. Australia, New Zealand reiterated support for waiver, with the latter suggesting applicability of waiver to vaccines only.

Sources also said that TRIPS Council chair, Norwegian Ambassador Dagfinn Sørli was cautious about way ahead and noted that members' positions have not deviated since previous meetings. But it is learned that he is optimistic on the discussions given the progress in bilateral consultations between members.

Discussions in the TRIPS Council are broadly being guided by the following objectives, Ambassador Sørli has said: engaging in text-based negotiations on the South Africa and India proposal, continuing deliberations in a small group format; urging "a compromise by members to move away from long held positions"; focusing on possible "points of convergence"; and aligning with the wider discussions in relation to the WTO response to the pandemic led by Ambassador David Walker.

He added that that if members reach a consensus at the TRIPS Council, it will contribute to other relevant processes in the context of the Ministerial Conference.

Interestingly he also added that the TRIPS Council will be informed if members meeting in another context are able to come to an agreement on this issue. "If members meet in another context and reach agreement, they will inform TRIPS Council...". This assumes significance in the context of bilateral discussions between the EU and South Africa.

While it is not "regular" to resolve intractable WTO issues bilaterally between members, (in this case, in Brussels) trade experts say that members do meet among themselves to resolve issues faster in ways that are not possible even in small group meetings that could have upto 20 members participating.

At the meeting South Africa said, "while the TRIPS waiver proposal should still be an integral part of any successful outcome at MC12, members should move beyond the binary approach between the waiver proposal and the declaration proposal submitted by the EU."

The next small group consultation is scheduled on October 26th. There will be a TRIPS council meeting ahead of General Council meeting in November 22-23.

TAI IN GENEVA

Meanwhile in a significant visit to Geneva this week, US Ambassador Katherine Tai also laid out the American vision for the WTO. On whether the US had wavered on the question of the TRIPS Waiver, Tai said:

"...It is something we continue to think about and work on because it is so important. From the outside it might look like silence. But I want everyone to know that the Biden administration's embracing and endorsement of the TRIPS waiver, and the proponents is about our commitment to the global COVID

response, the need to address what we are hearing from so many WTO members which is that we need more production of vaccines and a more equitable distribution of vaccines.

While we are making progress collectively there is a lot more progress that we need to make.

I want to put in context the endorsement of the waiver, in the overall efforts that the Biden administration is making, 1 billion doses committed, and to deliver on them.

To answer your question...because this is a Geneva crowd and I say this with the utmost affection that we are all trade nerds here, on the TRIPS Waiver, the challenge is how do you get consensus in the WTO, so that the WTO can look at the issue of IP rules and where they can be modified in the pandemic to increase production and for more equitable distribution of doses....It is such an important issue because of the time, because of the potential positive impact on the lives of people."

TAILPIECE: WTO DG ON THE WAIVER
Ngozi Okonjo-Iweala on the TRIPS Waiver speaking at Reviving the multilateral trading system:

"By focussing only on the TRIPS Waiver, people are missing a very important point and are not focussing on some very critical issues for solving this problem of access to vaccines. The simple fact was that the world was not equipped, did not have enough production capacity for producing vaccines in the first place. We were producing 5 billion vaccines in total prior to the pandemic – largely children's vaccines. And the pandemic came, we find that we need 10-15 billion doses. There was not enough investment in production capacity to begin with, to produce that number of vaccines. So, we must focus on that. So even you get the IP waive today and you do not have a factory or a manufacturing plant, you are not going to get anywhere. So, the attention on the waiver issue, yes, this

is important, but people have shifted attention from some of the other constraints...

So, you need to increase production capacity, you need to decentralise production, from the 10 countries. 80% of world export of vaccines come from these countries. In this crisis, that does not work..."

See also her remarks yesterday at the Peterson Institute for International Economics in Washington D.C., where she suggests that WTO members could find "a pragmatic compromise on the IP waiver which ensures equitable access to developing countries while preserving incentives for research and innovation."

Coming weeks will reveal who finally pays for a pragmatic compromise.

29.
THE EMERGING PATH TO THE TRIPS WAIVER (NOVEMBER 12, 2021)

With just a fortnight left for the 12th WTO ministerial conference, WTO members continue to diverge on the TRIPS Waiver proposal that many believe will bolster the response to COVID-19. But countries hope that they will be able to find convergence on a potential waiver to ensure a strong outcome on WTO's response to the pandemic on intellectual property issues.

Members are exploring ways in which vaccine manufacturers who are ready to produce, should be able to begin production of COVID-19 vaccines without worrying about patents. But it is unclear which route this could take – whether under existing TRIPS flexibilities or a waiver.

For the European Union, the way ahead is tightly signposted suggesting the use of existing TRIPS flexibilities such compulsory licensing. On the other hand, proponents of the waiver, led by South Africa continue to push for a waiver of obligations under a slew of intellectual property protections that go beyond compulsory licensing.

Time is running out. There could be potential political consequences for not only for WTO, but also its members. The growing expectations for deliverables for the ministerial, is putting pressure on the opponents to the waiver to work out a solution, diplomatic sources suggest. For the most part, after more than 12 months of pushing for a waiver, the proponents now seem to have more latitude to preserve the objectives in their proposal. Whether they will be able to retain key elements in their proposal is yet to be seen.

"The pressure is on others to row the boat, we are only steering the direction of the boat," a diplomat from a developing country told us.

This story tries to capture the state of play in these discussions based on multiple interviews with Geneva-based trade officials and diplomats.

THE CONTOURS OF THE EU POSITION VIS-À-VIS THE U.S. ON THE WAIVER

For the EU, any waiver-like solution must remain restricted to waiving provisions of Article 31 and Article 31*bis* that collectively regulate compulsory licensing – a mechanism which authorises the production of a patented product or process without the consent of the patent owner. (See our recent story which discusses these provisions.)

Sources familiar with these bilateral discussions between the EU and the proponents, said that the EU believes that the terms being offered "is very generous" and that the proponents must consider it.

"Using the US approach of restricting the waiver only to vaccines is useless. We need a waiver approach that will address other medical products including therapeutics and diagnostics. Therefore, the compulsory licensing approach suggested by the EU makes sense because it can apply to diagnostics and therapeutics and not just vaccines," a source from a developed country said.

However, observers point out that while the EU restricts the scope of intellectual property protections to the use of compulsory licensing only, the US, although limiting the waiver to vaccines, is more open to waiving other kinds of intellectual property protections going by the statement by the USTR on May 5.

A narrow, and as some would say, optimistic reading of the statement points to the use of plural in 'IP protections': "The Administration believes strongly in intellectual property protections, but in service of ending this pandemic, supports the waiver of those protections for COVID-19 vaccines," the statement had said.

"It is difficult to understand where the US stands and how far it wants to go. They have been very brief in their interventions in bilateral discussions and at TRIPS Council meetings," a diplomatic source from a developing country told us.

Earlier this week, Inside US Trade reported, that Katherine Tai, the US trade chief said that the US "had not proposed its own version of a waiver of some WTO intellectual property obligations for vaccines and other pandemic-related products." According to the report, she reaffirmed the support of the Biden administration to the waiver proposal and to "play our role at the WTO to facilitate that text-based negotiation." She acknowledged that the waiver was a "a very, very powerful message from the developing countries at the WTO that they need relief in this pandemic," the news report said. Sounding upbeat, on a potential outcome on the waiver at the ministerial, she is reported to have said, "We're going to bring our best game.... It is time to facilitate something that is going to work and is going to be meaningful and that can be accepted by the WTO," Inside US Trade reported.

Last month, Third World Network said in an update that the US had suggested a peace clause for disputes that could arise from the implementation of IPR (intellectual property rights) provisions in the WTO's response to the COVID-19 pandemic. Citing experts, the report noted that "...there is no clear legal basis for a peace clause and hence could create legal uncertainty and hesitancy with respect to its implementation. In contrast a waiver is rooted in Article IX of the Marrakesh Agreement. Unlike the peace clause there are also precedents for the adoption of waivers around intellectual property..."

ACCESSING TRADE SECRETS WITHOUT A WAIVER?

While the access to regulatory data and manufacturing know-how is key for the effectiveness of the waiver approach, suspending obligations to protect undisclosed information is a sticking point for the EU. The EU has been very protective about discussions on technology transfer, sources indicated.

Article 39 of the TRIPS agreement governs these areas, and the proponents of the waiver have asked for suspension of these obligations.

The EU is hoping to use the compulsory licensing regime to trade secrets, sources told us. According to an official aware of these discussions, the EU believes that the access to trade secrets is regulated under Article 39.3 of the TRIPS Agreement, and hence a waiver to enable access to trade secrets is not warranted.

This provision regulates undisclosed test data or other data submitted by the originator company for purposes of approving the marketing of the pharmaceutical product against "unfair commercial use", "except where necessary to protect the public" or "unless steps are taken to protect the data against unfair commercial use".

Article 39.3 reads as follows:

Article 39

3. Members, when requiring, as a condition of approving the marketing of pharmaceutical or of agricultural chemical products which utilize new chemical entities, the submission of undisclosed test or other data, the origination of which involves a considerable effort, shall protect such data against unfair commercial use. In addition, Members shall protect such data against disclosure, except where necessary to protect the public, or unless steps are taken to ensure that the data are protected against unfair commercial use.

But proponents argue that it has been difficult for WTO members to use such provisions, without facing political and commercial pressures. If the EU clarifies the use of compulsory licensing to access undisclosed information, these waiver discussions will have succeeded in pushing this further, sources told us.

"Developing countries have not been able to use these flexibilities, and therefore the need a waiver. Waiving 39.3 will help fast track the process and to get marketing approval," a trade law expert told us.

(Read here what an Indian lawyer told us, on how governments must get companies to share trade secrets within the scope of existing patent rules. Also, see language in EU's own directive on trade secrets that makes exceptions for public health)

DISPUTE SETTLEMENT: A STICKING POINT

During these discussions on the waiver proposal, some members have reportedly raised questions on the dispute settlement mechanism in the context of the implementation of a potential waiver.

On disputes, the proponents have said in their revised proposal: "Members shall not challenge any measures taken in conformity with the provision of the waivers contained in this Decision under subparagraphs 1(b) and 1(c) of Article XXIII of GATT 1994, or through the WTO's Dispute Settlement Mechanism."

There is no agreement on whether this potential provision will apply to all categories of medical products.

Experts have said that given the crisis around WTO's Appellate Body, filing disputes may be a non-starter.

However, in the context of the waiver it may be different. Back in March, a Geneva-based trade lawyer had told us, "The waiver discussion is very heated and it is aggravating the discussion on the EU's export restrictions. If the waiver succeeds, then the opposing members cannot do anything about it. So, they will be looking at other ways to beat up on behaviour they do not like on the COVID-19 front. Do not rule out disputes against supporters of the TRIPS waiver proposal, in case the waiver is adopted", the source added.

(See more on this in our earlier story: Could Vaccine Nationalism Spur Disputes at the WTO)

THE FINAL STRETCH TO CONSENSUS?
Despite the many conditionalities, what could consensus look like?

If the proponents were to accept any proposal by the EU, it will have to weighed against the objectives of the waiver, a source said. "The scope of the commitments expressed by the EU, even in the context of the limited approach to compulsory licensing, will have to meet the conditions the waiver seeks to achieve," the source added.

One diplomatic source told us that for the proponents, waiving Article 28.1 of the TRIPS Agreement, will be a key legal basis to arrive at a conclusion in these discussions. But it is understood that the EU is not in favour of this.

Article 28.1:

1. A patent shall confer on its owner the following exclusive rights:

a. *where the subject matter of a patent is a product, to prevent third parties not having the owner's consent from the acts of: making, using, offering for sale, selling, or importing (6) for these purposes that product;*

b. *where the subject matter of a patent is a process, to prevent third parties not having the owner's consent from the act of using the process, and from the acts of: using, offering for sale, selling, or importing for these purposes at least the product obtained directly by that process.*

In addition, the EU does not see that use of the waiver to be applicable to copyrights and industrial designs as suggested by the proponents. While these provisions continue to be on the table, some believe that certain intellectual property protections may be left out of a waiver and instead, find place in a non-binding declaration that could accompany a waiver.

THE QUID PRO QUOS AROUND THE WAIVER

Sources suggested in bilateral discussions between the EU and the proponents, that future collaborations could be at risk. So, in effect, the carrot of voluntary licensing deals is being used as a tool to get consensus on ways to agree on a narrower waiver.

However, for the proponents of the waiver, voluntary licensing approaches suggested by those to oppose the waiver, have failed to address the demand for COVID-19 medical products.

"The waiver does not pre-empt any collaboration. The waiver will be useful when these collaborations do not work," a diplomatic source from a developing country told us.

In addition, to understand the waiver discussions in a broader context, look at the discussions on the pandemic treaty at WHO. Spearheaded by the EU, the push for a pandemic treaty is now gaining more traction among developing countries, particularly in Africa. (South Africa is solidly in favour of a new legal instrument to address future health emergencies, even submitting a detailed proposal to secure commitments on equity in any potential treaty.)

HOW WTO MEMBERS LINE UP

While the EU continues to negotiate on behalf of a small group of countries who remain opposed to the waiver and those who have expressed reservations on the waiver, South Africa is leading the bilateral discussions on behalf of 64 co-sponsors of the waiver proposal.

Sources suggested that the UK and Switzerland remain opposed to the waiver, others including Brazil, Mexico, Japan, Norway, Canada and Singapore could eventually be brought on board towards a consensus. This week, Austria became the latest EU member state to express support for the waiver. This follows, Italy, Spain, Greece and France that have expressed support for the waiver.

(Note that in May 2021, the European Parliament passed a resolution and called on the EU to support the TRIPS waiver.)

Further, earlier this week, the European Parliament's Committee on International Trade (INTA) adopted resolution on Multilateral negotiations in view of the 12th WTO Ministerial Conference in Geneva, 30 November to 3 December 2021. This is expected to be submitted to the European Parliament for adoption. It called for "the establishment of a new permanent Committee on Trade and Health at MC12 in order to assist governments with implementing existing exceptions and flexibilities in international trade law and to lay the groundwork for a trade pillar for the negotiations on a future international treaty on pandemic response.."

TRIPS COUNCIL MEETING: 5 NOVEMBER

The WTO TRIPS Council Meeting met last week on November 5 both in a formal and an informal mode. While no major "breakthrough" has been reported yet during the consultations among WTO members on the TRIPS waiver over the past few weeks, sources said that countries are still hopeful of reaching consensus ahead of the 12th ministerial conference.

TRIPS Council Chair, Dagfinn Sørli, Norway's Ambassador to the WTO, has said, there was a "shared view" among countries, that those vaccine manufacturers which are ready to produce, should be able to begin production of COVID-19 vaccines without worrying about patents. However, delegations were divided on whether this can be done under existing TRIPS flexibilities or under a waiver approach.

The next TRIPS Council meeting is expected on 15 November. An oral status report on the discussions will be provided at the WTO General Council on that meets 22-23 November, ahead of the ministerial later in the month.

South Africa said during the meeting that the resolve of co-sponsors to the TRIPS waiver remains intact. It also expressed disappointment that a small minority of delegations continue to refuse to even engage in text-based negotiations.

The EU reported on working with several delegations to further its proposal on improving the compulsory licensing system. It is of the view that areas of convergence are emerging and has favoured bilateral consultations in the coming days.

BEYOND THE WAIVER: HOW THESE DISCUSSIONS TRANSCENDED TRADE POLITICS

Even as members continue to find areas of convergence on the waiver proposal, many believe the fight is already won even in terms of generating a discussion on making TRIPS flexibilities workable.

"The waiver discussion has implications beyond the ministerial conference. In some ways this is just the beginning in the long process to change the narrative on access issues," a trade expert told us.

"There are new stakeholders propelling this. These discussions have moved into a global, wider sphere transcending epistemic communities. There are new moderators in this debate and a new type of politics emerging that has democratized these discussions," the expert noted. This is truly multilateralism, for it also affects developed countries, the expert added.

To be sure, this debate has transcended trade policy.

This week, the International Commission of Jurists published an expert legal opinion: Human Rights Obligations of States to not impede the Proposed COVID-19 TRIPS Waiver.

In its conclusion, the opinion says:

"States should not impede the TRIPS Waiver proposal.

This opinion has set out States' obligations to guarantee the human rights to health, life, equality and science. These obligations include minimum core obligations of immediate effect that States parties to international Covenants are bound to prioritise in respect of marginalised communities and individuals. Furthermore, States are bound to refrain from obstructing the realisation of these rights; to regulate private actors, including businesses, to prevent interference with these rights; and, finally, to take proactive steps to realise these rights in full without discrimination of any kind.

State obligations in this regard also include extra territorial obligations – in particular the obligation to cooperate internationally to realise these rights. At the same time, a large majority of States parties to the ICESCR and ICCPR are member States of the WTO. These same States bear obligations to act in a manner that realises their human rights obligations. This extends to their activities at the WTO. The WTO 'covered agreements' contemplate this through the 'public health' objective in the TRIPS Agreements.

This opinion also explains that waivers of trade and intellectual property obligations are exceptional, but not unprecedented and discusses the waiver that followed the Doha Declaration as analogous to the proposed TRIPS Waiver in responding to a public health crisis.

Finally, this opinion explains that in concrete terms, under international human rights law, States have at the very least, a duty not to obstruct TRIPS waiver negotiations. By opposing the negotiations, as many continue to do, these States fail to perform their treaty obligations under international human rights law in violation of the rights to health, life, equality and science."

30.
IS THE 'WALKER PROCESS' AT THE WTO UNDERMINING THE TRIPS WAIVER? (NOVEMBER 19, 2021)

I n crafting a WTO response to the pandemic, not all members favor referring to a potential decision on the TRIPS Waiver. This, among other issues, threatens consensus around a broader declaration on what is being referred as the WTO response to the pandemic that builds on the trade and health initiative suggested by the Ottawa Group. (The group is a coalition of countries that first proposed a trade and health initiative in November 2020)

At stake is not only what members want as text in this declaration, but also the process of negotiating this text in the run up to the 12th WTO Ministerial Conference in less than two weeks from now. Fundamental questions are reportedly being raised by some developing countries and many quarters of the civil society on whether these deliberations seek to undermine not just the TRIPS waiver, but also whether the WTO is being definitively transformed from a rules-based institution to one dictated by powerful interests.

At the heart of what appears to be a somewhat festering discord, is the Walker process – an initiative led by New Zealand Ambassador David Walker to have a coherent approach to address challenges in the wake of COVID-19. There is a perception that the Walker process has been non-transparent and deliberately vague. Much of the discussion has been limited to small group meetings where developing countries and least developed countries have been excluded from these processes, sources said.

"It is understood that the Ambassador Walker has been threatening that if there is no agreement on the text, he will just go ahead and submit a clean text to the General Council on Monday, removing what he thinks will not fly", one source familiar with the process said. The WTO General Council meets next week 22-23 November.

A letter signed by more than 75 civil society organizations, sent this morning to the WTO director-general Ngozi Okonjo-Iweala and all WTO members, said:

"We are writing with great urgency regarding the abrogation of process leading up to the 12th Ministerial Conference of the WTO (MC12), and to reinforce that the absence of a meaningful outcome on TRIPS Waiver means that the WTO has failed to mount the required response to the ongoing COVID-19 pandemic that continues to devastate countries socially and economically...."

THE WALKER PROCESS – A RECAP

When Ambassador Walker was appointed in June this year, WTO had said in an update that delegates felt there was a need for all pandemic related issues to be channelled "into a horizontal, multilateral process". Choosing a facilitator, "would not only help us streamline and organize our work but also ensure transparency and inclusiveness" GC Chair Ambassador Castillo had said.

In the past, WTO officials had stated that the Ambassador David Walker would not be focusing on the TRIPS Waiver since it is being addressed in the TRIPS Council under Norwegian

Ambassador Dagfinn Sørli who chairs the Council and is facilitating the waiver discussions.

It was said that the Walker process was expected to address trade policy issues and WTO DG Ngozi Okonjo-Iweala's 'Third Way'. The Third Way is loosely understood as approaches including voluntary licensing and using TRIPS flexibilities under existing WTO rules.

The Walker Process sought to include discussions on export restrictions, technology transfer, regulatory coherence, among others.

Some members are now reportedly not happy with the way consultations were conducted. Some allegedly are of the view that their suggestions were not considered, sources said. Members are now in the process of working on a consolidated text for a declaration on the WTO response to the pandemic.

In their latest statement, CSOs allege, "...the General Council Chair Dacio Castillo unilaterally selected Ambassador Walker of New Zealand to chair discussions on a declaration titled 'WTO response to the COVID-19 pandemic'. Ambassador Walker also unilaterally tabled a proposed text which is clearly not designed to resolve the pandemic. Rather, the draft text promotes the same liberalization demands made by developed countries in various fora and interventions that will further constrain regulatory space and policy tools available to WTO Members, while further entrenching corporate influence in the institution, drastically undermining the Member-driven character of WTO as mandated in the Marrakesh Agreement..."

THE DIVERGENCE IN THE WTO RESPONSE TO THE PANDEMIC

A document titled *"General Council Facilitator Process on the WTO response to the COVID-19 pandemic"*, seen by Geneva Health Files, illustrates the divergence among members on several issues including notification, transparency, export restrictions, trade facilitation, regulatory coherence, the role of trade in services, and a framework of future preparedness.

A consolidated text dated 15 November, reflects some of the suggestions on these matters made by developing countries. Whether there will be consensus on these issues remains to be seen.

Apart from the EU, Argentina, India, suggestions were also made by Egypt, Pakistan, South Africa, Sri Lanka, Uganda, Egypt and Venezuela. These latter group of countries are co-sponsors to a proposal (referred as *278 co-sponsors*) in October 2021: *WTO Response in Light of The Pandemic: Trade Rules That Support Resilience Building, Response and Recovery to Face Domestic and Global Crises* (a restricted WTO document JOB/GC/278). (See Third World Network's analysis on this)

The co-sponsors of 278 have suggested text referring to intellectual property barriers, staggering inequities to access to COVID-19 medical products and the concentration in the production and supply of these products.

INTELLECTUAL PROPERTY
Specifically, India suggests:

"[Taking note of the decision of the General Council to waive certain provisions of the TRIPS Agreement, in relation to health products and technologies including diagnostics, therapeutics, vaccines, medical devices, personal protective equipment, their materials or components, and their methods and means of manufacture for the prevention, treatment or containment of COVID-19;]"

The co-sponsors of 278 also suggest a new paragraph on intellectual property.

The original para suggested in the Facilitator text:

1.3. bis [We recall the Doha Declaration on the TRIPS Agreement and public health of 2001 and reiterate that the TRIPS Agreement does not and should not prevent members from taking measures to protect public health. We reaffirm that the Agreement can and should be interpreted and implemented in a manner supportive of WTO members' right to protect public health and, in particular, to promote access to medicines for all.]

Suggestion by 278 co-sponsors:

1BIS.1. We recall IP/C/W/669/Rev.1 and affirm the General Council decision granting a Waiver from Certain Provisions of the WTO Agreement on Trade-Related Aspects of Intellectual Property Rights ("the TRIPS Agreement") for the prevention, treatment and containment of COVID-19. This decision is central to the WTO's Response to the COVID-19 pandemic and we urge WTO Members to rapidly implement and give effect to this decision.

1BIS.2. We also agree that beyond COVID-19, resilience building, response, and recovery to face future health emergencies or other crises, also requires WTO Members to address issues and concerns with respect to intellectual property including the difficulties faced by developing countries and LDCs in using flexibilities of the TRIPS Agreement to protect public health.

1BIS3. In accordance with existing WTO rules, we further agree that Members shall not directly or indirectly, prevent or discourage, another Member(s) from fully utilising the existing flexibilities of the TRIPS Agreement or in any way limit such flexibilities.]

NOTIFICATION AND TRANSPARENCY

The text also shows divergence among members on notification and transparency matters. Critics are of the view that notification requirements though important, could be burdensome on countries fighting the pandemic. They also raise the lack of transparency on questions around licensing to produce COVID-19 medical products.

So, the EU for example has suggested the following:

New para. 2.2: We stand ready to consult with any other affected Member which considers that a given measure may seriously disrupt supply chains or discourage exports, and consequently affect that Member's access to essential medical goods, including COVID-19 vaccines, therapeutics, diagnostics and related vaccine materials.

The 278 co-sponsors have suggested this:

New para. 2.6: Members recognize that opaque contractual conditions in licensing arrangements for manufacturing and procurement agreements have greatly contributed to inequitable access including vaccine inequity. Members will encourage transparency by making public these contractual terms to facilitate equitable access to COVID-19 products especially vaccines, therapeutics and diagnostics.

EXPORT RESTRICTIONS OR PROHIBITIONS

Export restrictions used by both developed and developing countries are a key sticking point in these deliberations.

India suggests the following language:

"While considering issues relating to export restriction, Members shall also keep in mind that export restrictions are symptoms of acute supply side constraints, and till we address such constraints, exports restrictions will continue to surface one way or the other. In fact, in a supply constrained environment, export restrictions can check limited supplies being cornered by a few, resulting in crowding-out effect on developing countries, including LDCs. We have seen that this has helped

in ensuring a more equitable distribution and access during the current pandemic."

Argentina suggests "exercising restraint in the imposition of any new export restrictions and prohibitions and have recourse to export restrictions and prohibitions only as a last resort, recognizing the need to review regularly all existing export restrictions and prohibitions on essential COVID-19 products with a view to assessing their continued justification and removing them as soon as possible"

THE EU AND THE WALKER PROCESS

Several civil society organizations who have been familiar with the discussions in these forums suggest that the Walker process is being orchestrated by the European Union.

Civil society groups are of the view that Ambassador Walker is rushing ahead with negotiations on WTO's Response to COVID-19 Pandemic to advance the agenda of the Ottawa Group including the EU aimed at promoting more liberalization and regulatory constraints under the guise of responding to the pandemic.

The EU mission to the WTO in Geneva did not wish to respond to our query on this. Diplomats did not want to comment since "discussions are underway".

Even as the EU conducts bilateral consultations with South Africa on the TRIPS waiver, no breakthrough has been reported yet, although both sides acknowledged progress in these consultations at a TRIPS Council meeting this week.

To be sure, the WTO has consistently stated that the Walker process is separate from the discussions at the TRIPS Council. But activists point out, why a declaration for the Ministerial – overseen by Ambassador Walker – should not mention the TRIPS waiver proposal – the centrepiece of the IP response to the pandemic. Afterall, with 64 co-sponsors, the support for the waiver proposal should not be disregarded in WTO's response to COVID-19, activists said.

CRITICISMS TO THE WALKER PROCESS

Ambassador Walker, it was pointed out by WTO officials in recent months, has been one of the most able and respected ambassadors in town, who had steered the membership as chair of the General Council and the Dispute Settlement Body.

Unusual in staid trade policy debates, several civil society organizations have criticized his role in very serious terms.

"Meanwhile the EU and several other developed countries such as Norway, UK, Switzerland continue to block progress on the TRIPS Waiver proposal through various strategies and tactics, working with Ambassador Walker to side-line the TRIPS Waiver proposal. These procedural manoeuvres are deplorable. What is clear is that the WTO discussions on COVID-19 response is a sham process and a distraction from addressing the real barriers to scaling-up production and supply....", one activist said.

"New Zealand's Ambassador David Walker is facilitating a broader Covid-19 recovery plan that has become skewed towards the interests of richer countries, especially the "Ottawa Group" that includes New Zealand. Reports from Geneva show the so-called "Walker process" has become a Trojan Horse to introduce a raft of new obligations through the back door. Least developed and developing countries, and their priorities, have effectively been excluded" Emeritus Professor Jane Kelsey, at the University of Auckland in New Zealand said.

Activists pointed out how the Walker Process has been crafted to put developing countries at a disadvantage.

"Without a meaningful TRIPS waiver there cannot be a meaningful WTO response to the pandemic. This is recognized and reiterated by a broad base of WTO developing and least developed Members, but their calls have been repeatedly ignored. Instead, Ambassador Walker set up a process that keeps the majority of WTO Members outside the negotiation room and is using multiple pressure tactics to push through his agenda and that of countries that want to use the pandemic to repackage old liberalization and deregulatory wishes. Their attempts to set up a future work plan and new body on the WTO response to the pandemic, based on the same premises, is only promising more of these tactics to continue post the 12th Ministerial Conference and could in effect bring an end to any remaining hopes that the WTO could deliver to developing countries and LDCs on any developmental elements, such as in agriculture and special and differential treatment, promised back in 2001 under the WTO Doha Development Agenda", Sangeeta Shashikant, legal advisor to Third World Network said.

THE TRIPS WAIVER UPDATE THIS WEEK

At a formal TRIPS Council meeting at WTO this week, members agreed to continue consultations on the IP response to the pandemic ahead of the 12th Ministerial Conference (MC12)

While there is no consensus yet on the TRIPS Waiver, discussions will remain "open" on the agenda of the TRIPS Council. Sources say discussions on the waiver could continue up until MC12.

At another meeting on 18 November, members adopted a status report that will be submitted to the WTO General Council on 22-23 November. As before, the text presents a factual overview on the status of the discussions on the South Africa-India waiver proposal and a proposal by the EU for a draft General Council declaration on the TRIPS Agreement and Public Health in the circumstances of a pandemic. The status report recognizes the differences among members on using the waiver approach as the IP response to the pandemic.

South Africa said there is "enough goodwill and pragmatism" to reach a meaningful outcome. Given the continuing divergences, the EU asked members to "move from their initial positions". Discussions will continue bilaterally, members said.

(Last week we reported that pressure is building on the EU to reach a consensus on the waiver proposal in consultation with the co-sponsors.)

Norwegian Ambassador Dagfinn Sørli, TRIPS Council Chair is reported to have said that "The role of IP in the context of the pandemic has become the centre of attention in the run-up to the ministerial conference," underscoring the need to arrive at an outcome in time for the ministerial. He reportedly asked members "to leave no stone unturned in exploring all available options" to find a common intellectual property (IP) response to COVID-19.

Ambassador Sørli reportedly said that ministers cannot be expected to draft a solution on a blank piece of paper during the ministerial and would push for a solution agreeable to all members.

The TRIPS Council will remain in session beyond the General Council next week. In addition, a formal meeting is scheduled for the 29th, ahead of the Ministerial Conference. EU trade ministers are also scheduled to meet in Geneva on the 29th.

At the meeting, India said "We cannot fathom an outcome at the ministerial on the WTO in response to pandemic that does not contain an article on this element. We hope that the naysayers could show solidarity with the demand of the majority of the WTO membership and we could formulate some concrete and effective recommendations to the Ministerial Conference on this issue."

Nigeria reportedly asked for clarity on whether the EU proposal is a replacement of the waiver request proposal or a complementary initiative. According to sources, Ambassador Sørli said that the question of whether the EU proposal is to be seen as a replacement or an alternative will have to resolved by members themselves.

In previous meetings, Ambassador Sørli had emphasized that the Walker process would not resolve the differences between members within the TRIPS Council.

BEYOND THE MINISTERIAL

Critics are also concerned about what comes after, once the dust around the ministerial settles. Of worry is the push for a Work Plan on Pandemic Preparedness and Resilience for not only COVID-19 but future crises. This is being discussed under the aegis of the Walker Process.

In addition, plans for a new working group on WTO reform has also met with some concern. Some key issues include normalizing "Joint Statement Initiatives (JSIs); matters linked to self-designation of developing countries and related implications for the access to special and differential treatment to many developing countries and LDCs.

"The reform narrative is also being utilized by some developed countries to inject into the WTO agenda issues that will further constrain the policy tools available to developing countries and open up more space for big business to influence the WTO agenda," civil society organizations said today.

They have also called out the "Different preparatory processes towards MC12 are being convened in a way that excludes the vast majority of WTO Members, while over-privileging the participation of developed country members." Exclusionary "Green Room" processes should be anathema to WTO Members and must be eliminated, activists said.

[In the WTO milieu, green room is the informal name of the director-general's conference room which is often used to hold

informal "deal making" meetings between a small group of select delegations to tackle intractable issues, instead of involving all 164 WTO members. Green room meetings can happen
anywhere and does not need to be in the DG's fold.]

One Geneva-based trade official told us, that if members
cannot agree on the text of such a declaration, then WTO's
response to the pandemic could be at risk. "If some countries
are unable to ensure the inclusion of the TRIPS waiver in this
declaration, then this declaration would not be possible," the
official said.

**The WTO is expected to hold a press briefing later this eve-
ning ahead of the General Council Meeting next week. This
report will be updated subsequently as relevant.

31.

WTO MINISTERIAL: AT WTO, SOME DEVELOPING COUNTRIES: "NO WAIVER - NO WALKER" (NOVEMBER 26, 2021)

With just days left for the 12th WTO ministerial, members are yet to reach a decision on the TRIPS waiver – one of the most important deliverables for this meeting. While the waiver decision may hold the key to the success or failure of this event, it is emerging as a key bargaining chip for developing countries in trying to steer the overall outcomes from this ministerial, according to trade diplomats.

There was already pressure building on the opponents to the waiver as hours towards the ministerial get smaller. In a dramatic turn of events, the rise of a new variant detected by South Africa, adds once again an urgency for the resolution of this stalemate which has plagued WTO for more than a year. For once, could raw epidemiology trump cold-blooded calculations of trade and economic considerations that have dictated countries' position on the waiver proposal?

Even at this juncture though, major members including the US, EU and others, are holding on to their cards, to weigh the waiver in the larger context of other considerations at WTO particularly future reforms of the WTO, the deal on fisheries, among others, according to multiple trade sources familiar with the fast-changing dynamics of these discussions.

Too WTO officials had said in a briefing last week that the outcome on the waiver could likely be negotiated at the political level at the ministerial conference (30 November- 3 December.)

Diplomatic sources told us that while the EU may be willing to move, discussions have been inconclusive with the US so far. Recall, that it was however the US that first lent support to a limited-waiver on the production of vaccines in May 2021.

(See also, KEI letter to USTR on TRIPS waiver negotiations highlights the three issues)

"The U.S. is apparently waiting to make a decision on the waiver after considering other issues such as future WTO reform, discussions on Joint Statement Initiatives among other matters on the table," a trade diplomat said.

The EU has been in bilateral discussions with the proponents of the waiver and is said to be moving towards a "landing zone". Sources indicated that one of the suggestions of the EU on applying compulsory licensing mechanism to trade secrets could be gaining traction and is being seen as "pragmatic" in some quarters. (It is not clear how wide is the spectrum of compromise on these issues among proponents.)

There are suggestions of a political declaration to accompany any waiver decision. Such a declaration could address those elements on which there is likely to be disagreement between members. This is to "send a political signal to jurisdictions" on what options are possible for countries to use.

Sources also suggested that waiving of Article 39 that governs undisclosed information, could come with conditions. (See our earlier story where we discussed accessing trade secrets without a waiver.)

A key demand from the proponents has been the access to regulatory dossiers that could help in the production of medical products to fight the pandemic.

It is not clear what the contours of a potential compromise can look like.

Knowledge Ecology International an influential advocacy group fighting for the access to medicines, for example has suggested "an unconditional waiver of Article 39."

"If this article is not included in the waiver, measures involving patents by themselves will be insufficient to address the need to accelerate and expand access to safe, affordable and effective vaccines and some other countermeasures. Allowing a waiver of Article 39 will also remove any doubt that countries can waive or choose not to recognize or enforce exclusive rights in data used for the registration of products, which is particularly important when such provisions have terms from 5 to 12 years, and lack the type of exceptions that exist for patents on inventions," KEI said in a letter to USTR last week.

"NO WAIVER – NO WALKER"

The Walker Process that has been established to script the WTO response to the pandemic, is now also increasingly under pressure to adequately address questions on intellectual property. (See our earlier deep dive on the recent concerns on this process: Is the 'Walker Process' at the WTO undermining the TRIPS Waiver?)

"Mere protestations against the waiver have not helped. The Walker Process should now be addressed decisively," a developing country diplomat said determinedly.

If there is no decision on the waiver, we will not allow any outcome for the ministerial, the source added. "No Waiver – No Walker" seems to be the view shared by some developing countries.

But what could be an acknowledgment to the limits to the Walker Process, is perhaps indicated by the involvement of Deputy Director Generals including Anabel González.

The FT reported *(Talks to waive patents on Covid vaccines are 'stuck', WTO head warns)* that the DG suggested that discussions on the waiver were stuck. "If we take an all-or-nothing attitude, then it means potentially we all walk away with nothing," the DG told a select group of journalists. (Geneva Health Files was not a part of this group.)

She is also reported to have said, "The WTO's work is not just defined by the IP waiver," she said. 'If you get the waiver but you don't have manufacturing capacity, you can't use it. If you have manufacturing capacity but no technology transfer, you can't use it."

Earlier this week, DG Ngozi Okonjo-Iweala briefed Civil Society Organizations on the upcoming ministerial.

THE PLAN AHEAD:
"Walking away with nothing" is indeed a driving concern for developing countries in the context of the Walker process.

"We do not want the discussions on the waiver process to conclude with the ministerial. If no decision is taken on the waiver, we will be left with nothing", a developing country diplomat said.

Diplomats fear that simply having "place-holder" on the TRIPS Waiver in the WTO response to the pandemic is not sufficient. "The place-holder will simply languish without a legal decision", the diplomat said.

Some countries are now working on tying up the technical work around the waiver, so that a political decision can be taken at the conference by the ministers. "The idea is once the building blocks of this decision is finalised at the political level at the ministerial, details can be concluded following the ministerial within a limited period," according to a source familiar with these discussions. Experts have said that most of the decision on waivers have been taken by the WTO General Council.

THE PRESSURE IS BUILDING – ON THE OPPONENTS

In the meantime, the heat on the EU and other members, is only rising with new and old constituencies putting pressure on these discussions.

The European Parliament passed a resolution earlier this week [25 November 2021 on multilateral negotiations in view of the 12th WTO Ministerial Conference in Geneva, 30 November to 3 December 2021 (2021/2769(RSP)], reiterating its earlier decision by stating, "recalls that the EU should actively participate in text based negotiations on a temporary TRIPS waiver; calls, in that regard, for the EU to support the granting of a temporary waiver from certain provisions of the TRIPS agreement for COVID-19, in order to enhance timely global access to affordable COVID-19 vaccines, therapeutics and diagnostics by addressing global production constraints and supply shortages."

Separately, Devex reported *"How Germany's new coalition could change the fate of the TRIPs waiver"* .

While IP academic, former heads of state and Nobel Laureates have already lent their heft to the proposal, human rights lawyers have now threatened legal action against governments that are opposing the waiver, specifically, Germany, Norway and Canada for "obstructing global efforts to increase access to COVID-19 vaccines and other healthcare technologies." See, *Human rights advocates eye legal action against UK, Canadian, German, and Norwegian governments over global COVID vaccine inequality.*

(Also see from before: the International Commission of Jurists published an expert legal opinion: Human Rights Obligations of States to not impede the Proposed COVID-19 TRIPS Waiver.)

PART V:

THE EMERGENCE OF THE QUAD GROUP (DECEMBER 2021 – MARCH 2022)

When the ministerial conference was postponed at the last minute, questions began to be raised on the future of the WTO. The TRIPS Waiver proposal then transformed into a bigger policy question than merely a trade response to the pandemic. From that moment on, it became about saving the reputation of the WTO, as an institution that was still relevant for its members.

This altered how negotiations were structured and how it eventually determined outcomes. One of many strategic turning points in these discussions, involved WTO DG Ngozi Okonjo-Iweala bringing four key members the US, the EU, South Africa and India, in mostly non-transparent, high-level political dialogues where deals were struck. This had deep consequences not only for the outcome on the TRIPS waiver, but also what this would eventually mean for diplomacy and coalition building between countries.

32.
TRIPS WAIVER AT THE WTO: THE FIGHT TO KEEP IT ALIVE (DECEMBER 3, 2021)

Days after the postponement of WTO's ministerial conference at the cusp of its convening, the proponents of the TRIPS Waiver are fighting to keep it front and center even as the emergence of a new variant has cast a spotlight on the WTO to resolve the waiver discussions to meet new challenges in the on-going pandemic.

Depending on who one speaks to, it seems that the new variant gives urgency to both the opponents and the supporters of the waiver.

One trade diplomat from an opposing group told us that the variant has underscored even more the role of the intellectual property framework in meeting the demands of this pandemic.

"The problem is not supply but distribution. The world will have 12 billion doses of vaccines by the end of 2021," the source added. If new kinds of vaccines are needed to fight new variants, we will need IP protection, the diplomat said.

For the proponents of the waiver, the emergence of the new variant further threatens access to medical products. Much of the developing world has already been left behind with more than 80% of the vaccines being administered in richer countries. The variant could worsen these inequities, diplomats cautioned.

Despite the growing urgency to address the pandemic, WTO members have been hobbled by process and politics to arrive at a decision on the waiver.

Some believe that the postponement of the Ministerial Conference declared the end of any expectation on the waiver in 2021. Western trade diplomats suggest that the discussion on the waiver is deeply inter-linked to the wider WTO response to the pandemic. This process driven by Ambassador Walker had deeply divided countries in the run-up to the now post-poned ministerial.

Proponents of the waiver suggest that any decision of the waiver can be taken independently of the convening of the ministerial. Experts have pointed out that many previous deci-sions on waiver have been taken by the General Council, the highest decision-making body at the WTO.

Geneva-based trade officials concede that the decision of the General Council has enough legal weight. Procedurally nothing stops the WTO from taking a decision on the waiver at the GC, a trade diplomat told us.

But politically this may be far from what members prefer.

By taking a decision on the waiver in isolation, members in-stantly lose leverage with respect to other deliverables that are pending at the ministerial including on fisheries and agriculture.

"Seven billion people are waiting for us on TRIPS and pan-demic response. And 260 million people are waiting for us on fisheries subsidies," DG Ngozi Okonjo-Iweala said at the WTO informal Heads of Delegation this week. She asked members to "conclude agreements on the WTO system's response to pandemics as well as on curbing harmful fisheries subsidies by the end of February 2022 to pave the way for approval by ministers."

SO, WHAT IS HOLDING UP THE WAIVER?

Some opponents to the waiver believe that the decision can only be taken at the political level and not at the technical level. Therefore, the postponement of the ministerial was a blow to the waiver process.

"Political leaders need to meet to find compromise. It is not possible to find compromise at the technical level", a western diplomat suggested.

Seasoned trade officials agreed that reading body language, informal discussions in the corridors, all contribute to breaking impasse and finding compromise. Without an in person ministerial, this is not possible, they suggested.

It is understood that India has suggested an intensive meeting to discuss the waiver, like one-day meetings conducted in the context of the fisheries negotiations to encourage discussion and consensus. (Over the last months, several sources indicated that India was committed to the elements of the waiver proposal and did not wish to compromise.)

DISAGREEMENT ON WHAT CONSTITUTES TEXT

Undoubtedly the pressure to find resolution on the waiver is growing not only on the opponents to the waiver, but on the WTO itself.

"People with well-known addresses have been pushing for a waiver. It is highly political and everybody is watching. There is a lot of pressure and until a solution is found WTO will be in the spotlight," a Geneva-based trade official said.

Members have been asked to find a "pragmatic" consensus on agreeing on the WTO response to the pandemic, that also necessarily includes the waiver.

The emphasis now is on moving to text-based negotiations to arrive at a consensus. However, it seems that there is no agreement on the text of the waiver and hence there is no scope to begin discussions, TRIPS Council Chair, Norwegian Ambassador Dagfinn Sørli is reported to have indicated.

But proponents to the waiver have argued that countries had agreed to begin text-based discussions on the revised proposal of the waiver earlier in the summer. What followed has been reluctance on the part of some countries to engage on this version of the text.

"There is no consensus on any text before negotiations begin. It is ludicrous to suggest that there needs to be consensus on text before discussions begin," a civil society trade expert told us.

If the EU does not agree with the text, they should come forward an alternate proposal, or indicate what is it that they do not agree with in the text provided by the co-sponsors to the waiver, the expert suggested.

The EU and South Africa have had bilateral consultations. But diplomatic sources told us, that there was no agreement reached during these discussions. "There is no text from the EU, for consideration by the 64 co-sponsors of the waiver proposal," a source familiar with these discussions told us.

It was also pointed that the EU proposal on compulsory licensing, cannot be seen as an alternative text to the waiver proposal, since it is essentially drafted as a General Council Declaration.

Sources also suggest that the TRIPS Council chair had suggested for text-based negotiations in June 2021. This is now disputed in some quarters although minutes to such meetings show the push towards text-based discussions.

In all of this, the role of the US has been mysterious, sources said. Despite commitment to the waiver at the highest political levels, it seems the technical team in Geneva has no mandate to negotiate, one trade source told us.

A COMPROMISE POSTPONED?

In the run-up to the ministerial, it was hoped that a political decision on the waiver will be forged by the ministers. Absent ministerial, the waiver proposal was suddenly left in the lurch. But come the Omicron variant, the waiver proposal has got an inadvertent push for resolution. Both these developments happened hours of each other on 26 November.

"The postponement gives all sides an opportunity to recalibrate, including those who first tacitly agreed to engage on text-based negotiations and then, did not", a developing country diplomat told us.

Some suggested that a compromise on the waiver was close. (We have been unable to confirm this.) Therefore, this additional time because of the postponement of the ministerial, may in fact give the co-sponsors greater leverage to preserve waiver proposal, diplomats hope.

But the narrative is completely different from the point of view of the opponents. "By mid-2022, the world will have enough vaccines. We do not need a waiver," a diplomat from a developed country told us.

This week, stories were recounted on a previous waiver decision at the WTO. "After a group of 17 delegations from African countries pleaded for a waiver in 2003, the opposition simply fell away", a trade official said.

We asked experts whether a waiver in 2021 is a possibility at all. "Anything can happen at WTO", the expert said.

33.

POLITICAL DIALOGUE LIFTS TRIPS WAIVER TALKS, GENEVA TRADE BUREAUCRACY UNDERMINES IT (DECEMBER 17, 2021)

In August 2021, discussions on the waiver had to be stalled because Geneva was going on a summer break. Now, nearly half a year later, with a raging infectious variant of SARS-CoV-2 and on the wreckage of anticipation around a ministerial conference that now stands postponed indefinitely, discussions on the waiver are stalling again because of the Christmas break.

Upwards of five million deaths from COVID-19 have failed to dislodge entrenched positions on intellectual property at the World Trade Organization. Some critics believe that the WTO is on the brink of irrelevance, that can somehow in a curious way be salvaged by the temporary suspension of legal rules of one of its multilateral agreements – the TRIPS agreement.

So dire is the crisis, that the inaction on decisively addressing this crisis, led to the postponement of the WTO ministerial conference - consumed by the very flames lit by this pandemic, which the TRIPS waiver proposal seeks to quell. It upended negotiators' travels on both sides of the debate.

But many wonder, given the acute crisis and unprecedented events, can the organization not adapt to the realities, to negotiate and agree on taking a decision on the waiver in a virtual manner? Why can't ministers be brought together on thematic issues, in the absence of a ministerial, some ask.

Developing country negotiators are of the view that the Geneva trade bureaucracy has contributed to stalling the progress on the discussions for the waiver even at this delicate hour.

It is important to meet in person to negotiate and agree, say those who believe that informal consultations between members would help achieve consensus and breakthroughs.

At the time when the ministerial conference was cancelled and postponed indefinitely, there was a lot of momentum between members to push for an urgent decision on the TRIPS waiver. That was three weeks ago. "Precious time was lost. We are being shown process considerations, to get an agreement on the waiver", a developing country negotiator told us.

THE HIGH-LEVEL POLITICAL DIALOGUE

Under pressure to deliver, sources suggest that DG Ngozi Okonjo-Iweala is making efforts for a swift resolution on the waiver discussion. She helped organize a ministerial level discussion on the waiver between the key players, South Africa, India, the US and the EU. This discussion over two different days was structured to help move the process forward. Countries mostly stuck to their previously stated positions.

"Things have not moved in the TRIPS Council, so it made sense to bring higher level deliberations on this. The goal was to find areas of convergence and close the gaps," a source familiar with the discussions told us.

It has been pointed out, that procedurally any decision on the waiver can be taken by the General Council, without waiting for the convening of a ministerial conference.

THE FAILURE OF THE DISCUSSIONS AT THE TRIPS COUNCIL?

Developing countries are also now contending with the alleged partisan approach with the TRIPS Council Chair, Norwegian Ambassador Dagfinn Sørli. "By denying that no consensus on the text exists, the Chair has failed to facilitate discussions on the waiver." **(**See our earlier story: TRIPS Waiver fights to stay front and center at WTO)

"We do not know why he is doing this," a senior diplomat told us expressing frustration that no consensus can be achieved on a proposal even before negotiations begin.

Sources also pointed to the "unbalanced" nature of the fisheries' text prior to wider agreement between members. "It is by negotiating that consensus can be achieved," a diplomat told us citing the fisheries negotiations at the WTO.

Unable to have got the two sides together, to sit and negotiate in some ways can be read as a failure of the chair to facilitate dialogue and discussion, observers say.

The impasse within the Council continues with co-sponsors pushing for text-based negotiations, and others unwilling to participate in these discussions as long as fundamental disagreements persist.

Remember that in the context of the Walker process that was put in place to formulate the WTO response to the pandemic, members were led to believe that any outcome on the intellectual property response will be within the TRIPS Council.

Therefore, impasse at the TRIPS Council at this stage of the discussions raises questions on the effectiveness of the council in addressing this key issue more than 12 months after the waiver proposal was first introduced. When more than 100 members are in favor of text-based negotiations, denying them a forum is undermining the legitimacy of this coalition of countries, mostly from the developing world.

THE TRIPS COUNCIL MEETING: 16 DECEMBER

The WTO TRIPS Council met this week, where members decided to continue their discussions alongside the high-level political dialogue.

While members supported the high-level dialogue between the ministers of key players, they also called for transparency in these discussions and to involve the wider membership of the WTO, trade sources in Geneva said.

As before, it was decided to keep the waiver proposal open on the agenda of the TRIPS Council. Also open on the agenda is the proposal by the European Union (IP/C/W/681) for a draft General Council declaration on the TRIPS Agreement and Public Health in the circumstances of a pandemic.

At the meeting, the countries participating in the high-level dialogue took the floor. South Africa and India underscored the need to start on text-based negotiations on the waiver proposal. India also pushed for a virtual ministerial conference on the TRIPS Waiver.

In its statement, it is understood that the EU noted areas of convergence on some elements of its proposal such as enabling WTO members under the TRIPS Agreement the possibility to authorize manufacturers to produce COVID-19 pharmaceutical products without the consent of the patent owner. (Proponents suggest such a provision already exists). (Sources said that the EU also received support from Switzerland on its proposal to ease the use of compulsory licensing approaches.)

The US is said to be open to continue engagement with others and look for areas of convergence. The US has reiterated its support for a waiver that is limited to vaccines only.

China, Australia, New Zealand and Colombia – took the floor to support waiving intellectual property rights on COVID-19 vaccines.

At the meeting, the UK said, "Ongoing uncertainties regarding emerging new variants only underline the vital ongoing importance of innovation in the fight against this and future crises.....Further, many delegations point to the risks a TRIPS waiver would carry for this and future pandemics. I would like to reiterate that the UK is one of those Members.... On this basis, the UK does not see how text-based negotiations based on 669/Rev.1 could lead to consensus, solutions, or pragmatic outcomes."

The chair of the TRIPS Council, Ambassador Sørli is understood to have said that high-level engagements must "continue and mature." Such discussions could "unlock" the situation in the Council and could contribute towards developing a consensus-based outcome. Parallel to the political process, Ambassador Sørli is understood to have urged all members to engage and show urgency in these discussions.

Sources said that Argentina became one of the latest co-sponsors of the proposal.

This week, an Irish Senator also pushed a motion in the upper house of the Irish legislature to support the TRIPS Waiver. Alice-Mary Higgins, an independent senator, reportedly said, "The motion from the Seanad tonight sends a clear message that we want the Irish Government to join other governments like Italy and Portugal in taking a stand in support of a TRIPS waiver and publicly calling on the European Commission to change position and allow for earlier and urgent scaling up of global supply of life saving vaccines," as cited in a report in Ireland's National Public Service Media.

THE WAY FORWARD

There are two ways to push discussions on the waiver, one by convening the General Council, the second by reaching a decision by a smaller group of members at the ministerial level, and then getting the decision endorsed by the wider membership, a Geneva-based trade official suggested. "Any decision can always be gavelled later," a trade source in Geneva said.

"We are less concerned by process. We just need the outcome," a southern diplomat told us.

Following the postponement of the ministerial, India had immediately suggested that a one-day meeting be convened similar to the approach during the fisheries negotiations, a top WTO official had said last month. However, that idea is being met with questions around process. It is understood that such a meeting can only be convened after getting a wider endorsement for such a move, from other WTO members. In effect, process and bureaucracy is getting in the way, of swiftly responding to the pandemic, the source pointed out.

Some believe that it is up to the EU and the US to speak to each other and come back with a common text that can be discussed with the co-sponsors of the proposal. "It is up to them to respond to the text submitted by the proponents," a developing country source suggested.

Diplomats noted that despite the postponement of the ministerial conference, there continues to be political pressure on both the EU and the US to respond to the pandemic, at a time when dose donations have fallen short.

In addition, vaccines' supply is expected to be constrained in the coming months because of hoarding for booster doses.

The FT reported this week, that there could be a shortfall of 3 billion doses in the first quarter of 2022 if richer countries expand their booster programmes. Citing a WHO official, the story said:

"There is a scenario where very aggressive consumption of doses by high- coverage countries to conduct paediatric vaccination and provide booster doses to all citizens... could lead to a constrained supply situation for the first half of 2022," said Tania Cernuschi, the WHO's technical lead for global vaccine strategy. *"The gap in the first quarter of 2022 could be of about 3bn."*

Financial Times

At a briefing organised by industry groups earlier this week, Thomas Cueni who heads IFPMA dismissed any projections in shortfall as "voodoo" economics".

Experts point out that to defer any decision on the TRIPS waiver, both - the countries blocking the waiver and the industry - are perpetuating the narrative that supply of vaccines are not a constraint, pointing to the projected production of vaccines in the coming months.

However, despite the estimated projection in the production of COVID-19 vaccines, there is no transparency on how and where vaccines are distributed, exacerbating a tight supply situation including for the COVAX facility.

The emergence of the omicron variant has swiftly changed these dynamics - with the industry increasingly facing questions on its rejection of the waiver proposal.

It is also evident that what is holding back the waiver is not the here and the now. It is what this breach of the fortress - suspension of IP rules at the WTO during a health emergency - can mean for the future.

This is what the fight is about. Therefore, no matter the emergence of new variants and bodies piling up, what is at stake is how intellectual property questions are addressed in the context of health.

The sheer evolution of this pandemic undoubtedly adds to the force of the waiver proposal. It is likely that the final blow to the resistance to the waiver, if it does come, will come from politics.

Cueni and colleagues attributed vaccine inequities to political failure. To an extent it is true. To be sure, commercial opportunism met political short-sightedness to create the scarcity that we witness today.

Will political leaders transcend commercial pressures and forge a decision on the waiver? After all, they are eventually answerable to their constituencies, irrespective of pressure from the industry.

34.

EFFORTS TO LIMIT THE IMPLEMENTATION OF THE TRIPS WAIVER, PROPOSALS TO EXCLUDE INDIA & CHINA (FEBRUARY 4, 2022)

A small group of WTO members deliberating on the TRIPS Waiver, are discussing suggestions to limit the geographical scope of the implementation of the waiver - plans that seek to exclude India and China, sources familiar with the process say. These discussions among the US, the EU, South Africa and India, are still fluid and are likely subject to other diplomatic considerations outside of the waiver. India has been a lead co-sponsor of the TRIPS waiver proposal along with South Africa since October 2020.

While it appears that India will likely not accept such a proposal, and yet, it is not entirely clear whether such a limitation will be a clear red line for the proponents of the waiver. We did not receive responses from Indian authorities to our queries by the time this story went to print.

Observers also point to India's pharmaceutical industry which has not favoured the waiver approach to address the supply challenges for COVID-19 medical products.

These on-going talks among these select members have been a part of the high-level quadrilateral process led by the WTO DG. Such an exclusive process limited to four WTO members has reportedly been criticized by other WTO members including the UK and Switzerland, for the selective nature of engagement, Geneva-based trade sources told us. Some members have even called this process a "breach of trust".

TRIPS WAIVER: WHAT HAS BEEN ON THE TABLE?
These high-level discussions led by WTO DG, Ngozi Okonjo-Iweala, have continued for the last two months following the indefinite postponement of the WTO ministerial at the penultimate moment late last year.

Sources tell us that discussions have mostly continued the following matters: on the scope of intellectual property protection that can be waived; the scope of products that can be included in such a waiver; on the geographical scope in the implementation of the waiver and on the duration.

THE LIMITATION ON THE GEOGRAPHICAL SCOPE
It is understood that the US and the EU have, in their own ways favoured a limited application of such a waiver. Some suggestions include restricting the waiver only to African countries, or to exclude India and China among other possibilities.

The EU has announced several bilateral investments in Africa to boost vaccine manufacturing and regulatory capacity and often points to its role around mRNA hubs for example. See this also in the context of the upcoming EU-Africa summit. (Politico: *Macron says EU and Africa seek vaccines deal at February summit*)

Sources indicated that the proposal to exclude India and China from the geographical scope of the implementation of a potential waiver was suggested by the US.

Even though India has defended the waiver proposal, paradoxically, there is also a perception that India may be open to compromise, sources familiar with the discussions indicated. We did not receive any comment on this from Indian authorities. *(We explore this further later in this story)*

To be sure, in recent days, Indian trade minister Piyush Goyal has defended the trade policy space of developing countries:

"A robust WTO response to Covid-19 and pandemic preparedness must necessarily show deference to the views of large number of WTO members...A successful resolution of the TRIPS Waiver must, therefore, be at the core of the WTO response to the pandemic. The TRIPS Waiver proposal by India, South Africa, supported by more than 100 other developing countries, provides a useful way forward to confront some critical health-related aspects of the Covid-19 pandemic effectively. This is both a health and a moral imperative for all of us collectively," commerce and industry minister Piyush Goyal told mini-ministerial meeting.

He cautioned that developing countries should not be asked to vacate their trade policy space.

As reported in The Times of India

The proponents of the waiver have resisted a limited implementation that would only include African countries, for example, sources told us. Efforts are being made to ensure that the wider WTO membership also stands to gain from the possibility of a global implementation of the waiver. The waiver proposal has the support of over 100 WTO members, including Latin American and Asian countries who are co-sponsors of the proposal.

It is understood that the US is keen on also excluding China from being able to implement the TRIPS Waiver. Remember that China is already the largest exporter of COVID-19 vaccines. (See Airfinity data on this.)

Also in the works, are discussions on potential opt-out mechanisms for members wishing to use escape clauses on certain aspects on the waiver. There are also suggestions to tie in conditionalities and load preferential terms on opt-in requirements. Details are scant. Experts fear that having a waiver with too many conditions would defeat its purpose.

It is learned that there has been no change in the US position on the waiver – the US continues to limit the discussion to waiving IP protection for vaccines, and not therapeutics and diagnostics.

While the EU is said to have shown more latitude, it continues to remain reluctant to waive obligations on patent protection, sources told us. Some western diplomats point to "successful" voluntary licensing initiatives by the Medicines Patent Pool on Merck's Molnupiravir, to underline the futility of a waiver on patents.

A NARROW IMPLEMENTATION OF THE WAIVER:

AFRICA SECURE BUT THE REST?

If indeed the discussions result in a limited scope to include only African countries, according to some elements in the on-going discussion, it would be a diplomatic win for developed countries and for Africa.

South Africa has been driving these discussions on behalf of the co-sponsors and has been perceived as willing to go the distance to negotiate an outcome with the EU.

As we have pointed out before, do also read this in the context of increased EU-Africa investments to build regulatory and manufacturing capacity in Africa, and ostensible alignment on new rules to govern health emergencies, including on a new legal instrument.

But observers say that a limited application restricting only to Africa will simply not be acceptable to the wider WTO membership that has fought long and hard alongside the lead proponents for a waiver.

THE INDIAN POSITION

Western diplomats suggest that India has not truly been in favour of the waiver proposal. (Even though India has led and co-sponsored the proposal for over two years.)

But this must be read keeping in mind legacy issues including the developed world's general distrust of India produced medicines dating back several years. Seasoned trade experts also cautioned us about narratives against India that have been routinely deployed by developed countries.

During the last few months, India was also seen as having an "extreme" position on securing the original elements of the waiver proposal, without being open to a "compromise" as suggested by the EU.

Between these two diametrically opposing narratives, India's position is somewhat unclear.

We tried to understand the dynamics operating within India that might have led to such perceptions gaining around.

Several diplomatic sources have raised questions and concerns on India's position that has, at a minimum, led to confusion, and worse, could lead to a potential loss of credibility for India in the global south, observers say. Some have questioned whether India is using gains from the waiver negotiations as a bargaining chip to trade for other objectives.

Experts familiar with New Delhi's policy flip-flop over the last two years, believe that health issues have seldom been systematically incorporated into foreign policy considerations. The lack-lustre response from the Indian industry is also brought up.

In a conversation with us this week, Murali Neelakantan, Principal Lawyer, amicus, and former Global General Counsel, at Cipla, told us:

"To me, it seems that India has not engaged in serious and tenacious diplomacy to garner support for the TRIPS waiver. I suspect that the Indian government may now be using the gains from the TRIPS waiver as leverage elsewhere. This was a great opportunity for India to articulate a foreign policy

vision or aspiration by demonstrating leadership on a global issue, but it seems like this opportunity was missed.

As time passed, with the increase in domestic production for vaccines and medicines on the back of voluntary licenses from originator companies the waiver proposal seems to have become less significant for India's national interest.

The waiver should have been framed as progress from Doha (2001) to achieve a paradigm for the future. India has not been to articulate any effective policy informing India's support for the waiver proposal.

The waiver is not seen as an expression of India's national interest. There has been no expression of support from the Indian pharma industry for the waiver. This suggests that the big Indian pharma players do not see a business opportunity in the waiver. The waiver may benefit the second rung of Indian pharma to build capacity, but they don't seem to have a voice in India's policy. For a few years now, Indian pharma industry has been co-opted by big pharma and is happy winning licenses whether it is for Sofosbuvir, Tocilizumab, Remdesivir or Molnupiravir and opposition to the waiver seems to be consistent with that approach."

(See also our expansive interview with Neelakantan from August 2021: Where does India truly stand on the TRIPS Waiver)

At this point, if India still has to make the most of the waiver proposal, it will have to achieve nothing short of a diplomatic feat of walking the tight rope, to ensure that it can have a big moral win for the sake of the developing world, a trade expert was of the view.

Also recall that India is part of the Quad partnership with Australia, India, Japan and the United States. Bilateral dynamics between India and the U.S. will also be in play here.

THE WTO MINISTERIAL & THE DYNAMICS IN GENEVA
Outside of these high-level discussions between select WTO members, a wider WTO response to the pandemic continues to take shape in Geneva. This month saw informal meetings of the General Council. The heat is on at WTO to forge a response to the pandemic of which IP will be a central element.

The process of finalizing the WTO response to the pandemic is now being dealt with by out-going General Council chair, Ambassador Dacio Castillo from Honduras. As the new facilitator for the trade and health response, he will work with the Walker text on the response to the pandemic. (New Zealand's Ambassador David Walker is now no longer associated with the process since his term concluded.)

Sources suggested that the US has not been in favour of the Walker text, since it is reluctant to sign up for any potential legal obligations arising from a declaration on the pandemic response. The EU and others have cautioned against reopening the Walker text.

WTO'S CREDIBILITY AS A TOOL FOR NEGOTIATION
Clearly, there is pressure on the WTO to deliver. WTO continues to be perceived as a 'rich country' club. "Developed countries are keen on getting the WTO to deliver. It is in their interest to do so," a southern trade negotiator told us.

Southern countries believe that WTO's credibility rests on a deliverable on the TRIPS waiver. And that has become a negotiating tool now. Proponents of the waiver are counting on this to push through commitments on the waiver and tying it into the wider trade and health response. "A commitment on the waiver will be a down payment for the rest of the trade and health package" a trade diplomat told us. *(See our earlier reporting on the Walker process.)*

WHATS NEXT?

The WTO DG has called for a conclusion on the discussions within the next few weeks. The next WTO General Council Meeting is scheduled for February 23. Several changes are expected. The General Council is now expected to be chaired by Swiss Ambassador Didier Chambovey. And for the Chair of the TRIPS Council, the name of Ambassador Lansana Gberie of Sierra Leone has been proposed, according to Geneva-based trade officials.

While there continues to be no agreement on the date of the next ministerial, some suggestions include July 2022 or towards the later part of the year in Geneva. Diplomats are also hopeful that if delegates in Geneva conclude much of the pending negotiations, a ministerial may also be convened virtually.

THE OMICRON IMPETUS

When Omicron destabilised the world in December 2021, waiver proponents believed that it potentially presented them with a "window of opportunity" and an urgency to push through the waiver proposal. However, in the past two months, WTO members have failed to arrive at a decision on the waiver.

One Geneva trade official told us, it was when EU diplomats were unable to travel to the WTO for the ministerial, the decision was taken to call it off. (Recall that Southern trade negotiators whose countries were slapped by travel bans were also unable to travel).

The efforts to scuttle the scope of a potential waiver have to be seen in the light of the far-reaching effects of Omicron, now also registering increasing deaths in many parts of the world.

Does this mean that the urgency brought on by Omicron has been lost? After all, these delaying tactics have had their impact. There are projections now of surplus vaccines' production in 2022.

The waiver proponents are still hopeful.

With the US witnessing high numbers of deaths, there is pressure not only for vaccines, but also for diagnostics and therapeutics. "The goal would be to catch Washington now", a trade source said alluding to the nearly 9,00,000 lives lost in the U.S.

While it is impossible to estimate the true cost of policy inaction, there may be growing recognition of this inaction.

Both sides are cautious about any long-term consequences brought on by a waiver: for the opponents, the waiver risks hollowing out the TRIPS agreement. And for the proponents, the waiver is a lever to widen the access to medicines not only during health emergencies, but a first step in rectifying structural barriers that have contributed to the current inequities. This tug of war explains the intractability of these negotiations.

TAIL PIECE
Even as compulsory licensing has become the new buzzword in Brussels during this pandemic, see this submission to the USTR, by industry lobby group Pharmaceutical Research and Manufacturers of America:

KEI's James Love

James Love ✓
@jamie_love

⋯

USTR has posted the Special 301 comments. The @PhRMA submission mentions compulsory licensing 125 times in a 273 page submission.

5:25 PM · Feb 1, 2022 · Twitter Web App

Also from MSF's Dimitri Eynikel:

Dimitri Eynikel
@DimitriEynikel

Pharma industry wants the EU (!) on a watchlist for putting at risk IP protection. Let this be a sign of the fanatic views in this industry and the questionable basis of these @USTradeRep and @Trade_EU watchlists (special 301 & IP enforcement report).

35.
EFFORTS TO NARROW THE TRIPS WAIVER CONTINUE: "ELIGIBILITY REQUIREMENTS" STILL ON THE TABLE (FEBRUARY 26, 2022)

The TRIPS waiver discussions at the WTO continue to teeter on the brink of a possible outcome that risks becoming too complicated to use.

More importantly, the discussions continue to be mired in narrow eligibility requirements that could potentially set conditions on the circumstances under which a waiver will be applicable. This essentially aims to achieve the lowest possible "impact" of a potential waiver, sources suggest. As we reported earlier, it is understood that these proposals continue to be pushed by the US and the EU.

No headway has been made on TRIPS Waiver discussions among key WTO members [the US, the EU, India and South Africa]. However, WTO members this week, agreed on a new date for the 12th Ministerial Conference during 13-17 June 2022. This might prove to be an impetus to push the waiver discussions towards a resolution, observers say. This week deliberations continued at the TRIPS Council and at the General Council at WTO. *(See details later in the story)*

Our extensive reporting this week suggests that there is no immediate pressure on either "sides" to conclude these intractable negotiations. While this may be a strategy, it is unclear how it will play out in the coming months.

The situation continues to be fluid, even as there is growing criticism to conclude and expand these "small group" discussions at the WTO.

STATUS UPDATE: TRIPS WAIVER TALKS
ELIGIBILITY REQUIREMENTS

Sources familiar with the discussions among the four WTO members, suggest that proposals on eligibility requirements are "still on the table" and are likely to be the most controversial. Eligibility requirements are understood as conditions under which a potential waiver will be applicable. It is learned that language could be crafted in a way that will effectively exclude countries such as India and China, without explicitly stating so.

The Hindu that followed up on our story, earlier this month, reported that India has rejected such a proposal. "Indian officials have formally opposed the geographic exclusion proposal that is part of a package of various options, but concede that until the negotiations conclude, they cannot be sure that this will be firmly ruled out," according to the report in *The Hindu*.

Indeed, supporters of the waiver who are familiar with the Indian dynamics, remain concerned on the pressure operating on India to accept these conditions. There are likely other potential bilateral factors between the U.S. and India, that could affect these discussions until the waiver negotiations conclude.

It appears that the proposal to exclude big, generic markets is a priority for the U.S., while the EU also stands to gain because of this suggestion, Geneva-based sources told us.

Experts also caution, that excluding countries like India from a potential waiver has deeper implications for the overall Special and Differential Treatment regime in WTO rules. What will this mean for discussions on other matters, they point out.

Africa continues to be a priority for the EU, and some suggest that the efforts to limit implementation of a waiver to the continent may be a part of this broader diplomatic goal. This also became obvious at the recently concluded EU-AU Summit, where despite the coming together of African and European leaders, the TRIPS Waiver continued to stick out as a major issue of disagreement.

RESTRICTIONS ON IP SCOPE: THE EU POSITION

Apart from restricting the implementation of a potential waiver to specific geographies, the EU and the US have suggested other limitations.

The EU has already made clear that their basic proposal of using existing TRIPS flexibilities such as compulsory licensing continues to be a priority.

In its statement at the General Council this week, the EU said:

"The EU is committed to finding a way forward on intellectual property. We have engaged constructively in the discussions facilitated by the DG and continue to believe that we can find a bridge between the positions of various Members, between those who advocate for a waiver and those of us who believe that the TRIPS Agreement provides enough flexibilities to ensure that the enabling qualities of intellectual property can be used to the maximum.

The European Union has shown utmost flexibility and moved its position significantly throughout this process. We have moved from the declaration we proposed in June 2021 towards a solution which would allow Members to authorise their manufacturers to produce and export vaccines in the fastest possible manner and without red tape, with maximum flexibility as to the legal instrument used to do so. But to find a solution flexibility is needed on both sides.

We are looking for a pragmatic solution that could facilitate production of vaccines and other essential health products in regions like Africa, while preserving incentives for innovation and investment that are key for responding to new variants of COVID-19, such as omicron or to new diseases."

This statement illustrates not only the importance the EU gives to existing TRIPS flexibilities, but also the importance of Africa in EU's engagement on this issue.

In their efforts at finding a "landing zone", the EU reportedly suggested attaching conditions to certain provisions. "It seems the EU does not like the word waiver. They are also seeking to suggest something that resembles a compulsory license (CL). If it walks like a CL and talks like a CL, it must be a CL," a trade official familiar with the discussions joked.

The EU remains opposed to waiving Article 28.1 of the TRIPS Agreement, which governs exclusive rights enjoyed by the patent holder.

Further, IP law experts also point out that every WTO member has the right to issue a compulsory license under the TRIPS Agreement. There are no eligibility requirements on who can use flexibilities. Therefore, if certain provisions of Article 31 of the TRIPS Agreement are waived (as is being discussed in the context of this proposal), with specific conditions that describe when such flexibilities could be used, it could hamper the use of such flexibilities. See here on the specific provisions under Article 31.

See below a footnote on Article 31*bis*[1] and why it resonates with the current discussions. Article 31*bis* is an amendment in the TRIPS Agreement, based on the waiver in 2003, that was supposed to have enabled a country to export medicines manufactured under a compulsory license to another importing country. Given additional procedures and notifications, the use of this mechanism has been cumbersome, it is widely acknowledged.

In a letter to the WTO DG Ngozi Okonjo-Iweala, CSOs said:

"We recall that even prior to the pandemic, the challenges of using compulsory licensing mechanism for exports (Articles 31(f) and 31bis) and the ineffectiveness to deliver equitable access were well-known. In addition, these CL provisions are only relevant to patents and do nothing to address other intellectual property barriers. For example, information related to manufacturing and quality control processes are often claimed by industry as trade secrets, even when this information bears clear public interests to boost the diversification and scale of production.

As such, a waiver of Article 39 of TRIPS on "Protection of Undisclosed Information" is essential and in the public interest. Further as elaborated in cosponsors document IP/C/W/684, copyright and industrial designs may also create obstacles for production and supply, and so these concerns also have to be addressed. While the specific details of the current consultations/negotiations are not public, we would like to stress that any Waiver outcome must create a clear pathway that provides potential manufacturers the full freedom to operate -- to manufacture, to import and export, and to commercialize needed COVID-19- related medical products -- without having to deal with procedural and legal IP requirements on a product-by-product basis. The waiver decision should also accord governments policy space to implement measures necessary to facilitate production, import and export of medical products and their components."

Supporters of the waiver want to go further and waive provisions that protect trade secrets, among others. Without a "freedom to operate", a waiver will be useless, access to medicines advocates warn. (See the unfolding discussion on the difficulties faced by South Africa's mRNA hub with respect to Moderna's vaccine patents.)

Legal experts and advocates have questioned the utility of a narrow waiver, especially, if it is also restricted to a small group of countries without adequate manufacturing capacities to be able to take advantage of a waiver.

ON RESTRICTING PRODUCT SCOPE

While the EU is unwilling to relent on IP scope, the US continues its stance on restricting the waiver to vaccines, effectively reducing the product scope of the waiver. But the importance of therapeutics and diagnostics in fighting the pandemic has been obvious, particularly in the face of rising variants of SARS-CoV-2. Using a successful test and treat strategy, hinges of having access to therapeutics and diagnostics.

Experts point to efforts by the US and the EU in snapping up supplies of therapeutics, just as they had done for vaccines.

At the WTO this week, officials suggested that there are efforts to have two track discussions on the TRIPS waiver, one on vaccines, and a second potential track on therapeutics and vaccines that could be addressed at a later stage.

But WTO observers are highly circumspect about putting off anything for later amid a health emergency. They cite to WTO's lengthy political processes that make difficult even on agreed provisions such as exempting least developed countries to apply the provisions of the TRIPS Agreement in view of their special needs and to accord them flexibility in creating a viable technological base.

THE IMPORTANCE OF AFRICA

As mentioned earlier, Africa has become a key strategic priority for the EU during the pandemic. The emphasis on EU's support to the South Africa mRNA hub is a case in point. (See *The Political Utility of The WHO mRNA Hub)*

In fact, at the TRIPS Council meeting this week, the EU, citing the recent EU-AU Summit, is reported to have said, "We need to enhance production of mRNA technology in Africa. We need to protect IP as the element necessary for research and development. That is why EU is supporting the mRNA hub." (This was also echoed by Ursula von der Leyen at the Summit last week.)

This statement by the EU is significant, when you also consider the conflicting signals from WHO and its partners: they have clarified that the mRNA hub will not roughshod over IP rights, even as the mRNA hub is constrained by a lack of technology transfer from Moderna. At the TRIPS Council meeting this week, South Africa also highlighted the IP barriers faced by the mRNA hub.

Sources familiar with EU's policy on mRNA hubs told us, "This is the only thing that will work" alluding to the alleged limitations of a waiver. Some point to the limited number of patents filed in Africa, again, questioning the effectiveness of a waiver.

To be sure, this is not only about helping boost African manufacturing capacities. When BioNTech announced its BioNTainers earlier this month, it was clear that the mRNA technology is crucial for other vaccines beyond COVID-19. And therein lies the crux. This also explains investments by European countries across facilities in Africa.

So, while investing in mRNA hubs in Africa might be a useful diplomatic goal for the EU, it is also an effective policy to deflect potential commitments in the TRIPS Waiver discussions that seek to decentralize and boost manufacturing capacities everywhere and not just in Africa.

Interestingly, there are no clear answers, on how limiting a potential waiver to Africa, will help address manufacturing needs in other regions including Latin American countries or other Asian countries (assuming the waiver could also exclude India and China).

What is also interesting to note is how the leadership at the WTO also pointed to EU investments in Africa as progress in fighting the pandemic.

THE INDIAN QUESTION

In our earlier story, we extensively discussed the dissonance between India's domestic policies on pharmaceutical intellectual property and its dominant flag-bearing role in the TRIPS waiver discussions on behalf of the developing world.

While ostensibly, India is fighting back on being excluded from its own proposal crafted with South Africa in 2020, there continues to be uncertainty to what extent India will be able to withstand the alleged pressure not only from the US, but also from its own domestic industry.

On the latter, experts point to the diversity in the Indian pharmaceutical industry. While big Indian companies have distanced themselves from the waiver, it is the smaller companies that will stand to benefit from the waiver based on the expectation that such a temporary suspension on IP rules will be help boost manufacturing capacities.

On India's bilateral relations with the US, seasoned observers are more cautious. It is not simply clear to what extent, India's foreign policy will be shaped by the US when it comes to the TRIPS waiver, even when faced with its traditional role as a leader of the developing world. Many believe that India might have effectively passed up the opportunity to lead the global south in the worst health crisis in a century despite its reputation as the pharmacy of developing world.

If India is unable to protects its interest in the TRIPS waiver discussions, it will be glaring failure not only for Indian diplomacy. At stake is also the support offered by more than 60 other co-sponsors of the waiver proposal at the WTO.

Indian commentators have questioned why India has "not developed a draft model law enunciating how it would implement the waiver. This would have not only fortified India's position internationally but would have also acted as a pressure point to influence the negotiations." They suggest that "the lesson is that for economic diplomacy to flourish, it should be backed by concrete actions on the domestic front."

WHAT HAPPENS IF THERE IS NO WAIVER?

To be sure, vast amounts of political capital has been invested not only by India, but also South Africa. To agree to a waiver that may not be very effective will risk the credibility of both leaders Narendra Modi and Cyril Ramaphosa. (The final declaration from the EU-AU Summit does not mention the word waiver)

After two years of discussions on this bold proposal, the risks of a waiver not being passed at all, is a possibility. We asked diplomatic sources what that would mean for WTO and the world at large. Some suggested bad blood between countries and "the digging of even deeper trenches".

THE DECLARATION OF THE END OF THE PANDEMIC AND THE WAIVER

Assuming that a narrow waiver proposal does get approved at the WTO, what will be the implications?

Supporters of the waiver believe that it could still be helpful to developing countries. They also suggest that when COVID-19 does become endemic, there will continue to be a need for a waiver to access medical products easily.

"If an end to the pandemic is declared, the developed world will likely forget about the disease in the developing world. The access to medicines will become even more acute. This is where the waiver will be useful," an access to medicines advocate told us. Better products will continue to be denied in the developing world, as is already being witnessed.

To be sure, the WHO has acknowledged that given the current projections of vaccine production it will likely be able to meet its goal of vaccinating 70% of the world's population by July 2022. But as it has been argued before, the TRIPS waiver discussions go beyond making vaccines available. The goal is to provide and enhance the access to manufacturing of therapeutics and diagnostics.

But key to the question on the declaration of the end of the pandemic, is how and when companies begin to enforce their patents. This also contributes to the urgency of the approval and implementation of the waiver, experts say.

GENEVA MEETINGS THIS WEEK

Finally, alongside the waiver discussions, members are also discussing the WTO response to the pandemic – a non-binding political declaration. This process has been taken over by former General Council Chair Ambassador Dacio Castillio from Honduras, and he has taken into consideration views from all members. Countries hope that this declaration, although a political statement, will be important in guiding and determining members' behaviour in implementing trade policies during future health emergencies. (Interestingly, it appears the WTO now distances itself from the contentious Walker text form last year, calling it "independent". That process allegedly did not consider views from developing countries.)

Geneva witnessed both the TRIPS Council and the General Council meeting this week *(See our updates from the meetings here)*. WTO members were updated on small group consultations. Several countries continued to express criticism and concerns on the small group process on the lack of transparency. WTO officials described "varying levels of grumpiness" among members on being left out of the group. These included, UK, Switzerland, China, Russia, Japan, Indonesia among others. It is understood that WTO leadership that is coordinating these meetings has sought patience from the quadrilateral process. An oral report from the TRIPS Council was presented at the General Council that described the status of the waiver discussions.

WTO DG Okonjo-Iweala also urged members to seek a resolution ahead of the proposed ministerial in June and not wait till the summer. But it appears delegates might take the time they need to arrive at the resolution of the TRIPS waiver.

Some developing countries had suggested that they would be unwilling to consider other deliverables for the ministerial, till an outcome on the waiver is reached. Whether this bargaining strategy will hold will remain to be seen. Officials believe that once an outcome is reached among the four members on the waiver, it will be taken back to the TRIPS Council, where the wider membership could tweak and carefully consider the implications of any potential outcome on the waiver.

Irrespective of the outcome, many believe the needle on the access to medicines has moved.

If developing countries begin using TRIPS flexibilities for cancer drugs, for example, will the EU or the US oppose such protected policies?

PART VI:

THE DG'S COMPROMISE TEXT (MARCH -JUNE 2022)

···

What can a compromise look like in a situation of a stalemate? In fact, how does a one-sided compromise look like? In a politically effective strategy, a version of the text being discussed by the Quad group was selective leaked in Brussels. This sowed confusion and set the tone for the last lap towards
the ministerial conference.

Far from the expansive TRIPS Waiver proposal, a text from the WTO DG was presented to the WTO membership. With less than 10 weeks to spare to the rescheduled Ministerial Conference, countries were asked to reach a consensus. The negotiations went on, literally till the last hour of the ministerial conference.

36.

A COMPROMISE ON THE HORIZON? TRIPS WAIVER TALKS IN THE 'QUAD' AT THE WTO (MARCH 11, 2022)

While the Russian invasion of Ukraine has upended trade diplomacy at the WTO in recent days, the TRIPS waiver discussions have proceeded among a small group of members and is likely nearing a compromise, although differences persist.

Sources familiar with the process told us about the technical deliberations among the quad that includes the US, the EU, India and South Africa, are now nearing completion.

These discussions are soon expected to follow at the level of the ministers of these four WTO members. "If the current text is acceptable by high-level decision-makers, it will then be taken up by the wider membership", a source said. It is understood that the process of taking the proposal to the wider membership will be brokered by WTO DG, Ngozi Okonjo-Iweala.

Considering the sensitivities in these discussions and the critical juncture at which it is poised, sources did not want to be identified.

THE QUAD PROCESS

According to sources the discussions among the technical experts in the Quad group on reaching a possible landing zone has nearly concluded. The ministers are expected to meet soon, some say, for the first time in two months, since these small group discussions first began in December 2021, following the abrupt postponement of the WTO ministerial due to the emergence of the Omicron variant. It also appears differences do persist.

"There is now compromised language on the table. We have defined a baseline in these discussions. It is now up to the high-level decision makers among the Quad to agree on a text," a diplomatic source said.

Meanwhile, this week, WTO members also met at a TRIPS Council meeting on March 9-10 *(see details below)* to discuss the waiver proposal among other issues. In parallel, the EU and South Africa had a flurry of bilateral consultations on the waiver over the last few days, on behalf of India and the U.S., it is learned.

While the EU and South Africa deliberated on the technical, substantive aspects of a potential proposal, the questions on product scope and beneficiaries were addressed by the US and India, sources told us.

WTO top officials had warned that a compromise will not make anyone happy but herded members towards finding what they had called a "pragmatic" solution to the waiver discussions. It was reasoned that if these four key members, representative of interests of other members, were able to reach a consensus, it would be easier to take such a proposal to the wider WTO membership.

Diplomatic sources did not sound elated on concluding these technical discussions but suggested that the talks had moved in the right direction. "The proposal as it stands now, is narrower than what was proposed initially. We had to make a difficult trade-off between what we need and what we want", the diplomatic source from a developing country said.

A developed country official said that the progress in the discussions has not been "too bad" but cautioned that discussions had reached a critical point in October 2021, before they fizzled out again.

A FEW SUBSTANTIVE ELEMENTS OF A POTENTIAL COMPROMISE

What the contours of a potential compromise will be is not yet, but it is understood that any waiving of intellectual property protections will, for now, remain limited to COVID-19 vaccines. A second track on therapeutics and diagnostics is expected to follow suit within a defined period, sources suggested. The U.S. has been insistent on restricting the discussions to a waiving of IP protections around COVID-19 vaccines only, since its first limited statement of support in May 2021.

IP experts also suggest that current flexibilities in the TRIPS Agreement can also allow for the issuance of compulsory licenses, for example, to address the manufacturing of therapeutics and diagnostics. Some believe that those therapeutics that are based on small molecules can be accessed by using compulsory licensing flexibilities already available to all WTO members.

It is understood that the final decision will have a set of clarifications on waiving certain provisions in the TRIPS Agreement, and will also extend authorisations, setting conditions for such a waiver to be legally effective.

Overall, the proposed mechanism seeks to make possible an issuance of an executive order by a government to approve the manufacture of medical products. This is expected to the same effect as the issuance of a compulsory license, sources indicated.

For the EU, it's proposal centering on Article 31 provisions *(on Other Use Without Authorization of the Right Holder)* of the

TRIPS Agreement continue to be of priority in the context of these discussions.

Note that some of these elements are subject to negotiation at the high-level and may change as discussions proceed.

PROVISION ON EXCLUSIVE RIGHTS OF PATENT OWNERS

A key sticking point among the members, was the waiver of Article 28.1 of the TRIPS Agreement that governs exclusive rights given to a patent owner. The proponents had suggested a waiver of this provision, and the EU, among others were opposed to it. It now is understood that members could potentially find a way to extend authorization under this provision to enable the manufacture of medical products.

Article 28.1 reads as follows:

Rights Conferred

1. A patent shall confer on its owner the following exclusive rights:

a. *where the subject matter of a patent is a product, to prevent third parties not having the owner's consent from the acts of: making, using, offering for sale, selling, or importing (6) for these purposes that product;*

b. *where the subject matter of a patent is a process, to prevent third parties not having the owner's consent from the act of using the process, and from the acts of: using, offering for sale, selling, or importing for these purposes at least the product obtained directly by that process.*

2. Patent owners shall also have the right to assign, or transfer by succession, the patent and to conclude licensing contracts.

TRADE SECRETS

Proponents of the waiver proposal have long argued that the access to undisclosed information is key to speed up the production of medical products including vaccines. The EU had said that gaining access to companies' confidential information is difficult.

Several countries have domestic legislations to protect undisclosed information including trade secrets such as the EU's directive on the protection of trade secrets and American laws to protect trade secrets.

Prevailing laws that protect trade secrets, seek to discourage "unfair competition". However, during a pandemic, public non-commercial use trumps these concerns. Proponents of the waiver believe that legitimate public purpose that needs to be serviced is not in opposition to unfair commercial use.

So, while the TRIPS agreement does not explicitly prohibit the issuance of compulsory licenses for trade secrets, there is no mechanism that governs this, as we previously reported.

The proponents had originally suggested the waiving of Article 39.3 that governs protection of undisclosed information.

This reads as follows (Art. 39.3)

3. Members, when requiring, as a condition of approving the marketing of pharmaceutical or of agricultural chemical products which utilize new chemical entities, the submission of undisclosed test or other data, the origination of which involves a considerable effort, shall protect such data against unfair commercial use. In addition, Members shall protect such data against disclosure, except where necessary to protect the public, or unless steps are taken to ensure that the data are protected against unfair commercial use.

Efforts have now been made to clarify and expand the nature of "use" as read in this provision. This is expected to help in the acquisition, use and production of patented materials, sources explained. But to what extent it will make regulatory dossiers accessible is not clear yet.

(See our story from July 2021, that discusses this detail: *Countries wrestle with regulatory data, trade secrets and tech transfer: TRIPS Waiver discussions at WTO*)

THE CLAUSE ON A STANDSTILL ON DISPUTES
In addition, it appears that the proponents have, for the moment, also managed to safeguard one of the key elements of their original proposal – the standstill on filing disputes associated with the implementation of a waiver mechanism. The original proposal had suggested: *"Members shall not challenge any measures taken in conformity with the provision of the waivers contained in this Decision under subparagraphs 1(b) and 1(c) of Article XXIII of GATT 1994, or through the WTO's Dispute Settlement Mechanism."*

ON GEOGRAPHICAL LIMITATIONS
One of the most contentious aspects of these discussions have been efforts by the EU and the US, to narrow the scope of the waiver by insisting on eligibility requirements. (See *Efforts to Narrow the TRIPS Waiver Continue: "Eligibility Requirements" Still on The Table*)

We reported on February 4, 2022, that key developing countries including India and China, could likely be excluded from implementing the waiver. It now appears that India is now not a part of such a limitation, meaning that the country will be able to implement a waiver mechanism. Sources suggest that China may be excluded from the implementation of a waiver. It has been pointed out that with Chinese vaccines accounting for a significant portion of distributed vaccines globally, China may, in fact, favour the protection of intellectual property. (We were unable to specifically confirm this in time for the publication of this story.)

It is not clear whether Latin American countries will also be excluded from the implementation of the waiver. Developed country diplomats had pointed to existing capacities in Brazil and Argentina to meet regional demand for medical products.

(See MSF: Latin America: How patents and licensing hinder access to COVID-19 treatments)

ON THERAPEUTICS

Clearly a waiver of obligations to help production of therapeutics and diagnostics is important. There is now fresh evidence of rising IP protections for these categories of medical products.

A patent landscape report by the World Intellectual Property Organization launched earlier this week, appears to underscore the need for a waiver at the time of a pandemic. COVID-19-related vaccines and therapeutics reveals insights on related patenting activity during the pandemic. The report says, "Patenting activity related to COVID-19 vaccines and therapeutics is nearly equally distributed between companies and universities and research organizations, with companies having a slightly higher contribution." Companies accounted for 49% of the vaccines patent dataset and 44% to the therapeutics patent dataset. The rest was accounted for by universities and research organizations, and independent innovators.

Meanwhile, Moderna published a new Global Public Health Strategy this week.

Moderna:

"Moderna is now updating its patent pledge to never enforce its patents for COVID-19 vaccines against manufacturers in or for the 92 low- and middle-income countries in the Gavi

COVAX Advance Market Commitment (AMC), provided that the manufactured vaccines are solely for use in the AMC 92 countries.

In non-AMC 92 countries, vaccine supply is no longer a barrier to access. In these countries, the Company expects those using Moderna-patented technologies will respect the Company's intellectual property. Moderna remains willing to license its technology for COVID-19 vaccines to manufacturers in these countries on commercially reasonable terms. Doing so enables Moderna to continue to invest in research to develop new vaccines, prepare for the next pandemic, and meet other pressing areas of unmet medical need."

But negotiators working on the waiver proposal were not impressed. "This gives control to Moderna. They can suspend the pledge whenever they want to. This is not a solution", one source told us.

Also read Brook Baker's analysis of this: *Moderna's Global Public Health Strategy: Parsing the Hype and Shameful Access Gap.*

(Do also note the recent announcement earlier this week: *WHO and Medicines Patent Pool welcome US National Institutes of Health's offer of COVID-19 health technologies to C-TAP)*

WHAT'S NEXT
Some developing countries at the WTO are keen on pushing through discussions on the waiver proposal independently of other considerations. But the EU, and others are keen on linking these discussions to a political declaration on the WTO's pandemic preparedness and response. It is still not clear how these parallel processes will progress in time for the Ministerial conference now scheduled for June 2022.

"The waiver must be concluded expeditiously. And it will be a deposit of sorts, for other discussions at the WTO," a developing country trade diplomat told us.

The waiver will likely be a part of "a decision matrix", or referred to, in the wider declaration on the WTO response to the pandemic, sources said. Although the declaration political in nature, members expect it to have some legal effect and set a precedent for the trade response in future pandemics.

Diplomats hope that DG Okonjo-Iweala will be able to get the wider membership together to decide on a text on the waiver. The pressure is building on the WTO to deliver on this, sources said.

It is understood that if the American support to a waiver text is secured, there may not be serious opposition to the proposal in the wider membership. Although members such as the UK and Switzerland have clear positions on the process and content of these discussions.

Developing country diplomats hope that a General Council decision on the waiver can be reached ahead of the ministerial conference. But it is also possible that any consensus on the waiver will be subject to other considerations at the WTO.

"We expect the DG to use strong arm tactics to drive the process among the wider membership for an outcome on the waiver, unless there is a revolt in the palace", one diplomat familiar with these dynamics said.

The Russian war in Ukraine has certainly put the DG in a tough spot, adding to an already complex situation.

Inevitably it has drawn the WTO leadership into this evolving political crisis within the international rule-making body for world trade. Geneva-based trade experts point to the pressure on the WTO DG to condemn Russia. "There is pressure on the WTO DG to take sides in this conflict" a person familiar with these dynamics told us. Ngozi Okonjo-Iweala, the WTO boss, seen as many as being decisive and outspoken, allegedly drew criticism for tweeting a photograph with her Russian colleagues in solidarity, although she also tweeted in support of her Ukrainian colleagues.

RUSSIA AT THE WTO

Russia's war in Ukraine has muddied multilateralism, trade diplomacy and health negotiations in Geneva.

While there have been calls to expel Russia from the WTO, there have not been any formal proposals yet, sources said. Trade law experts suggest that there is no clear provision in the WTO, to expel members. Some point to previous political disputes at the WTO involving the US and Venezuela, for example. Ironically, a previous Russia-Ukraine dispute about national security is also being cited in the current context. (See *Russia - Measures Concerning Traffic In Transit)*

There is also a perception that the Ukrainian crisis has given greater ammunition to the U.S., the E.U. and others, that have used the geopolitical response to this crisis to neutralize discussions in contentious areas especially at the WTO.

"The Ukrainian crisis is a game-changer for Europe. And certainly, at the WTO. How can we talk about patents when there is a war? The implications from this, can be deep. We could be looking at an agricultural crisis in a few months, given the importance of Russia and Ukraine in food exports. By June, things could be very different," a developed country diplomat told us, alluding to the WTO ministerial.

Some Geneva-based trade diplomats are of the view that the EU, and the US have "weaponized" trade and economic policy to isolate Russia, while not willing to engage militarily in the conflict. These dynamics have now gone well past the concerns for the Ukrainians, this is also a trade war, many believe.

Take discussions on the TRIPS Waiver.

"It seems that there is a narrative that you cannot talk about the waiver anymore because there is a war in Europe", a developing country diplomat told us.

The Ukraine crisis is important, but with an estimated 15 million deaths from COVID-19 we cannot let this geopolitical crisis scuttle the waiver discussions, one developing country diplomat noted. (WHO has registered 6 million deaths in the on-going pandemic. But it is widely believed that the actual number of deaths could be two-three times the official records.)

Members realize that there is a small window to decide on the waiver. Competing political crises and opportunities, are already driving public attention away from the pandemic.

It is increasingly clear that the Ukrainian crisis has spilled over across plurilateral meetings, committees and other forums within the WTO, sources said. This was witnessed at the TRIPS Council meeting this week.

THE TRIPS COUNCIL MEETING THIS WEEK

At the TRIPS Council meeting earlier this week, Ukraine first took to the floor. Ukraine reportedly said it does not see how members can conduct economic relations with Russia at the WTO on a business-as-usual basis in the current circumstances. (See *Ukraine seeks Russia's suspension from WTO due to Moscow's invasion*: Third World Network.) It also thanked Developed Countries Coordinating Group at WTO that recently excluded Russia.

In addition, the EU, US, UK, Canada, Norway, New Zealand, Japan, Switzerland, Georgia, Trinidad & Tobago took the floor to condemn Russia's "unprovoked military aggression" against Ukraine.

These members underscored that "the WTO is predicated on certain values among these that a fair and just international order is one built on rules, reciprocity and transparency. The invasion of Ukraine is an attack towards what the United Nations, the WTO and Geneva as the capital of multilateralism stand for," according to sources present at the meeting.

Russia is reported to have said the WTO is a rule-based organization and regretted the efforts towards politicization of WTO and fragmentation of the multilateral trading system, sources said.

The meeting took stock of small group discussions among the quad members, but no details from these consultations were shared. South Africa said at the meeting that small-group consultations continue on "good faith" and spoke about the on-going efforts to find a landing zone. The EU said it was convinced that a bridge possible between waiver proponents and its proposal of using existing TRIPS flexibilities. India said that the discussions on the waiver should address the ongoing pandemic and restore credibility of the WTO. The US reiterated its support for waiver of IP protections of COVID-19 vaccines at the meeting.

Other members including the UK, Switzerland and the Africa Group sought transparency and inclusiveness in these discussions, sources said.

In its statement, the UK said:

".... the current process around waiver discussions is not transparent and means this Council is not informed of the substance of discussions. At this point, I would like to support the delegation of Tanzania, speaking on behalf of African group, in the call for a fuller briefing to this Council. This is needed to fulfil the mandate placed upon Members to engage with each other constructively. Simply put, we cannot be expected to progress towards an outcome on discussions which this Council does not know the details of.

While we recognise the urgency of taking forward discussion on the wider pandemic response, the United Kingdom will not accept an outcome when we have not been consulted or given sufficient prior notice to assess what is being proposed in writing. This is because getting it wrong could make both short and long-term pandemic preparedness worse. Members of this Council are entitled to digest, scrutinise, and discuss any outcome of these negotiations before we can reach consensus. As was made clear ahead of November's expected MC12, this process needs to happen before Ministers can agree an outcome."

Dagfinn Sørli, the Norwegian Ambassador at the chair of the TRIPS Council hoped that the small group discussions may lead to a platform based on which consensus can be reached by the wider membership, sources said. Both the original waiver proposal by South Africa and India, and EU's proposal focused on TRIPS flexibilities remain as open items on the agenda of the TRIPS Council.

TAILPIECE

One of the larger goals of the waiver proposal has been to attempt to define processes to quickly boost production to improve the access to medical products, steps that could be adopted during health emergencies. While current discussions on the waiver are limited to the COVID-19 pandemic, there are no specific provisions for *future* health emergencies. It is something that can be added once a decision is made, sources indicated.

At the WHO, in the context of the pandemic treaty discussions, developing countries wish for a waiver-like provision that could kick in automatically once a Public Health Emergency of International Concern has been declared.

These are surely ambitious targets, given the sustained resistance that any suspension of IP protections during this pandemic has generated. But diplomats believe that the process has been as important as the destination.

It is not entirely clear to the extent to which the proponents of the waiver are willing to compromise.

One Geneva-based diplomat has called any potential narrow waiver as only a "political souvenir". Small, but possibly significant?

37.

THE LOWEST COMMON DENOMINATOR: THE QUAD TEXT ON THE TRIPS WAIVER (MARCH 18, 2022)

A developing country ambassador told us a few months ago that the best outcome on the waiver proposal would be to persuade the Americans and Europeans to have a solution that would include all kinds of medical products not just vaccines and waiving all kinds of IP protections not just patents, underlining the positions of these key WTO members respectively. Now, as a potential for a compromise is beginning to emerge, it seems that the proponents of the waiver might have lost out on both accounts.

While scholars and access to medicine advocates have already panned the compromise text, these are early days, considering that the text will now be taken up by a wider WTO membership. For now, it may have helped let off steam steadily building in the WTO fuelled by unmet expectations and has given its members something to play around with, as they will embark on arduous negotiations, weighing quid pro quos in their consultations in the run up to the Ministerial Conference in June 2022.

What is also noteworthy is that the leading pharma industry association, the IFPMA has also "condemned" this text.

In our conversations with diplomats, it appears most of the Quad members are not happy with the text. But a compromise by definition is often an unhappy outcome.

A developed country trade diplomat told us that the certainty around patents must be preserved. "We have offered deep concessions," the source said.

Here is a quick analysis of the text based on views from relevant experts.

Experts are of the view that the proposal as it stands, does not go far enough in ensuring a freedom to operate by not addressing existing cumbersome authorization procedures. It is limiting on both accounts - the kinds of medical products can be included in a waiver (only vaccines), and the types of IP protections that can be waived (only patents). Worse, it also limits by countries that can benefit from a potential waiver (a function of vaccine exports and status). (See *WTO-IMF COVID-19 Vaccine Trade Tracker)*

As we first reported last week, the essential structure of this proposed text has two parts, one on patents, and the other on trade secrets.

TRIPS COVID-19 solution: dated March 14, 2022

1. *Notwithstanding the provision of patent rights under its domestic legislation, an eligible Member*[1] *may limit the rights provided for under Article 28.1 of the TRIPS Agreement (hereinafter "the Agreement") by authorizing the use of patented subject matter*[2] 2 *required for the production and supply of COVID-19 vaccines without the consent of the right holder to the extent necessary to address the COVID-19 pandemic, in accordance with the provisions of Article 31 of the Agreement, as clarified and waived in paragraphs 2 to 6 below.*

2. *For greater clarity, an eligible Member may authorize the use of patented subject matter under Article 31 without the right holder's consent through any instrument*

available in the law of the Member such as executive orders, emergency decrees, government use authorizations, and judicial or administrative orders, whether or not a Member has a compulsory license regime in place. For the purpose of this Decision, the" law of a Member" referred to in Article 31 is not limited to legislative acts such as those laying down rules on compulsory licensing, but it also includes other acts, such as executive orders, emergency decrees, and judicial or administrative orders.

3. Members agree on the following clarifications and waivers for eligible Members to authorize the use of patented subject matter in accordance with paragraphs 1 and 2:

a. With respect to Article 31(a), an eligible Member may issue a single authorization to use the subject matter of multiple patents necessary for the production or supply of a COVID-19 vaccine. The authorization shall list all patents covered. In the determination of the relevant patents, an eligible Member may be assisted by WIPO's patent landscaping work, including on underlying technologies on COVID-19 vaccines, and by other relevant sources. An eligible Member may update the authorization to include other patents.

d. An eligible Member need not require the proposed user of the patented subject matter to make efforts to obtain an authorization from the right holder for the purposes of Article 31(b).

e. An eligible Member may waive the requirement of Article 31(f) that authorized use under Article 31 be predominantly to supply its domestic market and may allow any proportion of the authorized use to be exported to eligible Members and to supply international or regional *joint initiatives that aim to ensure the equitable access of eligible Members to the COVID-19 vaccine covered by the authorization.*

f.   *Eligible Members shall undertake all reasonable efforts to prevent the re-exportation of the COVID-19 vaccine that has been imported into their territories under this Decision. All Members shall ensure the availability of effective legal remedies to prevent the importation into their territories of COVID-19 vaccines produced under, and diverted to their markets inconsistently with, this Decision.*

g.   *Determination of adequate remuneration under Article 31(h) may take account of the humanitarian and not-for-profit purpose of specific vaccine distribution programs aimed at providing equitable access to COVID-19 vaccines in order to support manufacturers in eligible Members to produce and supply these vaccines at affordable prices for eligible Members. In setting the adequate remuneration in these cases, eligible Members may take into consideration existing good practices in instances of national emergencies, pandemics, or similar circumstances.[3]*

4.   *Nothing in Article 39.3 of the Agreement shall prevent a Member from taking measures necessary to enable the effectiveness of any authorization issued as per this Decision.*

5.   *For purposes of transparency, as soon as possible after the adoption of the measure, an eligible Member shall communicate to the Council for TRIPS any measure related to the implementation of this Decision, including the granting of an authorization.[4]*

6. *An eligible Member may apply the provisions of this Decision until [3][5] years from the date of this Decision. The General Council may extend such a period taking into consideration the exceptional circumstances of the COVID-19 pandemic. The General Council will review annually the operation of this Decision.*

7. *Members shall not challenge any measures taken in conformity with this Decision under subparagraphs 1(b) and 1(c) of Article XXIII of the GATT 1994.*

8. *No later than six months from the date of this Decision, Members will decide on its extension to cover the production and distribution of COVID-19 diagnostics and therapeutics.*

HOW EXPERTS READ THE COMPROMISE TEXT:

ON PATENTS

Sangeeta Shashikant, Legal Advisor, Third World Network

"The text needs improvement. There are some shortcomings. For example, we need to know whether the waiver will be applicable when the situation is no longer a pandemic. Also, there is no clarity on whether the decision will apply to products that have pending patent applications. The text now limits itself to patented subject-matter. COVID-19 products have many pending patent applications.

The requirement that the authorization "shall list all patents covered" is TRIPS-plus. Article 31 does not require the listing of patents. It is often not possible to know the patent landscape because patent applications are confidential for the first 18 months. Similarly, the requirement in footnote 4 of the text, creates additional conditions with respect to use of Article 31 that do not exist in the TRIPS Agreement. These TRIPS-plus requirements have the potential to hinder effective use of the decision.

In addition, the approach to Article 39 is flawed for it fails to deal with protection of undisclosed information (Article 39) as an independent barrier irrespective of the patent status.

We also need a decision that only requires a one-time authorization on the part of the government that creates a certain pathway for follow-on manufacturers to enter the manufacture and enter the market for all COVID vaccines, therapeutics and diagnostics for the duration of the waiver decision.

(See below: Footnote 4 of the compromise text seeks additional details including on the authorized entity, the product(s) for which the authorization has been granted and the duration of the authorization. The quantity(ies) for which the authorization has been granted and the country(ies) to which the product(s) is(are) to be supplied shall be notified as soon as possible after the information is available.)

ON TRADE SECRETS:

Hyo Yoon Kang, Reader in Law, Kent Law School, University of Kent said:

The leaked text mentions TRIPS Art. 39 (3) which concerns the exclusive treatment of regulatory data about pharmaceutical and agricultural chemical products. But Art. 39 (3) is in itself not necessarily connected to existing patents. One can have data exclusivity of various time lengths of time in different domestic/regional jurisdictions separately from patent rights.

Also Art. 39 (3) already contains the provision of public interest protection: "Members shall protect such data against disclosure, except where necessary to protect the public". This is only relevant for jurisdictions which have a high level of data exclusivity in place, such as US and EU for example, but these countries would not be included in the proposed waiver compromise proposal in any case, because it would only cover self-declared developing countries, and even amongst those, being restricted to countries that have exported less than 10% of global vaccines doses in 2021. My sense is that very few countries would be affected by Art. 39 (3) in this carved out category in any case.

The issue of data exclusivity - from a legal point of view - is not necessarily connected to patents or to the practical and legal technical challenge to devise ways to mandate know-how and technology transfer. The leaked text offers no mechanism or a mandate to share the data available at a regulatory agency outside one's jurisdiction for making vaccines - the already existing public interest provision in Art. 39 (3) is not elaborated or expanded towards non-domestic publics. For example, there is no mechanism by which a generic manufacturer in India could access European regulatory data.

The leaked text does not mention Art. 39 (1) and (2) which are about undisclosed information more broadly and incorporate the provisions of the Berne Convention Art. 10bis regarding the *fair treatment of commercially valuable information. TRIPS Art. 39 (1) and (2) need to be understood in the broader contexts of the meanings of fair or unfair competition, confidential commercial information and trade secrets. There is nothing in the current draft compromise text which indicates that 39 (1) and (2) could be waived on grounds of countervailing public interest. This is a missed opportunity.*

WHAT IT MEANS FOR IMPLEMENTATION
A view from India: Murali Neelakantan, Principal Lawyer, amicus. Former Global General Counsel, Cipla

"This is a welcome move even if it is delayed. If this waiver doesn't happen, it would be an acknowledgement that the TRIPs flexibilities and the Doha Declaration were impotent. This waiver acknowledges that they are meaningful.

India will have challenges implementing this as stated for the following reasons:

1. Getting a list of all patents attaching to a vaccine, it's raw materials and everything else required to make the vaccine (consumables like bio reactor bags) will be a huge exercise especially when we don't have a list of all patents attaching to the vaccine or any product in India.

2. Indian patent law doesn't require that each specific patent is listed for CL or government use during an emergency. This waiver now restricts the flexibility.

3. There is no mention of trade secrets being shared. Given the poor quality of disclosure in Indian patents, the patents in themselves may not be adequate to produce vaccines.

In effect, this waiver doesn't add to the TRIPs flexibilities. In fact, limiting it to vaccines and the requirement to list all patents for each product adds restrictions to Indian law incorporating the TRIPs flexibilities.

Finally, without a waiver for diagnostics and treatment would be a huge loss for patients in these negotiations"

WHAT COMES NEXT

It is unclear when the next TRIPS Council meeting is scheduled. But the Quad members are cautious about the response to the text from the wider WTO membership. Not only will vociferous opponents to the waiver proposal such as the UK and Switzerland will fight to protect their positions, but diplomats are also wary about countries such as China, excluded from the current proposal of the waiver, and even other developing countries that are manufacturing hubs.

Media reports suggest that following the leak of the text, some WTO members met to discuss the compromise text. There are efforts to link the outcome on the TRIPS Waiver to other deliverables at the WTO.

CAN THE TEXT BE STRENGTHENED?

Supporters of the waiver would like to see the compromise text be strengthened. But it may be difficult to introduce new features to the existing text at this stage. If anything, the possibility of this text to be watered down further is very real.

Nevertheless, nostalgic trade observers look to the past. In the decades old fight to improve the access to medicines, a few suggestions are often cited. Experts and activists suggest other provisions in the TRIPS Agreement that could offer more efficient ways to boost local manufacturing of medical products. One such route is the use of Article 30, and not Article 31 that the current text features. Some countries have said in the past that Article 30 is more substantive in nature, as opposed to Article 31, which is more procedural. These provisions seek to qualify the limits to exclusive patent rights available under the TRIPS Agreement.

Article 30, advocates believe offers an elegant solution. It simply states:

Article 30 Exceptions to Rights Conferred

Members may provide limited exceptions to the exclusive rights conferred by a patent, provided that such exceptions do not unreasonably conflict with a normal exploitation of the patent and do not unreasonably prejudice the legitimate interests of the patent owner, taking account of the legitimate interests of third parties.

Other alternatives to the existing approaches include the use of Article 44 that governs the use of injunctions when a patent has been infringed. This has also been brought up in the context of discussions at WIPO.

No matter what the outcome, the TRIPS waiver talks have entered a defining phase. The next few weeks will be crucial to see how the other co-sponsors of the proposal step in to shape these negotiations at the WTO.

Also see:

'Quad' raise hopes of a COVID-19 deal and revival for the beleaguered WTO: Trade β Blog

The WTO Touts Progress in Covid Vaccine Waiver Talks but No Agreement Yet: Bloomberg

WTO DG Okonjo-Iweala welcomes breakthrough on COVID-19 vaccine waiver: WTO

QUAD's tentative agreement on TRIPS and COVID-19: Knowledge Ecology International

Statement: Leaked Proposal on COVID Medicines Waiver Helps No One But Floundering WTO: Public Citizen

1. For the purpose of this Decision, an "eligible Member" means any developing country Member that exported less than 10 percent of world exports of COVID-19 vaccine doses in 2021.

2. For the purpose of this Decision, it is understood that 'patented subject matter' includes ingredients and processes necessary for the manufacture of the COVID-19 vaccine.

3. This includes the Remuneration Guidelines for Non-Voluntary Use of a Patent on Medical Technologies published by the WHO (WHO/TCM/2005.1)

4. The information provided shall include the name and address of the authorized entity, the product(s) for which the authorization has been granted and the duration of the authorization. The quantity(ies) for which the authorization has been granted and the country(ies) to which the product(s) is(are) to be supplied shall be notified as soon as possible after the information is available

38.

CURRENT COMPROMISE TEXT ON THE TRIPS WAIVER WILL UNDERMINE VACCINE DONATIONS (APRIL 1, 2020)

Global health is determinedly governed in silos. Occasionally though, policy questions seep through these porous boundaries. Somewhat problematically for powers that be.

Take the so-called compromise text - a result of discussions on the TRIPS Waiver proposal between four WTO members.

A provision in the current text that was creatively leaked a few weeks ago in Brussels, seeks to curtail re-exportation of unused doses. This, as it stands, will undermine vaccine donations – a key policy for Gavi's COVAX Facility. Donations have also been an important geopolitical and diplomatic tool for many countries, especially those that hoarded more vaccines than they needed, often without having specific plans on how to donate.

Gavi - The Vaccine Alliance has never fully supported the TRIPS Waiver, in line with its most powerful backers including the US government, and the Bill and Melinda Gates Foundation. It is therefore interesting to see that this shrunken form of the TRIPS Waiver, as it currently stands, will threaten an important facet of Gavi's strategy to meet the unmet demand for COVID-19 vaccines – namely donations of doses.

This flies in the face of the original TRIPS Waiver proposal, that sought to boost local manufacturing of COVID-19 medical products. It is striking that this version of the compromise text impedes even the less-than-preferable policy option such as the donation of vaccine doses. (Also note that donations have not really had the intended effect, mired with problems of short-shelf lives of vaccines and logistical problems.)

A Gavi spokesperson responded to our queries:

"Gavi, as an international private-public partnership, does not have a role in a TRIPS waiver process which is a decision for WTO Member States to take. Gavi welcomes any decision by governments that expand global equitable access to COVID-19 vaccines.

We also recognise the importance of countries' commitments to ensure free movement of vaccines and removing any barriers that get in the way of equitable access. Therefore, we urge that all countries also support technology transfer efforts so that not only IP but also know-how is put to use to diversify manufacturing and boost global production, both in the mid-term and in preparation for the next pandemic."

Legal experts have pointed out that the current text has several TRIPS-plus provisions (provisions that seeks to impose stronger obligations to protect intellectual property than those mandated by the WTO TRIPS Agreement).

HOW DOES THE COMPROMISE TEXT THREATEN DONATIONS?

In the leaked text, a provision reads:

"3 (d) Eligible Members shall undertake all reasonable efforts to prevent the re-exportation of the COVID-19 vaccine that has been imported into their territories under this Decision. All Members shall ensure the availability of effective legal remedies to prevent the importation into their territories of COVID-19

vaccines produced under, and diverted to their markets inconsistently with, this Decision."

A Geneva-based legal expert who has parsed through the legal implications of the leaked text told us:

"The prevention of re-exportation can prevent donations of unused doses imported under this decision by an eligible member. This will also prevent re-exportation of such doses to COVAX."

Sources familiar with the discussions suggest that this provision was favored by the EU and by the US. (The Quad process brokered by DG Ngozi Okonjo-Iweala since December 2021, involved discussions between the EU, US, India and South Africa)

Explaining the EU's support for the provision, the expert suggested:

"The EU has sought to waive Article 31(f)[1] [of the WTO TRIPS Agreement], and may perceive this as an implied waiver of Article 31bis and its annex[2]. In that context, they probably also wanted to not waive the clause in 31bis prohibiting re-exportation under that system." *(See footnotes on text of Articles)*

Article 31(f) says such authorizations will predominantly be for the supply of the domestic market of the country that authorizes the use without the consent of the patent holder. The current text waives this provision. However, by seeking to prevent re-exportation it defeats the purpose of waiving this Article 31(f) and introduces the restriction on re-exportation which does not exist in Article 31(f).

As a result, the implication is that if an eligible member exports any part of the vaccine batches produced under a regular compulsory license in accordance with the waiver of Article 31(f), the limitation on re-exportation under Article 31*bis* will still apply on the importing country, the source explained.

Article 31bis is a mechanism for compulsory licenses for exports, with conditions, such as on eligible importing Members - countries with insufficient or no pharmaceutical manufacturing capacity. This mechanism has proved to be cumbersome and mostly an unworkable arrangement for WTO members.

Activists say that the current text runs counter to the reality of the current pandemic where speedy transfer of unused doses through re-exportation will be critical to save lives given the speed at which variants have spread.

The current text also "creates a business opportunity for the patent holders to undermine the system through their little donations and platforms that promote such charity business," the expert said.

Another expert suggested that such a provision will also affect procurement of vaccine doses by smaller countries, especially those that procure in bulk for a region.

This provision illustrates one of the many shortcomings of the current text. (See: MSF comments on the reported draft text of the TRIPS Waiver negotiation)

THE CURRENT STATE OF PLAY IN THE DISCUSSIONS AT WTO

At an informal meeting of the WTO General Council earlier this week, it emerged that there is no agreement yet on the leaked text. Apart from the EU, other members of the Quad text appear hesitant to lend their names to this leaked proposal.

South Africa is reported to have suggested that the current proposal is being internally assessed.

Reuters reported earlier this week, that there was no agreement on the compromise text citing comments from US Trade Chief Katherine Tai. She was responding to questions from the members of the House Ways and Means Committee.

"Tai called the text the "concept" of a compromise developed during discussions facilitated by WTO Director General Ngozi Okonjo-Iweala between the United States, the European Union, India and South Africa," according to Reuters.

In the meantime pressure continues to build on the EU and the WTO to reject the current text. Civil society groups called to "refrain from rushing WTO members to rapidly adopt a purported proposal on intellectual property rights and COVID-19."

"The text under consideration by some WTO members contains problematic and contradictory elements and remains largely insufficient as an effective pandemic response. Further negotiations are needed to ensure an effective outcome in a multilateral manner, responding to the needs expressed by many WTO members and civil society," the letter said.

Activists are also calling for an immediate inclusion of therapeutics in the current text that is now limited only to include a waiver of patents on vaccines. They also suggest that access to trade secrets is key for both therapeutics and vaccines.

THE ALLEGED MOTIVATIONS AROUND THE LEAKED TEXT

Observers in Geneva said that the purported leak was meant to discredit the co-sponsors of the TRIPS Waiver proposal, and to put pressure on India and South Africa to own the proposal before it is taken to the wider WTO membership for consideration.

The leaked text continues to be discussed in small groups at the WTO. "Perhaps one strategy is to let countries let the steam off, in such small group meetings, before bringing this proposal to the wider membership at the TRIPS Council", one developing country diplomat told us.

"At the TRIPS Council, such deliberations are public, and often have a record. They want to avoid an ugly debate at the

Council, and hence the process has been deliberately slow." The diplomat added.

With more than 60 WTO members supporting the original TRIPS Waiver proposal, there is pressure now to widen these discussions and bring the outcome of the Quad process to the TRIPS Council.

"This text should now be brought forward as a facilitator's text and should be open for debate and negotiation among all members. The DG must own this and bring it to the wider membership", a lawyer working on the access to medicines told us.

In the meantime, dates for the WTO 12th Ministerial Conference are now scheduled for June 12-15th. This could in turn give an impetus to conclude the resolution on these discussions.

(Proponents of the waiver proposal have maintained that the mechanism can be approved even without a ministerial conference. A General Council decision can be adopted by WTO members. However, for some members, this complicates and lessens the leverage with quid pro quos across other deliverables that typically characterize such negotiations around a ministerial conference.)

TAILPIECE

Observers anticipate deep implications for developing country alliances at the WTO. It is arguable if it was a strategic error on the part of the co-sponsors, and other members of the WTO, to let the discussions within the Quad proceed for nearly four months.

But recall that discussions at the technical level even between these four members had reached a dead-end by mid-2021. While there was momentum in these discussions in the run-up to the Ministerial conference in December 2021, the abrupt postponement of the event put a spanner in these negotiations. A window to push these discussions to a political level among the four key members, was then opened by the DG. This, observers say has contributed to the weakening of the original proposal.

"Geneva-based diplomats were shut off from the process, and they decided this at a political level. It resulted in a *fait accompli*" one observer said.

"What signal does it send for future negotiations in the trade diplomacy?" the person asked.

It is likely that other co-sponsors could pressure to widen these discussions and improve the text, even as opponents to the waiver proposal will also make their displeasure known.

(The Ukrainian crisis also continues to muddy the waters for discussions at the WTO. The Geneva Observer reported that the BRICS countries are fighting back.)

What is clear is that the discussions on the TRIPS Waiver are far from over. Hardened activists anticipate negotiations to "go down to the wire" in the coming weeks. "This is the period where deals will be done", MSF's Leena Menghaney said this week.

"We cannot settle with a bad outcome, for it sets precedence. The waiver proposal is an "open agenda item" at the TRIPS Council. There is should be no pressure on the co-sponsors to agree to a weak proposal" an activist told us.

What happens at the WTO on the waiver proposal, will have implications beyond the pandemic and have echoes in other forums. Most immediately, at the WHO in the context of the pandemic treaty discussions where developing countries want a waiver-like approach to ensure access to medical products in the context of health emergencies.

1. Article 31(f), WTO TRIPS Agreement: Other Use Without Authorization of the Right Holder

Where the law of a Member allows for other use (7) of the subject matter of a patent without the authorization of the right holder, including use by the government or third parties authorized by the government, the following provisions shall be respected: (f) any such use shall be authorized predominantly for the supply of the domestic market of the Member authorizing such use;

2. Art. *31bis and annex: "3. In order to ensure that the products imported under the system are used for the public health purposes underlying their importation, eligible importing Members shall take reasonable measures within their means, proportionate to their administrative capacities and to the risk of trade diversion to prevent re-exportation of the products that have actually been imported into their territories under the system. In the event that an eligible importing Member that is a developing country Member or a least-developed country Member experiences difficulty in implementing this provision, developed country Members shall provide, on request and on mutually agreed terms and conditions, technical and financial cooperation in order to facilitate its implementation."*

39.
WTO DG TO TAKE COMPROMISE TEXT ON TRIPS WAIVER TO THE WIDER MEMBERSHIP (APRIL 14, 2022)

Ngozi Okonjo-Iweala is expected to take the compromise text on the TRIPS Waiver to the wider WTO membership, sources told Geneva Health Files this week. It is learned that some members of the Quad (the US, the EU, India and South Africa) have not signed off on the text.

The leaked compromise text between the four members of the Quad group has struggled to get endorsement and ownership from the US, India and South Africa. It is understood it is only the European Union, that has so far lent support to the current version of the compromise text on the TRIPS waiver proposal. (The current text resembles EU's original proposal on clarifying rules around compulsory licensing)

While internal consultations continue within countries at the national level, the reasons for not supporting the text vary between these key members. The reasons for not endorsing the text are strategic for the proponents of the Waiver given the deep concessions compared to their original proposal.

As we reported earlier, some WTO members and other stakeholders have been pushing for this text to be presented as a facilitator's text for consideration by the wider membership. After weeks of impasse during which the proponents of the waiver were allegedly asked to sign off on the compromise text, the DG is now expected to take this text to the wider membership, without such a sign off, diplomatic sources said. She had steered the discussions among this small group of members since December 2021.

So far, discussions on this compromise text have not been considered formally within the WTO. No TRIPS Council meetings have been scheduled, by the time this story went to print. The WTO ministerial is less than three months away, and an outcome on the TRIPS Waiver continues to be seen as a short-term panacea to save the relevance of the WTO. (See Politico: *WTO faces 'slow motion train wreck' amid Ukraine war chaos*)

Drowned by the Ukrainian crisis, the policy attention to the pandemic is already waning, not only at the WTO. Observers point to the glut in the production of vaccines, further complicated by a range of factors including vaccine hesitancy and logistical challenges in immunization programs in many countries. (Earlier this week, Airfinity, the life science analytics firm *downgraded global COVID-19 vaccine revenue forecast*)

However, considering that, nearly 3 billion people remain unvaccinated against COVID-19, and the need for therapeutics and diagnostics has not diminished, the relevance of the TRIPS Waiver continues to remain important, activists say.

Some point to the on-going developments with respect to the challenges in using TRIPS flexibilities (the EU's preferred policy approach as opposed to the waiver). Last month, Knowledge Ecology International, reported about *Pfizer's March 18, 2022 opposition to the KEI request for a compulsory license in Dominican Republic for Paxlovid.*

What next for the waiver proposal, and for the WTO?

The coming weeks will witness how these negotiations will progress at the WTO. After months of these discussions taking place, outside of the usual, formal processes of the WTO, the compromise text is now likely to be debated among the 164 members.

Sources also suggested that without a formal forum to discuss the compromise text it is difficult for other WTO members to make their positions known. "It is not clear to what extent, other co-sponsors of the waiver proposal, will take this forward."

Some delegates indicated that if the compromise text "dies a natural death", there would be scope for improvement on the current text or negotiation on the original waiver proposal. But the appetite for WTO members, especially that of many powerful ones, for engaging in lengthy discussions on the waiver, may be low, also given the political exigencies around the Ukrainian crisis.

It is learned that China has protested vociferously on being excluded from the implementation of a waiver as understood in the criteria suggested by the current compromise text.

For the proponents, the efforts will be to fight eligibility criteria that seeks to narrow the scope of implementation'; pushing to bring in therapeutics and diagnostics into the product scope of any waiver; and, to challenge the requirement for listing of patents as described in the current text, sources familiar with deliberations told us.

Developing countries are keen to have an outcome on the waiver proposal, failing which they would make conditional their support for the wider WTO response to the pandemic, diplomatic sources indicated. This is even as some opponents to the waiver seek to link the waiver discussions to issues such as food security.

Geneva-based sources also suggested that the small group approach used in these waiver discussions are now being suggested as an approach for negotiations on other WTO matters including on fisheries and agriculture. The small group deliberations have been criticized for being opaque and non-inclusive.

Whatever the outcome, time is running out. And it has also shown the reluctance of many countries to address the issues of equity in any meaningful manner at the WTO.

"If the DG wants to save the WTO, she must bring the compromise text in her role as a facilitator", one developing country diplomat told us.

And in the event the compromise text is dead in the water, activists around the world may be relieved, since many see the current text as setting a bad precedent.

Tailpiece: Industry Groups Beat up Waiver Proposal

In one of the most strident criticisms till date, on the alleged ineffectiveness and the limitations of the TRIPS Waiver, pharma industry group, IFPMA brought together CEOs of large companies, to articulate the contempt for the proposal at a briefing earlier this week.

Drawing attention to a glut in vaccine production and alleging high vaccine hesitancy in developing countries as reasons for low vaccination rates in some parts of the world, industry leaders repeatedly attacked the idea of a TRIPS Waiver. Some even called it "toxic".

Thomas Cueni, Director General of IFPMA said that he was stunned that countries continue to debate the TRIPS Waiver.

The timing of the outrage from the industry on the waiver proposal is hard to understand, given that even after 18 months of deliberations, what is now being discussed is a significantly reduced form of the original proposal.

As these negotiations come down to the wire in the coming weeks, such expressions of outrage will continue to feed headlines.

40.
WTO DG SERVES UP PROPOSED NEW TEXT ON THE TRIPS WAIVER TO A DIVIDED HOUSE, TENSE NEGOTIATIONS EXPECTED (MAY 6, 2022)

This week WTO members were given access to a letter that was described as an outcome document based on the discussions between select members. This letter was sent by the Director General Ngozi Okonjo-Iweala to the Chair of the Council for Trade-Related Aspects of Intellectual Property Rights, Ambassador Lansana Gberie of Sierra Leone, describing the progress of the informal discussions on the TRIPS Waiver proposal. The letter also shared a proposed text by the DG on the waiver discussions.

Although the document does not specifically mention the quadrilateral group (comprising the US, the EU, India and South Africa) it is understood that this text that was shared with the wider membership, is based on the discussions between these key members.

In her letter to the TRIPS Council Chair, the new text is presented to the WTO membership under the DG's ownership.

DG Okonjo-Iweala says in the letter, "What was evident was the need for additional impetus to the TRIPS waiver discussions given the impasse in the TRIPS Council. I therefore informed Members that I would be reaching out to various Ministers for needed input. In this regard, working with DDG Gonzalez, we have tried to support an informal group of Ministers to come together around what could be a meaningful proposal, without prejudice to their respective positions, that could provide a platform to be built upon by the membership."

The letter further says, "I assured Members that whatever outcome emerged from this informal process would be put forward transparently to the full Membership for discussion in the TRIPS Council".

Why is this important?

Sources say that this so-called outcome text has struggled to get endorsement and ownership from the US, India and South Africa. The EU has supported the text. In the meantime, even as these three countries have not completed internal consultations on the text, as has been suggested, pressure continued to build on the DG to make the text public, albeit without the endorsement of all the members of the Quad.

Today, 6 May, WTO members discussed this text at a formal meeting of the TRIPS Council. A General Council meeting of the WTO is scheduled next week on 9-10 May.

THE CONTENTS OF THE "OUTCOME DOCUMENT"

The "new" proposal in the DG's letter is similar to the leaked text (March 2022) on the discussions between the four key members. Similar to the EU's proposal, this text essentially clarifies and waives certain provisions regarding the issuance of compulsory licenses with respect to patents over vaccines. We reported earlier that this leaked text has been panned by critics and civil society organizations who believe that such a proposal could set a negative precedent for the access to medicines.

There are two changes in square brackets (suggesting lack of agreement), compared to the leaked text: one addresses the definition of eligible countries; the second, on the requirement to list each patent in non-voluntary authorization, Knowledge

Ecology International said in an update when this document first became public this week.

ON THE ELIGIBILITY OF COUNTRIES

A policy brief by South Centre has systematically analysed the proposal by the DG. "Footnote 1 of the draft has two parts in separate square brackets. The first part makes all developing country Members eligible but encourages such Members that have capacity to export vaccines to opt out of the decision. The other formulation in the third sentence of footnote 1, in square brackets, excludes developing countries that have exported more than 10 percent of COVID-19 vaccine doses in 2021," the analysis by South Centre says. This, experts say, is to exclude China based on vaccine production numbers.

It is understood that China has expressed reservations on such a potential outcome. Experts believe that such an exclusion might affect China even outside of these negotiations. This might also have implications for other developing countries.

Sources familiar with the discussions suggest that efforts could be made to persuade other developing countries to forfeit the use of such flexibilities intended through a waiver proposal. "There could be quid pros quos offered by powerful members in exchange for not taking advantage for potential waiver provisions," a diplomatic source told us.

In a separate commentary, Third World Network (TWN) said, "It is sheer common sense that during a public health emergency, there can be no place for criteria that deliberately excludes countries with production capacity from using the system to support other countries. From this perspective, the inclusion of a criterion that arbitrarily excludes any developing country WTO Member that exports more than 10 percent of world exports of COVID-19 vaccine doses in 2021, and all developed countries from using the proposed system not only as importing countries but also exporting countries is reprehensible. Clearly, petty politics are in play."

"Such a criterion is a major step backwards for addressing global public health concerns and a significant departure from the Doha Declaration on TRIPS and Public Health adopted at the height of the HIV/AIDS crisis that is applicable to all WTO Members. Even Article 31bis of TRIPS is applicable to all WTO Members, with countries having the option to self-opt out from using the mechanism for purposes of importing products. There is no exclusion of any country for purposes of exporting products," Sangeeta Shashikant, a legal expert at TWN said in her piece.

ON THE LISTING REQUIREMENTS OF PATENTS IN NON-VOLUNTARY AUTHORIZATION

The new text has the following square bracket suggesting a lack of consensus between the four members on this provision:

"3. Members agree on the following clarifications and waivers for eligible Members to authorize the use of patented subject matter in accordance with paragraphs 1 and 2:

(a) [With respect to Article 31(a), an eligible Member may issue a single authorization to use the subject matter of multiple patents necessary for the production or supply of a COVID-19 vaccine. The authorization shall list all patents covered. In the determination of the relevant patents, an eligible Member may be assisted by WIPO's patent landscaping work, including on underlying technologies on COVID-19 vaccines, and by other relevant sources. An eligible Member may update the authorization to include other patents.]

Experts had already criticised this language for making it onerous to list all patents to produce vaccines. Authors of the South Center paper further say, "Interestingly, compulsory licenses have been granted in the USA in the past without the required listing, in relation to present and future patents."

(See: Third World Network, WTO DG's proposed solution unsuitable for global public health crisis)

THE PUSH FOR THE INCLUSION OF THERAPEUTICS AND DIAGNOSTICS

On the inclusion of therapeutics and diagnostics in the scope of a potential waiver, the current text says, "No later than six months from the date of this Decision, Members will decide on its extension to cover the production and distribution of COVID-19 diagnostics and therapeutics."

Sources indicated to us that developing countries will push for an inclusion of therapeutics and diagnostics in the current negotiations. "It does not make sense to put off a decision on the applicability of the waiver to other products later in the year," a diplomatic source from a developing country told us.

It is also understood that given the delay in the decision on the waiver, the goalposts have now shifted. The evolving epidemiology of the disease suggests that COVID-19 will become endemic in many parts of the world. "While vaccines have been incredibly helpful, the world now needs access to therapeutics. Vaccination continues to be very low in Africa, and diagnostic capacities across the developing world are inadequate," a developing country diplomat said underscoring the need to expand the product scope in any outcome on a potential waiver.

In his recent remarks, WHO DG Tedros Adhanom Ghebreyesus said, "We cannot accept prices that make life-saving treatments available to the rich and out of reach for the poor. This is a moral failing."

IS IT A BIRD OR A PLANE? ("Outcome" Vs "Agreement")

Apart from the substantive elements of the proposed text, that critics say has little in common with the original waiver proposal by India and South Africa, the process guiding the introduction of this new text also raises questions.

Earlier this week, there was confusion on whether the Quad group had indeed endorsed and agreed on the text.

Sources familiar with the process indicated that the DG has been under pressure to introduce the text to the wider membership. It is understood that the US was keen that an official text be brought to the membership to begin formal consultations on the text. Other members at the WTO, have also been hesitant to make public statements on their positions on the text, because till today's (May 6) formal meeting of the TRIPS Council, there was no opportunity to discuss the new text.

It was only after the new proposed text was shared following the informal meeting on May 3, that members officially had access to the text. To be sure, ever since the text was leaked in mid-March 2022, members have discussed it informally, in small groups.

Efforts to suggest that an alleged agreement between the Quad has been reached, could indicate the pressure to reach a consensus on these highly sensitive and political discussions. In less than 6 weeks, trade ministers will gather for a ministerial conference, after nearly five years.

By the evening of May 3, the WTO published an update on the outcome document, that said, "After an impasse of more than one year in the TRIPS Council, DG Okonjo-Iweala, working with Deputy Director-General Anabel González, supported an informal group of ministers to come together around what could be a meaningful proposal, without prejudice to their respective positions, that could provide a platform to be built upon by the membership."

This suggests that negotiations will begin on this new proposed text as the basis. This also does not rule out any other proposals, or efforts by other WTO members to improve upon the text. Similarly, opponents to the TRIPS waiver, will express their positions on this approach to address the pandemic.

In an update, TWN said:

"Elements of the proposed outcome read out by the TRIPS Chair during the recent informal meeting, as prepared by the Secretariat, also mis-characterized the content of the proposed outcome, for instance, by suggesting that the proposal to "limit" Article 28.1 provides additional flexibility and that a patent waiver for vaccines is being offered. This representation is very far from the truth and reality. Experts and civil society groups globally have raised serious concerns over the contents of the WTO DG-led proposal.

There is consensus that the proposed outcome does not waive "patents" on vaccines. Instead, it introduces further conditions and uncertainties with respect to use of non-voluntary licenses of patents (also commonly referred to as "compulsory licenses") and contains harmful negative precedents on how to address global public health emergencies."

In addition, TWN pointed out:

"Nowhere is there any mention of any Quad Member or their agreement on any aspect of the proposal. In addition, reference to "whatever outcome" would suggest to include outcomes that have not been agreed to.

However, this did not prevent from the WTO Secretariat from issuing a public statement that misleadingly referred to the DG proposal communicated to the TRIPS Council as "Quad's outcome document".

(See TWN: WTO Secretariat misleads on status & content of intellectual property text, perpetuates confusion)

PRESSURE CONTINUES ON MEMBERS TO REJECT TEXT

This week MSF asked governments to reject the text. "This draft text being discussed at the WTO is simply not the effective intellectual property Waiver that more than 100 governments were asking for, and governments should reject it," said Yuanqiong Hu, Senior Legal and Policy Advisor for MSF›s Access Campaign.

On the provision in the current new text to delay extending any waiver applicable to therapeutics and diagnostics, Felipe de Carvalho, MSF Access Campaign Coordinator in Latin America said:

"It is particularly disheartening to even consider delaying a decision on treatments and diagnostics by an additional six months, especially when access to COVID-19 treatments remains a significant problem for people in many low- and middle-income countries, and particularly in Latin America," said Felipe de Carvalho, MSF Access Campaign Coordinator in Latin America. "The impact of the pandemic on people in countries in Latin America, including Brazil, Bolivia, Colombia and Peru, was *devastating, and access to affordable generic medicines would be crucial if another COVID-19 wave were to hit this region."*

More than 40 civil society organisations sent an open letter calling on the European Union to refrain from rushing WTO members to rapidly adopt the draft text.

WHAT NEXT

Today WTO members considered the new text at the TRIPS Council formal meeting. (This story will be updated later. We are following up on the discussions). It is expected that an update on the discussions from the TRIPS Council will be presented at the General Council Meeting next week on 9-10 May.

Bilateral meetings and small group meetings are expected in the coming days and weeks. "Members will finally begin text-based negotiations," diplomatic sources said. WTO members have not engaged in text-based negotiations on the original proposal from India and South Africa. In the past, a lack of consensus was cited as a reason, to prevent text-based negotiations among all the 164 members of WTO.

In addition, WTO members continue to discuss WTO's response to the pandemic that will also have an element on intellectual property. This process steered by Ambassador Dacio Castillo (Honduras) in his capacity as the General Council Chair's Facilitator. These discussions will address issues such as export restrictions, transparency, trade facilitation, transfer of technology among other issues. It also seeks to find a way on how WTO could work with other international organizations and how countries can preserve policy space during health emergencies.

Given the delay in the decision on the waiver, developing country diplomats also hope that they might be able to push for language that could be applicable for circumstances beyond the current pandemic. "We cannot be unprepared for the next emergency, there has to be an agreed understanding on WTO's response during health emergencies," a trade official said.

Undoubtedly, these are complex times. The DG has acknowledged that the ministerial in June 2022, is taking place against the backdrop of the COVID-19 pandemic, rising food and energy prices, debt distress, and war.

"This is not an ordinary Ministerial Conference," she said. The difficult context made reaching agreements both harder and more urgently necessary, she noted.

In the best of times, intellectual property issues at WTO have been thorny. With an estimated 15 million excess deaths associated with COVID-19, these are extraordinary circumstances that need innovative solutions. Will the WTO membership stand up?

41.

CHINA'S SPOKES WTO QUAD WAIVER TEXT, OFFERS TO SIDESTEP IF CONDITIONS MET (MAY 13, 2022)

China, one of the biggest exporters of COVID-19 vaccines, told WTO members this week that it has concerns on an exports-based eligibility criterion that seeks to exclude developing countries that export more than 10% of the world's vaccines – a condition that has been proposed as a part of the "Quad waiver text", now being negotiated at the WTO. China said that "using the criterion of export share to define eligible members will send a wrong signal to the outside world and also have systemic implications to the future negotiations".

China also offered that if its concerns on such criteria are addressed, it will not avail the flexibility in a potential waiver proposal. This was reportedly welcomed by the DG Ngozi Okonjo-Iweala and some members.

These discussions were a part of the General Council (GC) meeting earlier this week where the TRIPS Waiver was on the agenda among other matters. The Quad text is based on the discussions brokered by the DG, between 4 keys members – the US, the EU, India and South Africa.

HOW A FOOTNOTE CAME TO THE FORE
According to the Quad text (IP/C/W/688), presented by the DG to WTO members, a footnote specifies eligibility criteria for a potential waiver proposal. It says:

"Footnote 1: [For the purpose of this Decision, all developing country Members are eligible Members. Developing country Members with capacity to export vaccines are encouraged to opt out of this Decision.] [For the purpose of this Decision, developing country Members who exported more than 10 percent of world exports of COVID-19 vaccine doses in 2021 are not eligible Members.]"

China has expressed serious concern on this second square bracket in the above footnote.

After all, China has sent more than 2.2 billion doses of vaccines to over 120 countries and international organizations, a recent statement said.

In a statement made at the WTO TRIPS Council a week ago (May 6), China said:

"...For China, we can't accept the second brackets of footnote 1 which uses the criterion export share to define eligible members. Such an unreasonable and arbitrary criterion will send a wrong signal to the outside and also have systemic implication to the future negotiations. On one hand, this implies punishment to those who supplied a large number of vaccines to others even when they themselves were suffering from shortages. On the other hand, this constitutes a tolerance or even an incentive for members to adopt inward-looking policies and apply export restrictions in difficult times when we should resist such temptations. So, my question to everyone in this room is: is it a right signal that the WTO, a long-time advocate of free trade and multilateral cooperation, should be sending to the world? Should the contributions made by members during the pandemic be encouraged or discarded?

Compared with this second brackets language, the first brackets adopt a more positive approach, i.e. to encourage developing members who have capability to opt out from this decision. This is the right direction we should work to. However, as to what I just said on export criterion, we believe a more general language to encourage developing members who are in the position to opt out can be a solution."

At the GC meeting this week, China offered to not avail flexibilities as described in the Quad waiver text if its concerns on the export criterion is addressed.

China said:

"To further demonstrate our pragmatism and constructiveness and to better facilitate the negotiation (on the draft document circulated by the DG), China hereby announces that if our concern on the footnote is properly addressed, we will not seek to use the flexibility provided for by this decision."

The country was joined by other members in rejecting the proposed restriction on waiver eligibility to those developing countries that exported more than 10 per cent of the world's vaccine doses in 2021.

Here is why.

According to a policy brief by South Centre that has systematically analysed the proposal by the DG, such a criterion could set a precedent for other COVID-19 medical products. "This restriction creates a precedent of particular concern if the same criteria were to be applied to diagnostics and therapeutics in the future (in accordance with para. 8 of the draft) since developing country members with large potential to supply the world demand for those products would become automatically excluded as well," authors Carlos Correa and Nirmalya Syam argue.

But the fight to keep therapeutics and diagnostics out of the scope of the waiver is expected to be intense. Recall that it was the US that has been keen on limiting any waiver only to vaccines. It remains to be seen whether the EU and other WTO members will be amenable for such an inclusion to expand the application of any waiver to therapeutics and diagnostics. After all, the EU was reportedly open to considering a wider product scope in a potential waiver proposal.

This week, WHO DG Tedros Adhanom Ghebreyesus, asked Pfizer to improve access to its antiviral drug for COVID-19. He suggested that Pfizer must increase the geographical scope on the licensing it has signed with Medicines Patent Pool, keep drug prices affordable and transparent, have no additional contractual requirements that hamper or delay access, and support generic manufacturing for increased supply.

(See our exclusives: *Efforts to limit the implementation of the TRIPS Waiver, proposals to exclude India & China. Also, Pfizer Allegedly Pressured UNICEF to Keep Secret, Pricing for Anti-Viral Treatment Paxlovid. UNICEF Yielded.*)

THE GENERAL COUNCIL MEETING: 9-10 MAY 2022

In a statement on the General Council meeting this week, WTO noted, "....WTO members agreed that the outcome document emerging from the informal process conducted with the Quad (European Union, India, South Africa and the United States) opens the prospect for text-based negotiations on an intellectual property response to COVID-19." (See Members welcome Quad document as basis for text-based negotiations on pandemic IP response.)

Giving an update on the waiver discussions at the TRIPS Council, Chair Ambassador Lansana Gberie (Sierra Leone), reportedly said that it is not very helpful to speculate about the ownership of this document. He said the focus should be on the substance. He urged members to focus on this document because it is the only product, and the only game in town, given that the WTO ministerial conference is only a month away, WTO officials said at a press briefing this week.

"I think we should look at the document on its merits and see whether this is something that we can take forward to the stage of negotiation," he said. "I think it is important that we reflect on this because it is, frankly, the only product we have, the only game in town. We don't have a lot of time," Ambassador Gberie is learned to have said.

However, the ownership of the Quad text continues to raise questions among members. As we reported last week, there has been confusion on whether the Quad members have agreed on the text. Many media outlets have reported about the discussions as a compromise or an agreement, when in fact it is not. Apart from the EU, none of other members of the Quad group have supported it pending conclusive internal consultations.

This is important because at this critical stage of the negotiations, perceptions and numbers matter. WTO decision-making is ruled by consensus. So, although 64 members of the WTO have co-sponsored the original waiver proposal, it will remain to be seen if and how the quad text will unite or splinter this group of co-sponsors.

It is also learned that one of the existing co-sponsors could take a lead role in strengthening the quad text in the coming weeks, Geneva-based sources indicated.

Hectic negotiations will resume in Geneva with a small group of countries reportedly meeting today, May 13, to kickstart discussions on the quad text. We unable to get more details by the time this story was published.

In a blogpost this week, Deputy Director General Anabel Gonzales described the Quad text as follows:

At its core, the outcome document would confirm the right of developing country governments to issue executive decrees, emergency orders and other legal instruments, in addition to conventional compulsory licenses, to authorize a company to use the patents underlying the COVID-19 vaccines without the consent of the patent right holder, subject to a delicate balance of flexibilities and clarifications crafted within the general equitable principles set out in the framework of the WTO Agreement on Trade-Related Aspects of Intellectual Property Rights (TRIPS). Vaccines produced under these conditions may be exported, not only used to service domestic markets, and adequate remuneration to the patent right holder may take into consideration the humanitarian and not-for-profit purposes of these programs to support manufacturers to produce and supply vaccines at affordable prices. WHO guidelines also provide a helpful reference, given the lack of domestic experience in many countries. In addition, protection of clinical trial data would not prevent a government from effectively implementing these flexibilities. These provisions are to be applied for a period to be determined of between 3 to 5 years, and any measure taken in conformity with them would not be subject to the WTO's dispute settlement mechanism. Six months from now, WTO members would decide whether to extend this treatment to COVID-19-related therapeutics and diagnostics..

PART VII:

THE FINAL LAP AND THE RESIGNATION TO A LIMITED WAIVER (JUNE 2022)

....

As the ministerial conference drew closer, it became increasingly clear that many countries had little latitude to shape these discussions. The clock was ticking and there was not enough time to fight for everything that was once on the table with the original TRIPS waiver proposal. The approach then became to save the text from having "harmful" provisions that could impede public health goals. It is still debatable today, whether countries managed to prevent this.

While the ministerial bolstered the image of the WTO as being still relevant for its members, for the public health community, it was a moment of defeat, after a long, hard battle.

42.

TOUGH NEGOTIATIONS ON THE WTO'S IP RESPONSE TO THE PANDEMIC (MAY 20, 2022)

WTO members finally got their hands dirty with text-based negotiations on WTO's intellectual property response to the pandemic. Members met all week, at informal meetings of the TRIPS Council, and in smaller groups to consult and negotiate on the Director-General's TRIPS COVID-19 text. This text follows the discussions of the quad group that includes the US, the EU, India and South Africa.

Even before the negotiations began, the US fired its first shot, that some say, effectively drew the battlelines on these discussions.

At the General Council Meeting last week, China had offered to not avail flexibilities in a potential solution as being currently proposed, but rejected the restriction on the eligibility provision that seeks to exclude those countries that exported 10% of the total COVID-19 vaccine doses in 2021.

Soon after DG Ngozi Okonjo-Iweala was enthused about the constructive move by China.

However, on May 16, US effectively rebuffed the Chinese manoeuvre. Deputy US Trade Representative Maria Pagan told Bloomberg in an interview, "The second-largest economy in the world, which has Covid vaccines and mRNA technology, doesn't need the waiver... What we want is clarity."

Sources familiar with the discussions told us that China was clearly not happy with any provision that seemingly excludes it. China's offer to not use the flexibility in any decision at the WTO, did not cut it with the US. The repercussions of such positions are being felt and will undoubtedly have implications for any outcome on the WTO IP response to the pandemic.

The US position, many believe, reduces and characterises these negotiations to a geopolitical rivalry that threatens to bulldoze highly nuanced and complex positions on the debate of temporarily waiving IP protections to meet the demands of the pandemic.

One Geneva-based observer said, "The US is trying to make China "The Fall Guy", in the highly likely event that no deal is made". To be sure, the text as it stands now has not got endorsement from the US, India or South Africa.

China has highlighted the systemic implications for being excluded out of an agreement. This could also have an overall impact on developing countries at the WTO, in general, experts say.

Developed countries are keen on having language to address export restrictions during health emergencies in the wider WTO response to the pandemic. But by seeking to exclude China, one of the biggest exporters of vaccines, in any potential solution on a so-called waiver seems ironical.

THE TEXT: HEAVILY BRACKETED

The TRIPS Council chair, Sierra Leone's Ambassador Lansana Gberie reported that negotiations were held with a group of 30 delegations and group coordinators this week. The deliberations addressed questions on eligibility of members, the use of a single authorization and patent listing, on duration, review and possible extension of the instrument, and on the scope of the decision with respect to therapeutics and diagnostics.

Sources said that although developing countries favor the inclusion of therapeutics and diagnostics, there is pressure from developed countries to stick to the current articulation in the text. According to the current proposal, the expansion of the decision to include these medical products must be taken within six months from the date of the decision.

Increasingly, the text under consideration is being seen as a set of clarifications for the use of compulsory licensing to produce vaccines. Some delegates told us that "nothing is being waived. It is no longer a waiver", suggesting the distance of the current text from the original TRIPS Waiver proposal submitted by India and South Africa in October 2020.

In discussions this week, members also wanted to know more on the legal nature of the text, and whether it would be called a decision or a waiver. They also sought clarification on the WTO law it would be based upon. The TRIPS Council chair is understood to have said that content of the decision would determine the legal form and title of the document.

This week, members wrestled on questions of eligibility. Some members suggested deletions in the language on the "supply" of vaccines, on "distribution" in the existing text, which, if approved could substantially weaken the text, developing country sources said. There are also suggestions to delete a paragraph on patents listing that is being seen as onerous, that could make it more difficult for members to make use of existing provisions in the TRIPS Agreement.

THE PROCESS

Developing country delegates told Geneva Health Files this week, that members have been divided into small groups that have made these negotiations difficult. "Not all countries are invited to these discussions. Delegations have also been split. There is no clarity on who is agreeing to what, and this is being held against us", one diplomat said.

(See: *Green room politics and the WTO's crisis of representation:* Progress in Development Studies.)

According to sources closely tracking these negotiations, EU diplomats declared during this week, that they would not be open for new suggestions from outside the existing text. However, both the opponents to the TRIPS Waiver such as the UK, Switzerland, and co-sponsors of the original proposal are keen on bringing their suggestions to the text.

To be sure, TRIPS Council Chair Ambassador Lansana Gberie asked delegations to provide in writing any textual proposals for language in other parts of the text – that does not cover the bracketed text. He said that this can be done through the Secretariat, or through regional group coordinator to allow for structuring of the negotiations.

At the meetings this week, Switzerland is understood to have said that it cannot accept an outcome on IP and TRIPS only because also a meaningful outcome on trade and health is needed.

The UK noted that the timeline proposed to advance negotiations is ambitious and sought flexibility on the deadline. The UK is understood to have said that time pressures must not be used as justification for rushing given the need for substantial discussion of the text.

Tanzania, on behalf of the African Group, stressed its right to contribute to the discussion as any other member and reiterated that whatever outcome is achieved it should be sufficient in duration (a minimum of 5 years) without prejudice of prior manufacturing capacity in Africa. An outcome should result in the diversified production not only of COVID-19 vaccines but also of therapeutics and diagnostics, which should constitute a critical element of the final consensus, Tanzania said in its statement.

Geneva-based observers familiar with the proceedings are also questioning the lack of adequate coordination and engagement between co-sponsors to strategize on these negotiations.

THE WTO UNDER PRESSURE

Statements made by DG Okonjo-Iweala around these discussions suggest that the WTO is under tremendous pressure to deliver on an outcome on these discussions.

"We do not have the luxury of not getting an answer for MC12, it just does not exist, she said. We have ample time really to do it if we work on weekends, so please get your backpacks or your whatever you need to eat, we will be here all weekend," she told delegates. She is understood to have said this week during the TRIPS Council proceedings.

Some seasoned experts are already ruling out a deal on this text. "One just does not see the kind of momentum which is palpable when an agreement is nearing," an expert familiar with arduous trade negotiations told us in a late evening call this week.

There will be numerous late evenings and potentially all-nighters for Geneva delegates as the DG ups the ante on delivering a result to save the institution mired in an unlikely set of unfortunate circumstances of a war coinciding with a pandemic.

WTO's 12th ministerial conference is scheduled for June 12-15th. Negotiators are working round the clock in small group meetings. An informal meeting of the TRIPS council in scheduled for May 24. Small group meetings have resumed at WTO.

A block down the road, not far from the WTO, countries also gather for the World Health Assembly next week.

43.

IS THE DELAY THE DEFEAT OF THE TRIPS WAIVER DISCUSSIONS AT THE WTO? (JUNE 2, 2022)

With barely 10 days left for the WTO ministerial conference, countries are increasingly under pressure to arrive at a consensus on the text proposed by DG Ngozi Okonjo-Iweala.

Members have met in small group discussions over the last few weeks, that have included participation of up to 30 members. Countries with smaller delegations have been spread thin across multiple, parallel negotiations at the WTO in the run up to the ministerial conference (12-15 June 2022) including for disciplines such as agriculture, fisheries among others.

This analysis is based on the negotiations the version of the text dated May 30, seen by Geneva Health Files. We are unable to share the text. (But see a version of the text [May 25] published by Bilaterals.org.)

Supporters of the original TRIPS Waiver proposal say that current negotiations are mostly limited to vaccines, at a time when there is a surplus of vaccines production. And the text continues to have TRIPS-plus provisions, seeking stronger obligations than is currently mandated by the WTO TRIPS Agreement, some of which have been suggested by the UK and Switzerland, according to sources familiar with the discussions.

It is understood that the current text has a set of clarifications and a waiver of a single provision of the TRIPS Agreement.

THE POSITIONS AND THE POLITICS

Experts point out that the current text has several provisions that are being read as TRIPS-plus commitments including "necessity tests", anti-diversion measures and notification requirements. We look at some of the provisions in the current text.

ON ELIGIBILITY

The US-China dynamic on the criterion for eligibility to use any potential waiver could be the linchpin of these discussions, observers say. (See our earlier story on the eligibility question: *China's Spokes WTO Quad Waiver Text, Offers to Sidestep if Conditions Met*)

It is understood that the question on eligibility, specifically whether China will be eligible to use any potential waiver is expected to be addressed bilaterally between China and the U.S. The Chair of the TRIPS Council, Ambassador Lansana Gberie, has suggested this approach, while the membership continues to negotiate other elements of the current proposal.

Foot notes in the current text specify limits on eligibility requirements suggesting that developing country members "with capacity to export vaccines are encouraged to opt out", and further, that countries who exported more than 10 percent of world exports of COVID-19 vaccine doses in 2021 are not eligible Members. China has contested this latter formulation, alerting to implications for other discussions at the WTO and the potential for developing countries on benefiting from special and differential treatment in international trade rules.

Civil society organizations fear that if countries with production and export capacity are encouraged to opt-out, it could affect supply. In addition, such a decision could also translate into pressure on developing countries with capacity to export to stop using compulsory licenses – the exact intended effect of any waiver, particularly one that ostensibly seeks to make use of flexibilities easier. In addition, such a foot note could also affect future supply and production of therapeutics, experts fear.

Some believe that if both the US and China continue to stick to their stated positions on the eligibility footnote in the existing text, it may sink any outcome on these discussions. Observers say that these trade tensions are not limited to these negotiations. This is a consequence of a long history of mistrust between both parties, particularly at the WTO, Geneva-based trade sources said. *(See our earlier update: Tough negotiations on the WTO›s IP response to the pandemic)*

SOME KEY ELEMENTS OF THE TEXT

Sources point to the introduction of words such as "necessary", "essential", "required", into the current text, allegedly by developed countries. Legal experts say that this makes it difficult to use flexibilities. It is understood that developing countries are trying to fight such qualifications.

The first paragraph of the text [May 30th version] says:

[Notwithstanding the provision of patent rights under its domestic legislation,] [A][a]n [eligible] Member[1] may [limit the rights provided for under Article 28.1 of the TRIPS Agreement (hereinafter "the Agreement") by authorizing][authorize] the use of the subject matter of a patent[2] whenever necessary] [required for][for the purpose of] the production ~~and supply~~ of COVID-19 vaccines without the consent of the right holder ~~to the extent necessary~~ to address the COVID-19 ~~pandemic~~, in accordance with the provisions of Article 31 of the Agreement, as clarified and waived in paragraphs 2 to 6 below.

It is understood that Switzerland, for example, is not happy about text that says, "limit the rights provided under Article 28.1 If the TRIPS Agreement". This text is now in brackets. (Article 28.1 of the TRIPS Agreement governs the exclusive rights enjoyed by the patent holder)

As we reported earlier, some developed countries have suggested the deletion of the word "supply" in the current text, that purports to improve access to vaccines.

Concerns have also been raised on seeking to define "subject matter of a patent" in footnote 2 in the current text. Experts say that under Article 31 of the TRIPS Agreement compulsory licenses can be issued for any subject-matter. So, this footnote creates additional conditions that limits the use of compulsory license only for patented vaccines, ingredients and processes. In addition, it is often not easy to understand the patent landscape including for pending patent applications they say.

THE ONLY WAIVER IN THE DECISION
Members have reportedly spent a substantial amount of time discussing Para 3.c. of the current text, which is the only "waiver" in the decision.

a.   *"An eligible Member may waive the requirement of Article 31(f) that authorized use under Article 31 be predominantly to supply its domestic market and may allow any proportion of the [authorized use] [COVID-19 vaccine produced under the authorization in accordance with this Decision] to be exported to eligible Members and to supply international or regional joint initiatives that aim to ensure the equitable access of eligible Members to the COVID-19 vaccine covered by the authorization.*

(In the latest version of the text, there are other suggested footnotes clarifying that Article 31*bis* and the Annex will not be applicable, and that exportation is intended to supply only eligible members)

Experts say the waiver of this provision will only be applicable when a Compulsory License is issued to export much of the production under such a license. In addition, this waiver as currently articulated is applicable only for COVID-19 vaccines but not for exporting ingredients that may go into the production of such vaccines.

So, is such a provision of any use at all? Some believe that it might be useful to produce and export vaccines under limited conditions.

Recall that Article 31*bis* is an **amendment,** based on a waiver in 2003, that was supposed to have enabled a country to export medicines manufactured under a compulsory license to another importing country. Given additional procedures and notifications, the use of this mechanism has been cumbersome, it is widely acknowledged. *[See below our explanation[3] on this.]*

What the current suggested waiver intends to do is to do away with most procedures of Article 31*bis*.

"Article 31*bis,* as we have seen, is unusable. If indeed the TRIPS-plus provisions are removed from the existing text, this proposal may be useful for countries producing and exporting Covid vaccines under a compulsory license since it contains a waiver of Article 31(f) of TRIPS, the condition that compulsory license should predominantly be for the supply of the domestic market. Although, immediately extending the decision to therapeutics and diagnostics would make it more valuable given their importance in containing COVID-19." Sangeeta Shashikant, a legal advisor at Third World Network, explained to us.

INCONSISTENCY IN DECISION TEXT

The current text continues to have other problematic language (Para 3.d.) on re-exportation that could affect vaccine donations for example. *(See our earlier story: The Compromise Text on the TRIPS Waiver Will Undermine Vaccine Donations).* Experts point out the inherent inconsistency in the text between Para 3 c and 3 d - while the former makes provision for supply to international and regional initiatives such as The

COVAX Facility, built around pooled procurement mechanisms and dose donations, the latter lays down language on preventing re-exportation.

Para 3 d reads thus:

"Eligible Members shall undertake all reasonable efforts to prevent the reexportation of the COVID-19 vaccine that has been imported into their territories under this Decision. Members shall ensure the availability of effective legal means to prevent the importation into, and sale in, their territories of COVID-19 vaccines produced under this Decision, and diverted to their markets inconsistently with its provisions, using the means already required to be available under the TRIPS Agreement)"

ON TRADE SECRETS

Developing countries hope that they will be able to expand the scope in the current text on accessing undisclosed information, such as regulatory data, as governed under Article 39 of the TRIPS Agreement. The current text under negotiation however only refers to 39.3.

This provision (39.3) governs undisclosed test data or other data submitted by the originator company for purposes of approving the marketing of the pharmaceutical product against "unfair commercial use", "except where necessary to protect the public" or "unless steps are taken to protect the data against unfair commercial use".

The text currently under negotiation reads thus:

4. Nothing in Article [39] [39.3] of the Agreement shall prevent an [eligible] Member from taking measures [essential] [necessary] [to] [that would] enable the effectiveness of any authorization issued as per this Decision [without prejudice to the provisions of undisclosed information under Members' domestic legislation]. [Except as otherwise provided for in Article 39.3] [Nothing in this paragraph shall be interpreted as allowing the disclosure of undisclosed information submitted by the originator to the respective authorities of an eligible Member in a marketing approval procedure.]

Sources say that clarifications allegedly suggested by a developed country undermines the existing flexibility as articulated in the TRIPS agreement.

While the TRIPS agreement does not explicitly prohibit the issuance of compulsory licenses for trade secrets, there is no mechanism that governs this, we had reported earlier. Supporters of the waiver proposal, view undisclosed information as key to enabling access to information that could speed up the production of medical products including vaccines.

Prevailing laws that protect trade secrets, seek to discourage "unfair competition". However, amid a pandemic, public non-commercial use trumps these concerns, supporters of the waiver say.

A REFERENCE TO THE DOHA DECLARATION

The current text now also refers to the Doha Declaration on the TRIPS agreement and public health

"9. This Decision is without prejudice to the flexibilities that Members have under the TRIPS Agreement, including the Doha Declaration on the TRIPS Agreement and Public Health [and without prejudice to their rights and obligations under the TRIPS Agreement, except as otherwise provided for in paragraph 3(c)]"

But activists note that the limitations on eligibility as articulated in the footnotes in the current text, are a significant departure from the Doha Declaration on TRIPS and Public Health adopted at the height of the HIV/AIDS crisis that is applicable to all WTO Members.

THE OPPONENTS TO THE CURRENT TEXT

The UK and Switzerland continue to oppose key elements in the text, while bringing in tougher obligations, sources said.

"There is no logic in some of the demands made by the UK such as on the transparency requirement. They want a notification before a shipment takes place", a source said. Some suggest that the UK is only posturing and that it may finally yield to what the US and the EU decide. (It is understood that notification obligations regarding the use of the waiver were intended to be *post facto*.)

This week, civil society groups in the UK sent a letter to Anne Marie Trevelyan, UK Secretary of State for International Trade. It said:

"Since October 2020, we have strived to engage fully with the UK Government on this issue. We have met with the relevant UK Departments, namely the Intellectual Property Office (IPO) Department of International Trade (DIT) and the Foreign, Commonwealth and Development Office (FCDO) on several occasions, each time at our request. We expressed our views on the original TRIPS waiver proposal, as well as the new proposal currently being negotiated. We have consistently provided clear evidence for our positions, including the detrimental role IP has played in restricting supply and affordable access to COVID-19 health technologies, and the role the original TRIPS waiver proposal would play in overcoming this.

Despite this, engaging in a meaningful manner in these discussions with the UK Government has not been possible due to the way these meetings were conducted. For example, we have never been provided any clarity on the UK Government's position on the TRIPS waiver beyond the repeated assertion that IP rules were responsible for the rapid development of COVID-19 medical tools and do not present a barrier to access.

No evidence has been provided to support this claim, despite multiple requests."

Geneva-based trade sources say that an agreement is likely if the UK backs off. One delegate from an African country indicated that it is likely developed countries were working towards common positions in these discussions.

"Once the US makes up its mind on the decision, opposition from the UK will disappear," a developing country trade diplomat told us in a late evening call this week.

For members such as the EU, an outcome on the waiver will be used as a quid pro quo on other deliverables at the ministerial, a source familiar with other negotiations at the WTO said.

On Switzerland's position, some believe that ultimately the country would align with the EU.

TRIPS COUNCIL INFORMAL MEETING

At the TRIPS council informal meeting this week on June 1, the Chair, Ambassador Lansana Gberie is reported to have alerted the membership on the persisting differences during these negotiations.

The chair discussed points of convergence and disagreements between members. Countries have reportedly accepted text clarifying that exports to joint initiatives such as COVAX are intended to benefit eligible members only.

There are also efforts to make measures taken in accordance with the waiver decision to be applicable under rules of "non-violation" complaints (NVCs). (At stake will be whether countries will be allowed to bring NVCs because of measures taken under a waiver decision. NVCs enable countries to bring complaints against other countries even though there has been no violation of a WTO agreement.)

The Chair reportedly acknowledged the "gloomy" nature of the update but said that it reflected "the reality of the negotiations". He asked members to "exercise restraint, to be pragmatic, and to focus on those elements of the outcome text that would be absolutely essential or required to secure their delegation's approval," according to Geneva-based trade officials.

This week Third World Network also reported on the existence of a restricted TRIPS Council document (JOB/IP/58) called «Outcome Text - Revision» dated 23 May. Observers that it is unusual for two different documents on the same matter – a working document which includes all textual suggestions, and the other by the Chair.

OUTCOME OR NO OUTCOME?
Undoubtedly there is "waiver-fatigue" as the ministerial-fever reaches a high. While some are not optimistic about any outcome from these discussions, others believe that there are still chances for pulling through an agreement.

Apart from the US determining which way these negotiations could go – such as on the eligibility question – much depends on the importance of the TRIPS waiver relative to other deliverables for the ministerial conference.

"None of the other discussions at the WTO are closer to an agreement as these discussions on the waiver. There is an explicit pressure on the developing countries to compromise" a trade diplomat said.

Some have described the specter facing the WTO: being reduced to a playground for the two big multilateral trading powers, the US and China. While the US seems to have lost interest in the institution, China is keen on making WTO work, the Geneva-based diplomat added.

But it is unclear whether China will compromise on these waiver discussions to ensure an outcome for the ministerial.

Irrespective of the outcome, time has been lost, and consequently, lives.

"The delay is the defeat of the TRIPS Waiver," one global health law expert said. The time and the opportunity to act on the original waiver proposal, brought to the WTO 18 months ago, may have been squandered, and this has had irrevocable consequences.

This delay could also cost the WTO dearly.

44.

SO CLOSE, YET SO FAR: TRIPS WAIVER AT THE WTO (JUNE 11, 2022)

Proposed Waiver Text in Ministers' Hand, Key Differences Remain

Less than 24 hours before the 12th Ministerial Conference gets underway in Geneva – the capital of global health, and the seat of pandemic policy-making - WTO members continue to disagree on key aspects of the organization's response to the pandemic, including an agreement on a potential waiver of a provision of the TRIPS Agreement.

The discussions on the TRIPS Waiver remain on tenterhooks, as ministers will now consider a bracketed text, the WTO reported last night. Key differences remain on how to adapt international trade rules meant to protect intellectual property rights in response to the on-going pandemic. *(See more details below)*

The world's gaze turns to Geneva this week, as trade ministers gather after nearly five years for a ministerial conference of the WTO, its highest decision-making body. The conference will take place in the backdrop of a shift in geopolitics, war and health emergencies. It is being seen as one of the most significant events for the WTO, not only because the organization's legacy is at stake, but also as a barometer for international cooperation at a time when 15 million people globally are estimated to have died in the on-going pandemic.

And yet, 20 months on, from the date when India and South Africa, first brought a proposal to temporarily suspend IP protections to ostensibly, decisively, respond to the pandemic, members have not been able to reach agreement on the process to do so.

For an organization that runs on consensus, compromise is key. But activists have warned that compromising on a much watered-down TRIPS Waiver proposal would be detrimental and could even set bad precedent in terms of addressing countries' access to medical products.

While some countries remain boxed in their positions, activists continue to push governments to not only abandon their support to the current version of the text but are also pushing them to adopt a "full" TRIPS Waiver.

Even as pressure grows on countries to conclude an agreement, barricades had risen, earlier in the week, on the road approaching the WTO – the site of ministerial conference. Civil society organizations have now been barred entry on the first of the conference. "Please be informed that for unexpected security-related reasons, we are unfortunately unable to grant access to the WTO premises on Sunday 12 June", said a communication from the WTO to CSOs, earlier this week. Protests from Civil Society Organizations are no stranger to WTO ministerial. It is likely that this event will witness protests especially against the weak text on the TRIPS waiver, among other issues.

NEGOTIATIONS AT THE WTO: SOME "KEPT OUT", OTHERS "WALK OUT"

The weeks leading up to the ministerial generated much consternation as many developing country members continued to be excluded from smaller negotiating groups, called as "green room" meetings. While CSOs have cried foul on process, seasoned observers maintain that this is an effective strategy in forging solutions in smaller groups before taking it to the wider membership.

To be sure, process dictates outcomes. Take this: members such as Indonesia, reportedly keen on making textual proposals to the TRIPS Waiver negotiations were kept out of the green room processes. (On some occasions only Cameroon, Egypt, India, Nigeria and South Africa, were reported to be a part of these discussions.)

Geneva-based trade sources indicated that the "green room tactics" were allegedly used as forums to put pressure on developing countries including by DG Okonjo-Iweala. This has resulted in a chilling effect on the African Group, some have suggested.

An anonymous, but credible, twitter handle called "@ SouthEmpowering" has been sharing snippets of these negotiations at the WTO. The handle describes itself as a "Collective of individuals willing to work for Global South in International Relations".

In one of the tweets, @SouthEmpowering said: *"To propose textual amendments and negotiated is a Sovereign Prerogative. Attempts to silence developing countries in #TRIPSwaiver negotiations diminish @wto's legitimacy. #DG shud [sic] act without bias. #StopClusterNegotiations on #TRIPSwaiver. It is a classic "Divide and Rule" trick to isolate the developing country diplomats..."*

Even as mostly developing countries were kept out of deliberations, some developed countries including the EU, the UK and the US, have variously walked out of discussions, as a tactic to get countries to reach an agreement, Geneva-based sources said. (See more on this in the coverage by Third Network Network]

WHAT THE MINISTERS WILL NEGOTIATE: THE DECISION TEXT

The latest update from the WTO suggested, that negotiations at the technical level have now concluded and the decision text will now be considered at the ministerial level.

"What you have before you now is a text that will be submitted to ministers," TRIPS Council chair Ambassador Lansana Gberie of Sierra Leone told members. "We have come to the brink of our endurance, intelligence and creativity and we will give our ministers a chance to also take a shot, the final shot," according to the update from the WTO secretariat.

Ministers will also consider the draft text on the WTO response to the pandemic. This "sets out a series of trade-related pledges and objectives to support increased resilience to COVID-19 and future pandemics. These include general as well as specific provisions relating to trade facilitation, regulatory cooperation, intellectual property, services, food security and aspects of future work," the statement from the WTO said.

In his capacity as the facilitator on the WTO's response to the pandemic, Ambassador Dacio Castillo of Honduras is reported as saying, "Through the hard work and substantive contributions of delegations, in just a matter of three weeks, we have transformed the merged text of various proposals to a fully formed document for ministerial consideration at MC12."

Some of the documents related to the ministerial are now online.

THE WAIVER TEXT: JUNE 10 VERSION

Some of the bracketed text is discussed here:

According to the version on June 10 that was sent to ministers (seen by Geneva Health Files), the prickly footnotes qualifying eligibility requirements, remain in brackets. This might indicate that the bilateral negotiation between China and the U.S. on this question is yet to be resolved.

The necessity test in para 1 also continues to be reflected in the current text. *(... "an eligible Member may limit the rights provided for under Article 28.1 of the TRIPS Agreement (hereinafter "the Agreement") by authorizing the use of the subject matter of a patent required for the production and supply of COVID-19 vaccines without the consent of the right holder to the extent necessary to address the COVID-19 pandemic...")*

Para 3 c of the text is the only waiver in the text. *"An eligible Member may waive the requirement of Article 31(f) that authorized use under Article 31 be predominantly to supply its domestic market and may allow any proportion of the products manufactured under the authorization in accordance with this Decision to be exported to eligible Members, including through international or regional joint initiatives that aim to ensure the equitable access of eligible Members to the COVID-19 vaccine covered by the authorization."*

But experts wonder if the text is a backdoor method to bring back Article 31bis. (Article 31bis is an amendment, based on a waiver in 2003, that was supposed to have enabled a country to export medicines manufactured under a compulsory license to another importing country. Given additional procedures and notifications, the use of this mechanism has been cumbersome, it is widely acknowledged.)

The text continues to have language to protect anti-diversionary measures, that some say will cramp incentives for local production, and affect vaccine donations. (See *The Compromise Text on the TRIPS Waiver Will Undermine Vaccine Donations)*

Sources suggested that similar to the demand from the UK, Deputy Director-General, Anabel González, said offered an interpretation that said once the waiver period expired vaccine stock produced under the decision cannot be exported.

Countries can use it domestically or destroy them, she is understood to have said.

The rationale for such a measure is difficult to understand given the signs and learnings from the current pandemic. Experts believe that anti-diversionary clauses should be removed to enable importing countries to export what they do not need or use to other countries. This will help dose-sharing, regional procurement, and prevent dose wastage. Millions of doses of vaccines have been wasted globally - a hallmark of poor planning and a consequence of hoarding of vaccines during this pandemic.

(See Reuters: South Africa's Aspen COVID-19 vaccine plant risks closure after no orders, executive says, and The BMJ *Covid-19—How Europe's vaccine donations went tragically wrong)*

The language on re-exportation continued to be negotiated this week. This now has a new foot note.

"(d) Eligible Members shall undertake all reasonable efforts to prevent the re-exportation of the products manufactured under the authorization in accordance with this Decision that have been imported into their territories under this Decision.3 Members shall ensure the availability of effective legal means to prevent the importation into, and sale in, their territories of products manufactured under the authorization in accordance with this Decision, and diverted to their markets inconsistently with its provisions, using the means already required to be available under the TRIPS Agreement."

*Footnote 3: In exceptional circumstances, an eligible Member may re-export COVID-19 vaccines to another eligible Member for humanitarian and not-for-profit purposes, as long as the eligible Member communicates in accordance with paragraph 5.

(Para 5 in the text is on transparency requirements)

On duration the text reads:

An eligible Member may apply the provisions of this Decision [so that authorized uses continue no later than] [until] [3][5] [10] years from the date of this Decision. The General Council may extend such a period taking into consideration the exceptional circumstances of the COVID-19 pandemic. The General Council will review annually the operation of this Decision

Most problematic of all, perhaps is the fact that members have not reached a consensus on whether any potential solution will be applicable to therapeutics and diagnostics. "8. [No later than six months from the date of this Decision, Members [will][shall] decide [whether to extend this decision] [on its extension] to cover the production and supply of COVID-19 diagnostics and therapeutics.]" (Emphasis ours)

In addition, language on notification requirements also continue to exist in the text. Experts fear that this could result in potential injunctions, trade retaliation, political and commercial pressure on governments and local manufacturers that has often been witnessed.

(Also see our story from last week based on the text of May 30, that discussed some of the provisions of the text: *Is the delay the defeat of the TRIPS Waiver discussions at the WTO)*

PRESSURE TO DUMP TEXT BUILDS ON EITHER SIDE

Curiously the pressure on members to walk away from the text is building on both sides. This will come to a head in the coming days.

"CURRENT TEXT A REVERSAL OF THE DOHA DECLARATION": FORMER PRESIDENT OF SWITZERLAND

Earlier in the week, in a letter to WTO delegates, Ruth Dreifuss, former President of the Swiss Confederation, Celso Amorim, former Minister of Defence and Foreign Affairs, Federative

Republic of Brazil, Jorge Bermudez, Senior Researcher at the National School of Public Health, Fiocruz, Brazil; Member of the WHO C-TAP Technical Advisory Group, asked delegates to face their collective responsibility of "removing all barriers to diversified production of vaccines, tests, and medicines in the global South to ensure access in L&MICs."

The letter said:

"During the height of the HIV crisis, WTO members responded with the Doha Declaration, which stated that "the TRIPS Agreement does not and should not prevent Members from taking measures to protect public health". Without amendments, the current text under negotiation at the WTO is a reversal of the Doha declaration. It undermines the flexibilities in the TRIPS agreement that were emphasized by the commitments made by WTO members in 2001. Moreover, any agreement that adds new barriers could set a dangerous precedent for future pandemics."

THE ROLE OF THE LEAD SPONSORS RAISES QUESTIONS

Perceptions are rife in Geneva that lead sponsors of the original TRIPS Waiver proposal, India and South Africa do not seem to be leading from the front. *(See Have India and South Africa, Lead Sponsors of the TRIPS Waiver Proposal, Reconciled to a Weak Text?)*

In a story for The Wire, this week, I reported:

"A number of observers are perplexed as to why the lead co-sponsors are not bringing in elements from their original proposal to bolster the text under negotiation.

Diplomatic sources tell us that these lead sponsors have not been backed sufficiently by other developing countries. "We have led the way for 18 months, and ultimately it has to be taken forward by others as well," one official told us.

But this has been disputed. Seasoned observers ask where the coordination and leadership is among developing countries to make sure that the text is strengthened. "They have had no clear strategy," a source who works with developing countries told us."

To be sure, this is not only about India or South Africa. A weak text on the TRIPS Waiver could imply that although 100 countries supported the proposal, their negotiating leverage was not effectively deployed. This could alter the way negotiations will occur not only at the WTO, but also at WHO, experts say.

WHAT TO EXPECT THIS WEEK

Now that trade ministers will negotiate on bracketed text, activists fear that those ministers who are not technocrats can easily be pressured to toe the line without fully understanding the implications of what they are endorsing. And indeed, this has happened in the past, sources say, pointing to the Quad process earlier in the year. (There is a perception that the rich, arduous technical work done earlier came undone by pushing up the decisions to the political level.)

"There are three potential outcomes: one, that is a compromise where the final decision text will be weaker than it is now; second, that developing countries walk away from the text; and third, there might be some value in the political significance of any decision in an otherwise unworkable solution that the current text is," a person closely tracking these negotiations in Geneva told us last night.

Irrespective of the outcome, many believe that this process has shown that there is nothing sacrosanct about the TRIPS Agreement.

Indefatigable access to medicines advocates believe "that the fight is still on".

But another activist said, "the pharma industry could have the last laugh on this given the state of the current text."

(Also see: recent comments from USTR: *'Confident that India will be engaging with intentionality at the WTO meet.)*

45.

HAVE INDIA AND SOUTH AFRICA, LEAD SPONSORS OF THE TRIPS WAIVER PROPOSAL, RECONCILED TO A WEAK TEXT? (JUNE 10, 2022)

After more than 18 months of bringing their bold proposal at the World Trade Organization (WTO) to temporarily suspend some intellectual property protections to decisively address COVID-19 to enable local manufacturing capacity, sponsors India and South Africa do not seem to be leading from the front, Geneva-based trade sources say.

To be sure, the fight to preserve the original proposal has traversed a tortuous, circuitous path over many months, replete with leaks and other machinations that some say are typical of the international trade policy world.

Now, at the eleventh hour, when these negotiations could be coming to a close, these lead co-sponsors appear to have been locked into positions they cannot seem to get out of, sources closely following these discussions say.

How we got here

Recall that the original TRIPS waiver was discussed, formally and informally, over many months at the TRIPS Council at the WTO, where mostly developed countries, such as the US, the UK, EU countries and Switzerland denied the role of intellectual property being a barrier in the access to medical products during the pandemic. The WTO membership has not engaged in text-based negotiations of the original proposal, submitted in October 2020.

In what then seemed as a watershed moment in May 2021, the US lent limited support to the proposal by agreeing to consider a limited waiver for vaccines. This changed the discussions decisively.

Subsequently, India and South Africa had multiple bilateral consultations on their proposal with smaller groups of members for most of 2021. Later, South Africa and the European Union had long bilateral consultations in the latter part of 2021. While it seemed, they were close to a deal back then, the Ministerial Conference scheduled in December 2021 was unexpectedly postponed when trade negotiators could not travel to Geneva on account of the emergence of the Omicron variant of SARS-CoV-2.

Soon after, WTO Director-General Ngozi Okonjo-Iweala took the matter into her own hands, given the stakes for the beleaguered organisation she heads. The WTO's inability to respond effectively to the pandemic and to wider challenges in international trade have brought into question its effectiveness as a multilateral institution.

She brokered talks between India, South Africa, the EU and the US, assisted by Deputy Director General Anabel González. While the talks went on during the early months of 2022, these four key members were unable to reach consensus. This is where the story gets tricky.

What happened next appears to be deliberately obfuscated. A text, ostensibly called the 'Quad text' was leaked in Brussels. The text was a shadow of the original TRIPS waiver proposal and was, in fact, closer to the EU's proposal on essentially streamlining the compulsory licensing system. Attempts were made to present this text as an agreement. Diplomatic sources say this caused confusion among other WTO members not party to these discussions.

Without the ownership of the text by the US, India and South Africa, (the EU supported the text), Okonio-Iwaela brought her version of the text to the wider membership. This version reflected elements of the leaked text.

Finally, in May 2022, when the Ministerial was barely weeks away, WTO members began text-based negotiations.

What is currently under negotiation?

Activists have decried the current text as one that could set bad precedents, and which may potentially make it harder to make use of existing TRIPS flexibilities. There have been calls in India and South Africa to walk away from a bad outcome.

The current text has conditions on eligibility, a major source of contention between the US and China. It has limitations on exports of vaccines only to eligible members. Some believe that the text might be useful to produce and export vaccines under limited conditions.

But it also has elements that seek to qualify conditions of using any potential solution by having language such as "necessary", "essential", "required", allegedly inserted at the suggestion by developed countries. Legal experts say that this makes it difficult to use any flexibilities. It is understood that developing countries are trying to fight such qualifications.

At this stage, it is unclear if members will commit to expanding the scope of the waiver to also include therapeutics and diagnostics.

Are India and South Africa locked into compromises made by politicians?

Sources suggest that it was during the discussions between these four key members (the EU, the US, India and South Africa) in early 2022, that compromises may have been made at the political level. It is understood that the introduction of eligibility requirements, that essentially seeks to bar China from taking advantage of any waiver, was also made during this period.

Now, as countries scamper to negotiate text with the Ministerial Conference less than 72 hours away (when this story went to print), India and South Africa, are not the leading voices in these discussions, sources tell us.

"By not effectively pushing for strengthening the text at this stage, the lead co-sponsors appear to be endorsing the text by default," a trade law expert familiar with the discussions told us.

In fact, in recent days, India even made efforts to preserve the current text, essentially opposing suggestions from other co-sponsors. "Egypt, one of the 64 co-sponsors of the original TRIPS waiver proposal, brought in language to expand the scope of trade secrets in the existing text. But India resisted," a source aware of the deliberations told us.

A number of observers are perplexed as to why the lead co-sponsors are not bringing in elements from their original proposal to bolster the text under negotiation.

Diplomatic sources tell us that these lead sponsors have not been backed sufficiently by other developing countries. "We have led the way for 18 months, and ultimately it has to be taken forward by others as well," one official told us.

But this has been disputed. Seasoned observers ask where the coordination and leadership are among developing countries to make sure that the text is strengthened. "They have had no clear strategy," a source who works with developing countries told us. This is a far cry, from the days when India and others led coalitions of developing countries at the WTO, just a few years ago.

Undoubtedly, trade negotiations are complex. And this situation is no exception. Much of these parallel negotiations at the WTO (fisheries, agriculture, TRIPS waiver) have resulted in excluding and dividing developing countries and delegations, WTO watchers say.

Others point to inconsistent support from Delhi to the Indian mission in Geneva. Some have even suggested inadequate negotiating capacities to deal with the brazen ways of trade diplomacy in Geneva. One source also hinted that the change of guard at the commerce ministry in India has influenced India's willingness to go the distance.

To be fair, the question of negotiating capacity is particularly true of smaller countries and delegations. But as a perceived leader of the developing world; one that was bold enough to bring a waiver proposal to the WTO, supporters of the waiver ask: why was India was not adequately prepared and resourced to crack these negotiations?

As we reported nearly a year ago, experts believe that India did not seem to have a consistent position on even using TRIPS flexibilities domestically. This lack of coherence might have translated into insufficient diplomatic leadership during this crucial period, sources suggest.

Ultimately, the accountability of what has gone into these negotiations' rests with political leaders, experts believe. Activists say that irrespective of technical teams working hard in these discussions, a lot could be unravelled if deals have already been made at the political levels.

"If we have trade ministers who do not fully understand what they are signing up to, the work done by the technical teams is undone," a source closely involved in these discussions told us.

Trade circles in Geneva are abuzz with news of pressure being applied on developing countries who are "standing in the way" of reaching a consensus on some of the deliverables for the Ministerial. In several instances, developed countries have threatened to walk away from negotiations, *Third World Network* has reported.

Similarly, it is understood that the government of South Africa has also faced pressure. On several occasions, South African leadership has insisted on a full TRIPS waiver. A source familiar with the progression of these events told us that attempts were made to get South Africa to agree on a deal in a secretive manner. But after intervention from civil society organisations, the government allegedly reconsidered its position.

But this has not meant that South Africans are pushing for strengthening the text at this stage.

"The time for intervention may have been lost," one trade expert tracking these discussions ball-by-ball, told us.

Queries sent to Indian and South African authorities went unanswered.

The WTO Director-General's push for outcomes ahead of the Ministerial has also had an impact on developing countries, multiple sources said.

What are the implications on the Global South?

There is wide recognition of the unprecedented momentum and the intense discussions in furthering the access to medicines agenda because of the TRIPS waiver proposal. Irrespective of the outcome next week in Geneva, India and South Africa, with support from others, have permanently changed the complexion of these debates.

However, by getting boxed into a narrow set of clarifications, far from the expansive waiver proposal first suggested, these countries could have shrunk the negotiating leverage of the developing world at large, sources warn.

"By agreeing to a potentially bad outcome, these countries have shown that developing countries can be bullied into submission. This will have consequences for the future," one activist told us in Geneva this week.

In the context of these discussions, trade scholars are divided on whether the WTO is really a level playing field. After all, the 164-member organisation is driven by consensus. But it has been increasingly hard for the WTO to shake off the perception that it is run by – and for – the developed world.

"The pressure of negotiating with the rich world is palpable. It is not easy," one developing trade diplomat told us recently. A few blocks away at the World Health Organization, countries are getting deeper into negotiations for a new pandemic instrument. What transpires at the WTO will be a harbinger for what could follow at WHO, especially on the question of intellectual property and its impact on equity.

Meanwhile, it was reported that the US is "confident that India will be engaging with intentionality at the WTO meet". The *Hindu* quoted US Trade Representative (USTR) Katherine Tai as saying: "Now, India knows its own mind. India has a complex place in the world order to put it diplomatically."

"In terms of India's approach to trade and to the WTO, what I see is an increasingly strategic India when it comes to trade, and so, I am confident that India will be engaging with intentionality," she continued.

Her remarks had come in response to a question on India's track record in Ministerials being "not great".

This piece was first published in The Wire, India.

46.
"POWER" TRIPS THE WAIVER AT THE WTO
(JUNE 16, 2022)

No consensus yet hours before the close of MC12

The journey of the TRIPS Waiver proposal through the labyrinthine maze of trade politics at the WTO illustrates the larger story of the shrinking leverage of developing countries in multilateral institutions.

The current TRIPS Waiver proposal, the linchpin of WTO deliverables at its 12th Ministerial Conference, underway in Geneva, has become the problem child that no one is happy with – barring, perhaps, the European Union – given that the text mostly resembles its original proposal. On failing to reach consensus on a number of different deliverables, before the original date of June 15, the WTO decided to extend the conference by a day with the assumption that an agreement could be reached on some of the key objectives in fisheries, agriculture, or the WTO response to the pandemic, including on the TRIPS waiver.

When this story went to print, there were on-going negotiations on a potential TRIPS waiver outcome, and other deliverables. Trade sources also indicated attempts to craft an emerging package that would comprise an agreement negotiated horizontally across disciplines.

After an envious build-up of support that saw 100-countries supporting the original TRIPS Waiver proposal, there is reluctant appetite now to adopt a mostly unworkable text that no one is expected to use. Save the political significance of the current waiver proposal and the associated political declaration, there is no real excitement among the supporters. The declaration, the WTO's response to the pandemic, some say, is no response at all, coming in two and half years after COVID-19 hit the world and even as there is another health emergency already brewing on the margins.

Saddled with a text of a potential waiver solution that they do not want, developing countries are under pressure from several quarters to reject the text. If adopted, it is increasingly clear that a weak waiver text could become a reality. This will make some stakeholders happy including developed countries that have fought hard to allegedly preserve incentives for innovation and the pharmaceutical industry that has been keen to safeguard the protection that the status quo provides.

This story unpacks the discussions at the WTO Ministerial on the TRIPS waiver and the wider pandemic response, at the cusp of a potential agreement before the close of the conference on June 16. The possibility of countries walking back with no deal in hand has not been ruled out when this story went to print.

THE MINISTERIAL CONFERENCE – A GROUND VIEW

The Ministerial Conference that began on 12 June in Geneva, saw hundreds of delegates comprising ministers, diplomats, trade experts convene at the WTO to buckle down on tough negotiations to deliver on trade objectives on the back of a debilitating pandemic resulting in economic pressures having socio-political implications the world over.

In her opening speech at the conference, DG Ngozi Okonjo-Iweala, warned that the road to deliver MC12 will not be smooth. "Expect a rocky, bumpy road with a few landmines along the way. But we shall overcome them," she had said. Now with hours left before the close of the Ministerial, it is not clear whether the DG expected the kind of pushback from developing countries as has been witnessed this week.

Some countries continued to raise concerns on process particularly on the use of green rooms - the hallmark of WTO ministerial tactics. These are smaller group negotiations convened to forge quicker decisions, but allegedly at the expense of excluding developing countries. Earlier in the week, trade officials referred to TRIPS waiver, and other discussions as having "gone underground, in proverbial smoke-filled rooms".

DELIVERABLES FOR GLOBAL HEALTH AT MC12
Jerome Walcott, Minister of Foreign Affairs and Foreign Trade of Barbados was named as the facilitator of the discussions on the WTO's response to the pandemic and on the TRIPS Waiver. The past few days at the Ministerial saw several "green room" meetings making negotiations on these issues tougher, diplomatic sources and other experts closely tracking these discussions said.

At a thematic session discussing the WTO response to the pandemic and the TRIPS waiver, nearly 70 interventions were made by members. The political declaration on the response to the pandemic appeared to have a fair amount of support from members, Daniel Pruzin, spokesperson of the WTO indicated during a press briefing.

But unresolved differences on the current TRIPS waiver text remained as countries continued to negotiate on key elements. Sources told us that the political declaration had a placeholder for the TRIPS waiver. And it was foreseen that these two different tracks will have to be adopted together.

As days passed, it was obvious, that the TRIPS waiver will not be a stand-alone deliverable for many members including for some developing countries. At a press briefing on June 15, Federal Councillor Guy Parmelin, indicated that an eventual agreement could emerge because of negotiations across disciplines.

THE CURRENT TEXT OF THE TRIPS WAIVER
ELIGIBILITY

Members continued to disagree on several key elements of the TRIPS waiver decision text that has been considered by ministers and their delegations over the last few days. Worryingly, the question on eligibility had not been resolved between the US and China (Part of Footnote 1 in the text reads: "[For the purpose of this Decision, developing country Members who exported more than 10 percent of world exports of COVID-19 vaccine doses in 2021 are not eligible Members.") It was not clear whether bilateral consultations were held between these members to address the question. Queries sent to American and Chinese authorities were not answered.

Ministerial watchers say that this question alone could sink the waiver if either side do not change their position. But efforts were made to draft language to seek a compromise, sources said this morning.

THE SCOPE OF APPLICATION

Countries also disagreed on what should be included as the subject matter of a patent. While developed countries such as the UK have allegedly pushed for exhaustive language, developing countries have tried to keep the definition of subject matter as non-exhaustive.

The draft decision text – June 10 – reads thus:

"For the purpose of this Decision, it is understood that 'subject matter of a patent' [includes][means all finished COVID-19 vaccine products,]ingredients and processes [necessary] for the manufacture of the COVID-19 vaccine.

Alternative wording [For the purpose of this Decision, it is understood that 'subject matter of a patent' refers to [finished] COVID-19 vaccine products, and [ingredients][products] and processes necessary for the manufacture of the COVID-19 vaccine.]"

THERAPEUTICS AND DIAGNOSTICS

For developing countries, one of the few remaining elements in an otherwise weak text is the promise of including therapeutics and diagnostics to the scope of any potential waiver.

(The paragraph reads: *"No later than six months from the date of this Decision, Members will decide whether to extend this decision to cover the production and supply of COVID-19 diagnostics and therapeutics."*)

But countries have struggled with committing to discuss the scope of the waiver to include therapeutics and diagnostics. In a statement during the Ministerial, Indian minister Piyush Goyal made clear: "It is of paramount importance for us to commence negotiations on therapeutics and diagnostics. We cannot have a pandemic response which does not deliver an effective and workable document on TRIPS, nor can we agree to any pre-shipment notification requirements."

Swiss authorities indicated that the current text was a framework that limited the discussion to vaccines. A representative from the pharma industry told us on the side-lines of the conference, that the current text would be problematic for therapeutics.

One expert told us that the economics of therapeutics will be quite different from that of vaccines. And therefore, a similar framework of the current waiver text may not work for treatments.

Interestingly, access to medicines advocates also believe that the current text would prove to be too restrictive for therapeutics.

It is not clear whether this would be a red line for the sponsors of the TRIPS waiver proposal. Many fear that, in effect, this may never be discussed at the WTO.

In a scathing follow on statement made at a meeting of co-sponsors of the TRIPS Waiver, published late one evening this week, Minister Goyal of India is reported to have told co-sponsors, "So, my own sense is that what we are getting is completely half baked and it will not allow us to make any vaccines, they have no intentions of allowing therapeutics and diagnostics and if at all they try to say that we are the cause for its collapse, I think we should unanimously speak to the world and tell them that no we ideally we want a holistic solution including therapeutics and diagnostics."

DURATION

Hours before the close of the conference, the question on the duration of any potential waiver also remained unresolved. (Pre-dawn consultations on June 16, indicated that an agreement on this issue may be reached, sources familiar with the discussions said. No details are known yet)

The UK had allegedly sought to link the termination of a compulsory license with the end of the period of the implementation of the waiver.

Geneva trade officials also pointed to suggestions to link the duration of the waiver to the inclusion of the therapeutics and diagnostics.

The draft text had read: "An eligible Member may apply the provisions of this Decision [so that authorized uses continue no later than] [until] [3][5][10] years from the date of this Decision. The General Council may extend such a period taking into consideration the exceptional circumstances of the COVID-19 pandemic. The General Council will review annually the operation of this Decision."

ON NOTIFICATIONS AND ENFORCEMENT
The language on notifications and anti-diversion in the current text has also worried activists.

"The current text makes the enforcement right more of a public responsibility, rather than a private right," James Love of Knowledge Ecology International told us on the side-lines of the conference. Love has worked extensively on these issues.

The relevant provisions of the draft text, on these matters, said:

b. *An eligible Member may waive the requirement of Article 31(f) that authorized use under Article 31 be predominantly to supply its domestic market and may allow any proportion of the products manufactured under the authorization in accordance with this Decision to be exported to eligible Members, including through international or regional joint initiatives that aim to ensure the equitable access of eligible Members to the COVID-19 vaccine covered by the authorization.*

c. *Eligible Members shall undertake all reasonable efforts to prevent the re-exportation of the products manufactured under the authorization in accordance with this Decision that have been imported into their territories under this Decision. Members shall ensure the availability of effective legal means to prevent the importation into, and sale in, their territories of products manufactured under the authorization in accordance with this Decision, and diverted to their markets inconsistently with its provisions, using the means already required to be available under the TRIPS Agreement.*

(Associated footnote: In exceptional circumstances, an eligible Member may re-export COVID-19 vaccines to another eligible Member for humanitarian and not-for-profit purposes, as long as the eligible Member communicates in accordance with paragraph 5.)

As we reported earlier these provisions entail only waiver in the current text - of Article 31 (f)

In an update, Love shared on Thursday morning, he said:

"The three core elements of 31bis are notifications to the WTO, anti-diversion measures and eligibility. 31bis applies to drugs, vaccines and some diagnostic tests. It is permanent. It applies to all diseases.

The new text had marginally less problematic notifications, different anti-diversion requirements, more trade restrictions on eligibility for both imports and exports. It is temporary, only applies to vaccines and it only applies to one virus – COVID 19."

THE WTO RESPONSE TO THE PANDEMIC

Several countries appeared favourable to adopt draft Ministerial Declaration On The WTO Response To The Covid-19 Pandemic And Preparedness For Future Pandemics, given that it will set a precedent and will become a reference for the future on these issues, in addition to having certain elements that can be binding in nature.

Experts say that "the Declaration can have an effect on existing rights, obligations and flexibilities, particularly when applied as a subsequent agreement or subsequent practice." WTO ministerial declarations could operate as subsequent agreements, they said citing opinions of the WTO Appellate Body.

However, activists also told us, that the declaration was not strong enough to bring any real change to how trade policies could be adapted at the time of health emergencies.

One senior diplomatic source referred us to paragraph 23 of the declaration, as significant for the future:

"We underscore the importance of understanding how WTO rules have supported Members during the COVID-19 pandemic, and their role in future pandemics. We affirm the need to review and build on all the lessons learned and the challenges experienced during the COVID-19 pandemic, to build effective solutions in case of future pandemics including on balance of payments, development, export restrictions, food security, intellectual property, regulatory cooperation, services, tariff classification, technology transfer, trade facilitation, and transparency, in an expeditious manner."

In a brief sent prior to the ministerial, on the declaration India had said, "Certain developed countries (EU, US, UK, Canada) are seeking to include elements pertaining to limiting the scope for export restrictions, seeking permanent disciplines with respect to trade facilitation measures, increased market access and limiting the scope for TRIPS waiver. On other hand, developing nations [South Africa, ACP group, Sri Lanka, Egypt, Tunisia, Uganda, Jamaica] want the WTO response to address issues with respect to the supply side constraints, increased access for services, such as, healthcare and related services namely ICT etc, flexibilities with respect to export control measures, food security measures and limiting the scope for any additional disciplines."

"The declaration includes terminology that differentiates between developing countries, by using a qualifying term 'some' before 'developing countries' in multiple paragraphs of the declaration. This will potentially feed into the attempts to normalize differentiation among developing countries and their access to special and differential treatment. It sets a political precedent which is likely to make it more difficult to resist on-going attempts to differentiate amongst developing countries," a note from Third World Network said.

It was also reported that the UK and Switzerland sought to dilute the language on intellectual property in the declaration. But sources told us, that the declaration and the waiver decision were linked. It is not clear how the declaration can be adopted if there is no corresponding agreement on the waiver.

THE LINK BETWEEN THE WAIVER AND THE DECLARATION

In the thematic session on these issues, Minister Goyal of India said:

"India has made several compromises along the way to make this possible, like the TRIPS automaticity clause, which was not accepted, extensive dilution of the language on IP and tech transfer; a muted ambition on food security and economic resilience, compromises on a strong forward-looking agenda on these issues, resolution of the issue of developing countries and LDCs, acceptance of issues and language we have not been comfortable with in areas of transparency, export restriction, market openness and developing countries etc.

Therefore, disturbing this delicately poised document even slightly would unravel the months-long complex negotiations and will run the risk of failing an outcome we are close to achieving.

This document, however, has an inextricable link with the satisfactory resolution of the TRIPS document. One cannot go through without the other and they both should be finalized together. It is of paramount importance for us to commence negotiations on therapeutics and diagnostics. We cannot have a pandemic response which does not deliver an effective and workable document on TRIPS, nor can we agree to any pre-shipment notification requirements."

THE FATE OF THE WAIVER HANGS IN BALANCE

Although the WTO is a member-driven multilateral organization, ultimately the deliverables at the Ministerial depend on a few key members, such as China and the US for the waiver, the UK and Switzerland, also on the waiver, and India on the decision on public stockholding for food security, or fisheries.

Diplomatic sources indicated that many of the negotiations could also be the result of proxy wars between bigger members.

There is a clear anti-India narrative prevailing at the WTO, not unsurprising given India's positions in previous ministerial. However, diplomats also suggested that this was a convenient narrative to blame southern countries such as India.

It is also becoming evident, that while important, the waiver is not the priority for India, as much as its proposals for food security and fisheries. In a brief, ahead of the ministerial, India indicated, "The department of commerce has organized a few consultation meetings with the Ministries concerned and the industry stakeholders on this subject. The Indian pharmaceutical industry has acknowledged it though the draft text that emerged does not reflect India's envisaged outcome; still, it is a significant step to pressure the international pharma community to provide voluntary licenses for COVID Vaccines."

But another developing country diplomat told us that "vaccines will not be a sacrificial lamb for public stockholding for food security", indicating that for some countries an outcome on the waiver is key.

THE ROLE OF THE DG

Depending on who one speaks to, the role of the DG in the run up and during the ministerial, has evoked strong reactions.

While some have called her charismatic and determined, others have found her over-bearing in her zeal for the WTO to deliver outcomes.

Multiple sources told us that WTO DG Okonjo-Iweala has put a lot of pressure on developing countries to hasten negotiations towards conclusion. "This is about the image of the DG, rather than whether the current waiver text is suitable for countries," one diplomatic source said. Some believe that African countries would have participated better, without the determined role that the DG has played.

"This is a member-driven organization, she should leave this to the countries", the source added.

At the end of tense negotiations and discussions on the TRIPS waiver, among other issues, many WTO members may not be in any mood to give greater powers to fewer countries.

THE POST-WAIVER WTO
As we reported before, some believe that the delay is the defeat of the TRIPS Waiver discussions at the WTO.

There is pressure building on countries to walk away from the text. After pushing for a full TRIPS waiver for 20 months, hundreds of activists all over the world, say that they have recognized the futility of the current text. More than 150 CSOs called on countries to not accept current draft of Ministerial Decision on TRIPS.

But irrespective of the outcome on the TRIPS waiver, the discussions on the access to medicines have turned a corner at the WTO.

Felipe de Carvalho, Advocacy Advisor for Brazil, MSF Access Campaign, pointed out that irrespective of the outcome, the discussions on the waiver had generated a global debate on the issue of access and inequity, it showed the extent of the barriers posed by intellectual property. "For the first time we have discussed the barriers imposed by trade secrets, for example", he said at a briefing by CSOs. The discussions opened the way towards a transformative agenda in health, he said.

Compulsory licensing was expanded in Brazil, we had new laws for local production, we had new rules to pierce trade secrets using CLs, he added emphasizing the impact of the discussions in Geneva, in some countries.

Not everyone shares this view. Ellen 't Hoen, director Medicines Law & Policy, and a former head of the Medicines Patent Pool, said on the sidelines of the conference, "The waiver text as currently being considered risks doing a disservice, not only to the public the WTO is meant to serve, but also to the WTO itself. WTO IP rules offer a broad range of flexibilities without restrictions on type of diseases, products or countries that may apply them and those flexibilities risks being eroded by a restrictive waiver. For the WTO to be relevant in public health it needs to be much more ambitious. This is also why we support the proposal for a public goods agreement".

Experts recall another lost opportunity in the access to medicines journey two decades earlier and find echoes in the current situation.

Carlos Correa, the executive director of the South Centre, told us this week, "There is, in effect, a parallel. Like in the case of the waiver negotiated pursuant to the Doha Declaration on the TRIPS Agreement and Public Health, while implicitly admitting that patents can be a barrier to expand the supply and access to vaccines, developed countries delayed the needed action in response to the request by India and South Africa. They also drastically narrowed down the scope of the waiver and sought to impose conditions (e.g. notifications, restriction on re-exportation) that substantially limit its possible effectiveness. The story has been repeated after 20 years showing that solidarity and cooperation continue to be proclaimed by those countries but not practiced."

There is already introspection among developing countries and supporters of the waiver. The story of how an expansive proposal seeking to waive several provisions across the TRIPS Agreement, got whittled down to essentially the waiver of a single provision.

The negotiations have been very tough, several developing country negotiators told us. Speaking at an event in Geneva, alongside the Ministerial, Baone Twala, Legal Researcher, Section27, in South Africa said, "The immovable met with the unstoppable," alluding to developed countries as an immovable force despite the demand for a full waiver form more than 100 countries. The southern negotiators were unstoppable, but there have been limits to how much they could push for, she added.

THE VIEW FROM THE OUTSIDE: MC12
The pressure on the WTO to deliver especially in the face of the pandemic continues. An open Letter was sent from the Special Rapporteur on contemporary forms of racism, racial discrimination, xenophobia and related intolerance to the WTO.

That said:

"Systemic racial discrimination is embedded into transnational legal, economic and political structures, including the international intellectual property regime. These systems uphold racial inequality by constraining the possible solutions for challenging such inequality. In the context of the COVID-19 pandemic, this has meant that the burdens of the pandemic have been borne disproportionately by certain States, peoples and territories most harmed by colonialism and racism, while the mechanisms for reducing these burdens are controlled

almost entirely by States, peoples and territories which were the beneficiaries of colonialism."

But far from examining the politics underneath trade law, some believe that the WTO has come to assume a "negative neutrality" that has been unable to ensure a level-playing field for all countries.

In her opening speech, DG Okonjo-Iweala said:

"...A trust deficit dating back to the breakdown of the Doha Round and even before took its toll. The media coverage reflected this and was brutal, with uniformly negative headlines about a failing WTO and failing ministers.

Permit me to be blunt and say that Geneva has internalized many of these negative messages.

The negativism is compounded by the negative advocacy of some think tanks and civil society groups here in Geneva and elsewhere who believe the WTO is not working for people. This is of course not true, although we have not been able to clearly demonstrate it, but it worsens the trust deficit that I have noticed in these past 15 months. Despite this, ambassadors have been working very hard, trying to overcome, to work hard together, and work to deliver. I want to say a heartfelt thank you to all the ambassadors in Geneva. I hope as ministers you can work even better together to complete nearly completed deliverables so this organization can be put back on a results-focused trajectory. I would like you to spend just a little bit of the political capital you have stored for your bilaterals and regional deals, to support multilateral deals at the WTO."

Many critics of the WTO, including scholars and the civil society disagreed with the DG's assessment.

Negotiations continued till pre-dawn, the night before the last day of the ministerial. No agreement was announced with less than few hours before the close of the conference.

By the time this story went to print, it was not clear whether the waiver decision would be adopted.

Winnie Byanyima, UN Undersecretary-General, UNAIDS executive director, and Co-Chair of the People's Vaccine Alliance, urged developing countries to "persist, persist, persist". Unity is our only strength, she said this week.

47.
TRADE WON, HEALTH DID NOT. A SLIVER OF A WAIVER AT THE WTO. (JUNE 18, 2022)

There was jubilation and cheer after the landmark ministerial conference at the WTO which saw a raft of agreements between its 164 members, that some say, has set a new benchmark for success, a kind not witnessed in decades. The outcome also included a weak text clarifying the use of existing rules in the WTO TRIPS Agreement. For the 100-odd countries that supported the original TRIPS waiver proposal, and countless supporters globally, conference was a moment of resignation. It was the culmination of 20 months of a fight that saw sustained resistance from many developed countries that refused to waive intellectual property protection rules to boost manufacturing of COVID-19 medical products.

The performance of multilateralism at the 12th ministerial conference in Geneva was for the survival of international and domestic elites and failed the world's poorest, Hyo Yoon Kang, a scholar of intellectual property law tweeted, hours after the ministerial. For months, Kang and others, have highlighted the politics of the intellectual property legal regime and have shed light on the importance of waiving intellectual property provisions in the TRIPS Agreement to fight the pandemic.

But voices like Kang's have been too distant at the WTO that has been all too keen to preserve prevailing IP regimes even in the face of the worst health emergency in 100 years.

This week the WTO adopted a weak text that essentially, only partially waived a single provision of the TRIPS agreement. In fact, so far is this text from the original TRIPS waiver proposal led by South Africa and India, that activists tried hard, and failed, in persuading WTO members to reject the text.

The dust will eventually settle down in Geneva, after 20 months of intense and divided debate on the TRIPS waiver. But observers say, a dent has been made. And the efforts to make intellectual property rules accountable to public health interests, will undoubtedly continue.

This story tries to capture the final hours of negotiations around the TRIPS waiver discussions at the ministerial conference. We also try to understand what this will mean for the future.

THE DRAFT MINISTERIAL DECISION ON THE TRIPS AGREEMENT

At the penultimate hour before the ministerial conference drew to a close at 5 a.m. on June 17, 2022, WTO members adopted the clarifications to the use of TRIPS flexibilities and a partial waiver of a single provision.

Stubborn disagreements on key elements on the text continued well into the small hours of the final day, illustrating the hard-won negotiations the "waiver" discussions have been. While the trade community loosely refers to this text as the waiver text, supporters of the original proposal disagree with the description. "This is not a waiver", is the common refrain that is heard from the supporters of the TRIPS waiver proposal.

It is also politically expeditious, for both, the WTO and developed countries to refer to this as the waiver text. While semantics matter, in the light and sound that the ministerial has generated, this nuance has already been lost.

Medicines Law and Policy, a group of legal experts, clarified in an analysis, "This Decision is no longer a TRIPS waiver in the sense it was proposed by South Africa and India in October 2020, which was a more comprehensive waiver of TRIPS obligations to be able to produce and access Covid-19 countermeasures. The broad waiver characteristics were lost when the EU's counter-proposal from October 2021, which was centred around using the existing TRIPS flexibility of compulsory licensing, became the core of the draft that was put in front of the ministers to work with this week."

So, what WTO members adopted this week is a narrow legal mechanism, limited to developing countries, where they can override a patent related to the production of COVID-19 vaccines without the consent of the rights holder. The mechanism clarifies the issuance of compulsory licenses. This is expected to help exports of vaccines among eligible countries. But much of this already exists in the TRIPS Agreement, experts say.

In an analysis on the adopted text, Knowledge Ecology International said:

"The TRIPS agreement contains 73 Articles describing various obligations on WTO members as regards the granting and enforcement of intellectual property rights. The original waiver proposal would have provided a clean waiver of 40 Articles in the TRIPS, as regards the manufacturing and supply of any COVID 19 countermeasure. The new considerably scaled back agreement focuses on just one part of the agreement, the 20-word paragraph 31.f which limits exports made under a non-voluntary authorization, often referred to as a compulsory license."

Several key issues were resolved only in the final days and hours of this 20-month discussion. A number of delegations were not aware of the final outcome on some of these issues, even after the text was adopted. Essentially, many countries were not aware of what the wider WTO membership had already signed up to, sources familiar with the proceedings of the final hours, told us.

On eligibility

The most contentious of them concerned footnote 1 of the text, that now reads

"For the purpose of this Decision, all developing country Members are eligible Members. Developing country Members with existing capacity to manufacture COVID-19 vaccines are encouraged to make a binding commitment not to avail themselves of this Decision. Such binding commitments include statements made by eligible Members to the General Council, such as those made at the General Council meeting on 10 May 2022 and will be recorded by the Council for TRIPS and will be compiled and published publicly on the WTO website."

The US and China discussed this at length, literally till the final hour, sources tracking these negotiations said. And ultimately a work-around was crafted. However, experts feel that will set a precedent not only for developing countries such as China, but also have implications for how the developing world will access special and differential treatment at the WTO.

"If the goal was to help production of COVID-19 vaccines why punish the exporters?" a supporter of the waiver proposal said. Experts also worry what such a conditionality could mean to produce therapeutics in the future.

María L. Pagán, Deputy United States Trade Representative and Chief of the US Mission in in Geneva, said at a press briefing hours after the conclusion of the ministerial, "The waiver encourages developing countries that have existing capacity to manufacture COVID-19 vaccines not to avail of the flexibilities that are provided here. Our position with respect to China has been that you have the COVID vaccines and the mRNA technology, you are the second largest economy in the world. This is not for you. You don't need this. This is to enhance the manufacturing capacity in other areas of the world that don't have the capacity right now or need a little bit of help in boosting that capacity."

"The point is the encouragement to others, to also raise their hands and say, this is not for me because I don't need it. It is really for countries that don't have that capacity, to create...the economies of scale ...", she added, responding to our question on whether this language in the footnote could also potentially restrict countries such as India and others, from taking advantage of the new adopted text.

Footnote 2: "Subject Matter of a Patent"

There were also extensive discussions on footnote 2, primarily on account of opposition from the UK, sources said. This now reads as follows: "For the purpose of this Decision, it is understood that 'subject matter of a patent' includes ingredients."

Experts say that developing countries were able to push back and make this interpretation broader than what was discussed during the negotiations.

The lone waiver: Article 31 (f)

Overall, experts say that the only waiver in the text is of Article 31 (f) of the TRIPS Agreement [para 3(b) of the text). The fundamental difference between the waiving of Article 31 (f) in the current text and using the current Article 31*bis* mechanism that exists in the TRIPS Agreement, is that the use of this limited waiver will be "supply driven", where eligible members can export to all other eligible members, Geneva-based trade experts explained to us.

In Article 31*bis*, the use is "demand driven" where the importing country would first have to notify the WTO. Now any eligible member could technically produce vaccines, primarily for export, using this new adopted text.

[Specifically, experts point to the Annex to the TRIPS Agreement, 2 (b) (i), that says: *"only the amount necessary to meet the needs of the eligible importing Member(s) may be manufactured under the licence and the entirety of this production shall be exported to the Member(s) which has notified its needs to the Council for TRIPS".* Such conditions do not apply in the adopted text.]

Duration:

There were discussions on the duration of the applicability of this agreement, that was finally decided as five years, that experts say is too short.

On therapeutics and diagnostics

After much negotiation, there was consensus on paragraph 8 of the text that now reads:

"No later than six months from the date of this Decision, Members will decide on its extension to cover the production and supply of COVID-19 diagnostics and therapeutics."

While developing countries are not hopeful that this will be discussed at the WTO, it was nevertheless significant to have this language in the adopted text.

In a statement made at the ministerial, Indian trade Minister Piyush Goyal said:

"...with great difficulty we got the period of 5 years. But we all know that by the time we get an investor, get funds raised, draw plans, get equipment, and set up a plant, it will probably take 2.5-3 years to do that. After that, you will start producing and within 2 years, you will have to bring down your exports to the normal compulsory license level and your capacity will remain idle. Today, in India, we have vaccines which are expiring,

we have the capacity of vaccines which is idling and therefore, investors will not be easy to come by for this."

Responding to a question on this, Pagán at USTR said, that the US, like other WTO members, will consult stakeholders internally on the extension of the solution to therapeutics and diagnostics. "We are committed to looking at this decision...we will see where that takes us", she added. In the run up to the Ministerial, the US was one of the staunchest opponents to this paragraph.

But WTO DG Ngozi Okonjo-Iweala was more hopeful. "Now we have something in hand. Exciting to now be able to go to those factories that are being set up all over the developing world and to work with them and to see how this can be made real."

ON PROCESS
Apart from the weakness in the substantive elements of the text, what also caused consternation among developing countries, not only ahead of the ministerial, but also during the proceedings, was the lack of transparency and opportunity.

Sources familiar with the discussions indicated that there was not enough room or time for most of the delegations to fully understand the implications of the final text.

KEY STATEMENTS
The U.S.

It is widely acknowledged that the support of the US to these discussions in May 2021, gave impetus to the TRIPS Waiver discussions, although critics say that the US was not able to live up to the expectations it generated.

On the eve of the conclusion of the ministerial, a statement from US ambassador Katherine Tai on an intellectual property response to the COVID-19 pandemic, said, "This agreement shows that we can work together to make the WTO more relevant to the needs of regular people. During a global pandemic, under difficult circumstances, the WTO moved quickly to address a major global challenge and respond to the strong desire of our African partners to produce a meaningful outcome. Consultations with our stakeholders in the private sector and civil society, with Members of Congress and their staffs, and colleagues across the Administration, were critical in informing USTR's understanding of the nuances in the global market, production challenges, and the public health needs of the world's people."

THE UK

International Trade Secretary, Anne-Marie Trevelyan, said:

"Coming into discussions about the WTO's response to the pandemic, we were clear that the solution to the access of Covid-critical goods lay beyond Intellectual Property, such as principles in applying export restrictions, increased transparency supporting trade facilitation and tariff reduction. While we pressed for the WTO Declaration to go further, we welcome the fact that members found common ground and committed to keep working to improve our preparedness for future pandemics.

The UK is a long-standing champion of equitable access to vaccines. However, we could only accept an outcome on TRIPS that was operable and did not undermine the existing Intellectual Property framework. That is why the UK fought hard to clarify the exact intent and scope behind the TRIPS Decision. After intense negotiations, we are satisfied the final text is sufficiently workable.

Let me be clear: this is not about waiving IP rights. This decision should make it easier for developing countries to export the vaccines they produce within existing flexibilities."

THE EU:

"Ministers agreed on a Declaration on the WTO response to the pandemic and preparedness for future pandemics which affirms their commitment to transparency, timely and comprehensive information sharing, and restraint on imposing export restrictions. Responding to the exceptional circumstances of the COVID pandemic and to address the requests from developing countries, Ministers agreed on a waiver of certain procedural obligations under the TRIPS Agreement which allow for the swift manufacture and export of COVID-19 vaccines without the consent of the patent owner. At the same time, the agreement maintains a functioning intellectual property framework with incentives for investment, research and transfer of technology. This environment is indispensable for the development of new vaccines and medicines and should contribute to the strengthening of the production capacity of African countries."

THE INDUSTRY

"Pharmaceutical industry expresses deep disappointment with decision on waiving intellectual property rights adopted at the World Trade Organization Ministerial Conference

IFPMA, the body representing biopharmaceutical companies in Geneva, expresses deep disappointment with the decision taken to adopt a TRIPS waiver, despite intellectual property (IP) not being a barrier to vaccine scale-up and wide acknowledgment of vaccines surplus.

IP has enabled the rapid research and development of several effective vaccines against COVID-19 and underpinned the more than 380 voluntary partnerships; while trade barriers have severely undermined collective efforts to deliver vaccines to those who need them most.

Industry warns that such an "empty shell" and fact-free decision can have severe consequences on innovation and global health security."

MSF

In a statement following the ministerial, MSF said:

"We are disappointed with the inadequate outcome on waiving intellectual property for COVID-19 medical tools that resulted from more than 20 months of deliberations...

...Without agreement on a true global solution to ongoing access challenges, MSF now urges governments to take immediate steps at the national level to make sure people have access to needed COVID-19 medical tools. Governments should consider using all available legal and policy options, including suspending intellectual property on COVID-19 medical tools, issuing compulsory licenses on key medical technologies to overcome patent barriers, and adopting new laws and policies to ensure the disclosure of essential technical information needed to support generic production and supply."

DISSECTING THE NEGOTIATIONS

Several supporters of the original waiver proposal brought by South Africa and India, have already begun soul-searching on strategies that might have led to greater success.

"This is essentially the first waiver decision in 19 years. It was a lost opportunity. Why didn't the negotiators focus on treatments? Vaccines are harder. Why did they restrict the discussions only to COVID-19? The pandemic was an opportunity to widen these discussions", a prominent access to medicines advocate raised these questions, on the side-lines of the ministerial.

While some point to weak negotiating capacities of southern countries, other defend co-sponsors, suggesting that the blame for the weakening of the original proposal lie with the rich countries.

"These were very difficult negotiations. Southern negotiators were up against not only developed countries, but also forces outside of the room," a source following these discussions said. There could be external pressures operating on developed countries that ultimately shaped these discussions, the source added. "We will never know", the person said.

A senior diplomat, from a developed country, engaged with these discussions for many months, suggested that in most permanent missions of countries in Geneva, there was very little understanding of public health and public interest, indicating that missions mostly had patent experts trained in upholding the law and not in innovating with existing rules.

"It also did not help, that southern negotiators effectively blamed northern countries for deaths associated with COVID-19 deaths world-wide. That is not the way to engage in negotiations," he added.

These discussions also showed that developed countries had to acknowledge that IP was indeed a barrier in the access to medical products during COVID-19, he said.

Others reflected on how messaging and advocacy on the part of some CSOs might have contributed to confusion in the public. "They first said they want a waiver, then they said, they did not want it. This confuses the common man," a seasoned global health observer remarked.

But most agree, the well-funded campaigns supporting the TRIPS waiver galvanized communities across countries leading to greater engagement and participation in these issues.

As for the WTO, the diplomat closely involved in the waiver discussions said, "We did not expect the Quad to take so long in their discussions, and not reach an agreement."

Many believe that the strategy to divide the discussions in the Quad, unravelled the negotiating strategy for the global south. "India and South Africa should never have agreed to engage bilaterally with the US and the EU, respectively," an expert who was involved in access to medicines negotiations in the past, told us this week.

As for the activists, some hope to now focus on taking the fight to the capitals to influence national laws directly.

The challenges in addressing the access to medicines has already moved to WHO, where a new instrument to govern health emergencies is taking shape. The TRIPS Waiver discussions offer a cautionary tale, and many lessons to rework the playbook at WHO.

PART VIII:

WHAT'S AHEAD: TRIPS WAIVER 2.0. ON THERAPEUTICS AND DIAGNOSTICS (JULY 2022)

••

Given the circuitous path of the TRIPS Waiver discussions have taken, there is a fair amount of trepidation, on what the forthcoming negotiations on medicines and tests will be like. But battle-hardened negotiators are keen on approaching these issues afresh and are ready for the next round of difficult discussions, not the least because the COVID-19 tests and treatments hold the key for a variety of different health conditions. Another fight is on.

48.

TRIPS WAIVER 2.0 AT THE WTO: PROPONENTS BACK AT THE TABLE TO PUSH FOR THERAPEUTICS AND DIAGNOSTICS (JULY 8, 2022)

The embers from the WTO's 12th ministerial conference are still warm.

While the supporters of the original TRIPS waiver are still coming to terms with the remains of the 20 month saga that yielded a ministerial decision clarifying the rules of compulsory licensing for the production of vaccines, they are back at the WTO to stomach another fight. This time, to discuss the way forward to boost the production of therapeutics and diagnostics by seeking to extend the applicability of the June decision to these medical products.

This puts the co-sponsors, again, directly in opposition to industry interests where companies such as Pfizer alone are projected to make billions off a single drug to treat COVID-19.

At this week's TRIPS Council meeting, the first since the ministerial that ended on June 17th, WTO members gathered to discuss, among other policy matters, paragraph 8 of the decision that concerns therapeutics and diagnostics.

Recall that the text said:

"8. No later than six months from the date of this Decision, Members will decide on its extension to cover the production and supply of COVID-19 diagnostics and therapeutics."

In an "unofficial room" document that is classified as "restricted" (RD/IP/49), South Africa, India, Pakistan, Indonesia, Egypt and Tanzania, on behalf of the co-sponsors of the original TRIPS waiver proposal (IP/C/W/669/Rev.1), have suggested the rationale and the plan to conduct the discussions on therapeutics and diagnostics.

(According to the WTO, "documents issued in the RD series are not official WTO documents. They usually appear in their language of submission and will not be translated systematically into the working languages of the WTO. They are intended for use in WTO meeting rooms and are attributed an unofficial symbol for archiving purposes only".)

THE RATIONALE

The document cites WHO's analysis on the "the supply-side problems for tests and therapeutics, with insufficient funds and insufficient access" noting that developing countries have been most affected. The co-sponsors also cite two specific measures taken by the US and the EU in securing treatment courses – the test and treat initiative by the US for rapid access to COVID-19 testing and treatments; and the EU Strategy on COVID-19 therapeutics. It notes that the US has already "secured the purchase of 20 million treatment courses of Paxlovid and also procuring Molnupiravir".

The co-sponsors point out that there are four times as many patent filings related to therapeutics compared to vaccines. Already, more than 5,200 patent applications related to COVID-19 were published across 49 patent offices between 2020-21 according to the World Intellectual Property Organization (WIPO) Patent Landscape Report (PLR), the co-sponsors cite.

"Many of these patent applications are for repurposed drugs rather than innovative products developed to treat COVID-19. Government funding has supported a significant part of the research and clinical trial efforts," they say.

They argue that granting of patents could delay the entry of generic drugs, and in turn lead to price increases affecting access.

Although voluntary licensing approaches have been championed by the industry and other stakeholders, they point out that such terms are limited in scope. The example of voluntary licenses for Paxlovid and Molnupiravir, negotiated by Medicines Patent Pool has been cited.

"Under the high-profile agreement between the originator and the MPP, only 95 countries can benefit from the potential supply of generics. Even within those countries, only a limited number of companies have the capacities to access MPP under the strict requirements of the WHO Prequalification of Medicines Programme (PQWHO). Although the license will ultimately allow for generic production by companies that signed the license, it has been estimated that new generic companies may only be able to start supplying the treatment in 2023," the co-sponsors say.

On the importance of addressing the access to diagnostics, co-sponsors say that that by the end of 2021, of the more than 3 billion tests reported across the world, only 0,4% had been performed in low-income countries.

Because diagnostics has been mostly produced in high-income countries, over-reliance on imported diagnostics resulted in scarcity and high prices which restricted access in low- and middle-income countries (LIMCs), they say in their proposal.

THE PROCESS

They seek an extension of the policy tools provided in the June ministerial decision to therapeutics and diagnostics. This, they say, "will help developing countries to address IP barriers to the expansion and diversification of production".

The co-sponsors are pushing for a resolution on this matter within the 6-month period as worded in the ministerial decision. While some countries seek consultations on this over the coming weeks and months, they also want an update to be sent to the WTO General Council meeting that will convene at the end of this month. Another formal TRIPS council meeting is scheduled in October this year. They hope that the discussions are concluded by December 2022 as set out in the decision.

Sources familiar with the proceedings of the meeting this week said that several members made interventions supporting the engagement in these discussions including South Africa, Cambodia, Indonesia, Egypt, Zimbabwe, the EU, among others.

A few other members reportedly sought more time for consultations. (In the run up to the ministerial in June 2022, the US, for example, was keen on limiting the waiver to vaccines only. Top US officials have also indicated consultations with domestic stakeholders on this.)

In a statement made at the meeting, the UK said:

"...The UK will engage constructively and in good faith, being guided by evidence and noting the distinction between vaccines, therapeutics, and diagnostics. We welcome all Members' views and the opportunity to engage bilaterally on the matter. We are pleased to see the IP framework has been put in use by licensing partnerships for COVID-19 treatments underway, including via the Medicines Patent Pool....," the statement said.

"...Given the complexities of therapeutics and diagnostics, we will use the time available, and we call on others to do the same, to gather and analyse evidence and engage bilaterally during the summer months, so that we are able to deliver on the mandate via multilateral evidence-based discussions after the summer. We see the TRIPS Council, with you, Chair, at the helm, as the right forum to hold these discussions...."

For developing countries getting the text on therapeutics and diagnostics in the June decision was seen as a minor win, in a decision that effectively codified EU's initial proposal on clarifying rules on the compulsory licensing system. Whether developing countries will be able to extract commitments on this, is another matter entirely.

THE LINK BETWEEN THERAPEUTICS AND DIAGNOSTICS

While some global health experts believe that intellectual property is not a barrier for diagnostics, others say that both therapeutics and diagnostics are collectively important in fighting the pandemic.

WHO officials have decried the lack of adequate testing over the last many months. "We are flying blind," officials remarked at several instances on the decrease in testing systems even as variants of SARS-CoV-2 emerge. Diagnostics are vital not only for surveillance but to simply manage the pandemic, they say.

At an event earlier this week, the South Centre discussed the implications of the WTO ministerial decision on the TRIPS Agreement. Experts cited prevailing laws at the national level to demonstrate the link between these two categories of medical products.

Nirmalya Syam, a senior programme officer at the South Centre explained at the event that there is an intrinsic linkage between these categories. As an example, he pointed to provisions in the Indian patent law to demonstrate precedence on these issues.

Specifically, Section 92A in The Patents Act, 1970, on compulsory licence for export of patented pharmaceutical products in certain exceptional circumstances:

"...(3) The provisions of sub-sections (1) and (2) shall be without prejudice to the extent to which pharmaceutical products produced under a compulsory license can be exported under any other provision of this Act. Explanation. -For the purposes of this section, ‹pharmaceutical products› means any patented product, or product manufactured through a patented process, of the pharmaceutical sector needed to address public health problems and shall be inclusive of ingredients necessary for their manufacture and diagnostic kits required for their use."

THE COVID-19 DRUGS MONEY SPINNER

Given the evolution of the disease, having access to drugs to treat COVID-19 are critical. Treatment activists have long pushed for the inclusion of these medical products in any measures on waiving IP rights.

But if the last 20 months are anything to go by, this will be even more contentious than what we have already witnessed, observers predict.

Privately, some diplomats in Geneva express concerns on whether WTO members will be able to arrive at a decision on this. After all, it took 20 months to agree on a narrow waiver, and that too only for vaccines.

Much is at stake. In May 2022, it was forecasted that Pfizer's Paxlovid could be among the fastest-selling treatments of all time, with revenue of almost $24 billion expected in 2022, Bloomberg said in a report citing estimates from Airfinity.

In addition, drugs and diagnostics used for COVID-19 can also be adapted for use in fighting other diseases. There are efforts to optimise diagnostics to detect a range of infections.

The industry fears that waiving IP rights in the production of these medicines and tests would undermine innovation. Some industry leaders have varyingly referred to the waiver proposal as dangerous and toxic.

Thomas Cueni, of IFPMA reportedly said "It›s a Pandora›s box and sends completely the wrong signal for future pandemic preparedness», according to a Reuters story.

It is unclear whether the June decision will be applicable to therapeutics and diagnostics as it now stands. Neither the industry, nor civil society organizations want that.

Activists believe that a stronger framework should be applicable to this second category of medical products, because they see the many caveats and conditions in the current decision as affecting access.

This week WHO DG, Tedros Adhanom Ghebreyesus called on Pfizer to work closely with health agencies and countries to ensure its new oral antiviral is available quickly and effectively. To fight the pandemic, he said that it was important to make new oral antivirals and other treatments available to all.

"Working with Global Fund and UNICEF, WHO has developed an allocation mechanism to support countries as antivirals become available. So far, 20 countries have accepted allocations of Molnupiravir, which has moved into distribution. For Nirmatrelvir-Ritonavir, – or Paxlovid - 43 countries have expressed interest. However, our organizations are still trying to finalize with Pfizer the appropriate terms and conditions for low- and middle-income countries. This is delaying access and some countries may choose to wait for a generic version of the antiviral, probably available only early 2023 and this will cost lives. I call on Pfizer to work closely with health agencies and countries to ensure its new oral antiviral is available quickly and effectively."

TAILPIECE

Even as moves are being made to begin negotiation to waive or clarify certain provisions of the TRIPS agreement to enable access to therapeutics and tests, there are also efforts to increase the scope of IP protection.

In a proposal tabled by the US, the EU, Canada, Australia, Switzerland, China, the UK and others, (IP/C/W/691), member seeks to identify IP licensing opportunities to further intellectual property and innovation.

Proponents of this new proposal discuss the various kinds of licensing of IP in categories such as technology, publishing and entertainment, and trademark and merchandising. This can involve all types of IP assets, including patents, copyright, trademarks, as well as know-how, they explain in their proposal.

On licensing know-how, the proponents say "Know-how can include a range of IP-protected and non-IP protected assets, such as unpatented, technical information, trade secrets, data, specifications, procedures, studies, processes, or methods in the manufacture, sale or use of licensed products. For instance, the technology. Know-how can also be licensed separately from patents, as a distinct form of IP with different terms. For example, a license for know-how can be for an indefinite term, whereas a license for a patent may expire with the patent expiration date."

Access to technology has been central to the discussions not only at the WTO's TRIPS waiver discussions, but also at WHO.

Watch this space.

49.

DECONSTRUCTING THE TRIPS WAIVER DISCUSSIONS: THE SUSAN SELL INTERVIEW (AUGUST 5, 2022)

I n June 2022, the World Trade Organization adopted a decision at its 12th Ministerial Conference, that could potentially help facilitate easier production of COVID-19 vaccines. This was the outcome of a 20-month long discussion at the WTO on the so-called TRIPS Waiver. But ultimately what resulted was a rather narrow legal mechanism, essentially clarifying existing rules in the WTO TRIPS Agreement.

For many, this outcome was not entirely surprising. Susan K Sell from the Australian National University has long examined and explored the nature of the TRIPS Agreement and the politics at the WTO.

We spoke with Sell during her recent visit to Geneva in July 2022. She is a Professor at the School of Regulation and Global Governance at Australian National University and is Emeritus Professor of Political Science and International Affairs, George Washington University. She has published widely on the politics of intellectual property, including private power, public law, global governance, and public health.

During her recent visit, she had a session on *21st Century Capitalism and Intellectual Property: A Research Agenda*, at the Geneva Graduate Institute.

In this interview, Sell explains why words matter and how the waiver discussions, though disappointing, have broadened and shifted the conversation on intellectual property and public health forever. In her conversation with *Geneva Health Files*, Sell also says she is optimistic about discussions on a new instrument to govern pandemics at the WHO. Read on.

(Julia Dötzer contributed to the production of this interview.)

[Geneva Health Files: GHF] What do you think is the political significance of the TRIPS Waiver discussions that lasted 20 months, but eventually resulted in a rather narrow mechanism, essentially clarifying existing flexibilities. Given the historical role of the WTO as a citadel of IP protection, how bold was this proposal from South Africa and India?

[Susan Sell: SS] The proposal was very good. I thought it was timely. It was certainly well justified in the face of a global pandemic in which it wasn't just vaccines, that were a problem, but also shortages of personal protective equipment and all the things that they were asking: medical devices, therapeutics. So, I thought it was an extremely reasonable set of requests and I was quite hopeful that during a global pandemic, if there was going to be any movement on this issue, it would be with COVID-19.

We all lived through the HIV/AIDS negotiations, back in the late 1990s, early 2000s and what ended up as the Doha Declaration was very disappointing. It just clarified that countries could use flexibilities that were already in the TRIPS agreement. And it also created a very complicated, convoluted mechanism for exporting generic drugs to countries that did not manufacture them. That has only been ever used once... a very clunky mechanism. So that was very disappointing, but I did get my hopes up during COVID-19 when the TRIPS Waiver proposal was put forward.

I am, of course, very disappointed in the outcome, but I am also not at all surprised. Disappointed, yes, not surprised. But I do think apart from the language of the waiver, broadening the conversation is important. I think words really matter. You go back and look at the legacy of the failed efforts to get a strong mechanism for making affordable HIV/AIDS drugs available... and up through the Doha Declaration. Ever since those debates, you cannot talk about intellectual property without talking about Public Health. So, I think words matter. These things take a long time.

The power dynamics are very asymmetrical and you can't expect it to move in a day, but I think the conversation has shifted forever. And I think the broadening of the set of demands in the most recent negotiations has put them on a table in a way that it will be difficult to stop talking about them going forward. So that is a positive thing that the bigger conversation is there and can't be avoided. I am also a hundred percent sure, that there will be many more pandemics to come. Looking back at all the unnecessary death under COVID-19, I am hoping that policymakers and manufacturers will understand the gravity and the importance of the urgency of having better responses to avoid unnecessary deaths.

The numbers of unnecessary deaths from COVID-19 are just staggering. Multiple causes are behind that, but some of it does have to do with intellectual property and the right to exclude others from making, producing PPE. I think 3M has over 400 patents on their N95 masks. These are obstacles for rapid scaling up of production when it is urgently needed to save lives. So, I am hoping and I do believe that the broader conversations that have continued over these 20 months with a disappointing result will change the conversation going forward just as it did back in 1999/2001.

[GHF]: You suggested that some of the features of the TRIPS waiver proposal were strong. What according to you were some of the provisions you thought were progressive in that sense and, certainly out of reach eventually.

[SS]: Well, in particular, I would say the many asks behind it, all the things that the demandeurs wanted to have covered under it. It was the broader coverage, more comprehensive approach to a waiver, not just about producing generic medicines. It recognized the broader universe of necessary aspects to address a pandemic.

[GHF]: What do you think contributed to the failure of these negotiations? Are only rich countries to blame, given their staunch opposition to the original expansive proposal or do you think that developing countries should have adopted different negotiating strategies? You mentioned the previous crisis, were there any lessons from the past that could have been employed in these negotiations?

[SS]: I mean, from my perspective, I tend to look at asymmetrical power and structural imbalance. And from that perspective alone, I think that goes most of the way in explaining the failure, rather than a strategic or tactical error on the part of developing countries.

What I think is smart and what I think is promising as we saw... one of the lessons we did get at least that led to the Doha Declaration, was shifting forums. So, the Doha Declaration, even though it was weak, you know, in the big scheme of things, it still was an important discursive change, recognizing that something shouldn't get in the way of protecting Public Health. And patents in particular, even though didn't have much, I mean, the declaration didn't have much in terms of teeth. However, what it did show is that you can build a consensus in the World Health Organization that then could be brought into the World Trade Organization with more legitimacy. So, I think that forum shifting and the part of civil society actors in developing countries were smart.

By the same token now, I think the activities going on in the World Health Organization and negotiations on a pandemic treaty are also smart. The negotiations for a pandemic treaty have the potential to have more punch in the sense that, if you are addressing pandemics as a whole, and we are going to get a lot more of them, you really have to address a range of behaviours and a range of practices that go far beyond intellectual property. So, I think it is a possibility or it has potential for a more productive dialogue about what we all really have in common when it comes to trying to grapple with pandemics.

[GHF]: Big pharma companies have alliances with some of the domestic industries in developing countries, that might have had an impact on how even these countries, including the co-sponsors of the waiver proposal, the way they might have approached these negotiations with an emphasis towards voluntary licensing and so on. The world has changed since Doha. So, do you think that was a factor, why maybe some developing countries were not entirely convinced about a waiver of IP protection as an approach to solve the pandemic?

[SS]: Yeah, I mean, I think you are right, in the sense that the interests are much more conflicted now than they were back in Doha, where there are some places with domestic capability that, in the developing world, that may have different kinds of interests if they partner with pharmaceutical firms to develop their industries. Or countries like Jordan, the famous U.S.-Jordan FTA, where big American pharmaceutical firms were able to enter that market, not really transferring technology to Jordanians to have domestic capability, but certainly influencing their political lines and some of these issues. So, it is a much more variegated landscape than it was back in the day.

[GHF]: Despite the sort of limited outcome that we have had with the WTO ministerial decision with respect to this waiver issue, are there any lessons at all, that can be sort of distilled from the last 20 months, going forward, for the

access to medicines movement? Do you think, developing countries can transpose some of those lessons into pandemic treaty negotiations at WHO?

[SS]: I think one of the interesting things that has happened during the pandemic, is that several OECD countries, including Israel, the European Union and France...they either threatened compulsory licensing or issued compulsory licenses. They threatened pharmaceutical firms for withholding some necessary technology under abusive dominant market positions. And once that threat was there, they came through said and what is your need... So, the fact that the OECD countries are recognizing that these things can be impediment to an effective pandemic response, I think should give some powerful ammunition for developing countries to point out that, you guys realize it is a problem and you took action and we want to take the same kind of actions that you did. So, we share a view, that these things can be impediments to effective pandemic response.

[GHF]: Was the TRIPS waiver really a landmark in that sense? Also, in the context of the fact that the way capital moves, the way interests have changed, how do you see these discussions progressing? The term equity has to some extent been co-opted. And I think that the way we talk about equity will have changed forever after this pandemic. But how do you see this discussion evolving?

[SS]: No, I don't think it was a landmark. I am very disappointed. But I am not surprised, this doesn't look that different than what we have seen the last 20 years in terms of resistance to these kinds of openings. And I thought, if there was a moment in time where we could really have potential for a different approach to these issues, it was COVID-19. I was wrong, but there will be many pandemics down the pike, that is something we know for sure. Partly the fact that the whole world didn't get vaccinated, we are already seeing Omicron subvariants BA.4, and BA.5, which more transmissible. We don't know yet about their effects on long COVID, hospitalization, but, you know, the story isn't going away and it is going to get worse, whether it's COVID-19 or the next one. So, I think that the conversation is going to continue and I hope that some of the lessons we learn is that we really can't wait to address this in a much more effective way, which means compromise, in particular for IP owners.

[GHF]: Is there reason for optimism?

[SS]: I like to think so, otherwise I have a hard time getting out of bed in the morning.

[GHF]: Thank you so much.

CONCLUSION

One balmy evening during the 12th Ministerial Conference at the WTO in June 2022, an ambassador from a developed country recounted the journey of the TRIPS waiver discussions in the 20 months when it dominated optimism and activism during the pandemic of COVID-19. He said that the outcome of the discussions that had by then, mostly resulted in a narrow legal mechanism, was to be expected. "We could not have set aside the rule book", he said suggesting that whatever decision had resulted was very much within the framework of existing rules.

This essentially captured how constrained trade diplomats in Geneva were, in responding to the pandemic, very much straight-jacketed by the rules set in the TRIPS Agreement. Never mind the underlying politics and circumstances that came together to bring about these rules.

So although the TRIPS waiver discussions did not become the litmus test that demonstrated the imagination of policymakers in creatively responding to the pandemic of COVID-19, from my limited perspective, it surely galvanized not just activists but also many different epistemic communities, as one trade negotiator articulated. It is not often that scholars, Nobel laureates, civil society organizations, students, governments, unionists, nurses and world leaders come together to campaign for a cause. And failed.

When was the last time, that matters of copyright and trade secrets, were even on the table while discussing the access to medicines in the context of trade and health? While it may not have succeeded in finally gaining the critical mass to introduce a wide-ranging international legal mechanism that could have been adopted globally, these discussions did challenge power asymmetries in trade diplomacy that had mostly become normalized.

But we know from the ubiquitous impact of the pandemic that few things will ever be the same again. These discussions challenged the status quo and some say, this is just the beginning.

It will not only be interesting to watch the forthcoming discussions on extending the ministerial decision to therapeutics and diagnostics, but how potentially the waiver of certain intellectual property rules will be used as an instrument to deal with future health emergencies in general. Look no further than the on-going negotiations towards a pandemic accord at the World Health Organization, that might draw inspiration from these discussions at the WTO.

TIMELINE

October 2020: The introduction of the TRIPS Waiver proposal by South Africa and India

November & December 2020: TRIPS Council discusses proposal

Spring 2021: The stalling of the TRIPS Waiver proposal at the WTO due to resistance by few members

May 2021: The US decides to extend limited support to a patent waiver on vaccines

June 2021: The EU's counter proposal to the TRIPS Waiver

Fall 2021: Bilateral Consultations between the EU and South Africa

December 2021: The 12th WTO ministerial deferred on account of travel bans due to the Omicron variant of SARS-CoV-2

January & February 2022: Quad Group Discussions between the EU, the US, India and South Africa

March & April 2022: A text is leaked, eligibility requirements surface

May 2022: Emergence of the DG's compromise text on the waiver proposal

June 2022: The 12th WTO Ministerial Conference in Geneva, a limited waiver is adopted

REFERENCES

1. The WTO TRIPS Agreement, 1994

2. The WTO Marrakesh Agreement, 1994

3. Minutes of the WTO TRIPS COUNCIL MEETINGS (Unrestricted documents) [October 2020 – June 2022]

4. The Making of the TRIPS Agreement, *Personal Insights from the Uruguay Round Negotiations*, WTO

5. The General Agreement On Tariffs And Trade, 1994

6. The Doha Declaration on the TRIPS Agreement and Public Health, 2001

7. Decision of the General Council of 30 August 2003, WTO

8. Implementation of paragraph 6 of the Doha Declaration on the TRIPS Agreement and public health, September 2003, WTO

9. Amendment of the TRIPS Agreement Decision of 6 December 2005 (WTO, General Council)

10. Trade In Medical Goods In The Context Of Tackling Covid-19: Developments In 2020 (WTO)

11. Intellectual Property And Public Interest: Beyond Access To Medicines And Medical Technologies Towards A More Holistic Approach To Trips Flexibilities, *Communication from South Africa* (WTO IP/C/W/666) [July 2020]

12. Human Rights Obligations of States to not impede the Proposed COVID-19 TRIPS Waiver. Expert Legal Opinion November 2021 (International Commission of Jurists)

13. DIRECTIVE (EU) 2016/943 OF THE EUROPEAN PARLIAMENT AND OF THE COUNCIL of 8 June 2016 on

the protection of undisclosed know-how and business information (trade secrets) against their unlawful acquisition, use and disclosure

14. Examples Of IP Issues And Barriers In Covid-19 Pandemic Communication From South Africa, November 2020 [WTO, IP/C/W/670]

15. Declaration from Members of the European Parliament to urge the Commission and Member States not to block the TRIPS waiver at the WTO and to support global access to COVID-19 vaccines [February 2021]

16. Meeting the Global Covid-19 challenge: effects of waiver of the WTO TRIPS agreement on Covid-19 vaccines, treatment, equipment and increasing production and manufacturing capacity in developing countries [June 2021]

17. DS199: Brazil — Measures Affecting Patent Protection [WTO Disputes Settlement, July 2001]

18. Strengthening local production of medicines and other health technologies to improve access [WHO resolution May 2021]

19. Review of the Intellectual Property Rights Regime in India [July 2021] *(Department Related Parliamentary Standing Committee On Commerce Report No. 161)*

20. In The Supreme Court Of India Civil Original Jurisdiction Suo Moto Writ Petition (C) No.3/2021 In The Matter Of:- In Re : Distribution Of Essential Supplies And Services During Pandemic *(Affidavit Dated 09.05.2021 On Behalf Of The Union Of India)*

21. Thambisetty, Siva and McMahon, Aisling and McDonagh, Luke and Kang, Hyo Yoon and Dutfield, Graham, The TRIPS Intellectual Property Waiver Proposal: Creating the Right Incentives in Patent Law and Politics to end

the COVID-19 Pandemic (May, 2021). LSE Legal Studies Working Paper No. 06/2021

22. Pharmaceutical manufacturers across Asia, Africa and Latin America with the technical requirements and quality standards to manufacture mRNA vaccines, December 2021 (MSF & Access IBSA project)

23. Special 301 Report, April 2020, Office of the US Trade Representative

24. 2021 Special 301 Report, Office of the US Trade Representative

25. Pauwelyn, Joost, Export Restrictions in Times of Pandemic: Options and Limits under International Trade Agreements [April, 2020].

26. The Commission's pharma echo chamber, Corporate Europe Observatory [May 2021]

27. Analysis of the Outcome Text of the Informal Quadrilateral Discussions on the TRIPS COVID-19 Waiver, By Carlos M. Correa and Nirmalya Syam, South Centre [May 2022]

28. Open Letter from the Special Rapporteur on contemporary forms of racism, racial discrimination, xenophobia and related intolerance to the World Trade Organization's Twelfth Ministerial Conference [June 2022]

29. WTO-IMF COVID-19 Vaccine Trade Tracker

30. International Federation of Pharmaceutical Manufacturers and Associations (IFPMA)

ACKNOWLEDGEMENTS

I am especially grateful to the legal experts at Third World Network and South Centre who helped clarify my understanding of the politics in these discussions. My gratitude to the wider access to medicines community including activists at Médecins Sans Frontières and Knowledge Ecology International, among other organizations. I am also grateful to trade negotiators of both developing and developed countries. The staff at the WTO also helped facilitate my reporting on these discussions. Numerous IP academics have illuminated my understanding of these complex topics. Their scholarship and generosity have informed this journalistic work. Above all, I thank the readers of *Geneva Health Files*, who engaged with this reporting at every stage of the process.

My copy editor Tushar Behl, an international arbitration lawyer who worked on the manuscript in record time, helped push this project into completion. My designers Hammad Khalid and Oladimeji Alaka brought this book to life.

My colleague, Julia Dötzer, a student of public health, who interned with Geneva Health Files in 2022, was instrumental in putting this compilation together. She also helped me every step of the way in the often intimating journey of self-publishing a book.

Finally, my husband Aditya Kumar, supported me during this entire period, including by putting our young son to bed on many nights. I also thank my childcare providers in Switzerland who enabled me to keep up with the demands of an unforgiving reporting life. And of course, my parents, who taught me to question and write.

ABOUT THE AUTHOR

Image Credit: Lakshman Varanasi

Priti Patnaik is the Founding Editor of the Geneva Health Files, a weekly investigative newsletter that tracks power and politics in global health. In her twenty years in journalism, she has reported on global health, international trade, finance, and illicit financial flows. She has worked as a reporter in Geneva, New York City, and New Delhi. Outside of journalism, she has worked at a UN public health agency. Priti has a master's degree in Development Studies from the Geneva Graduate Institute and a master's degree in Business and Economic Reporting from New York University. She also has a bachelor's degree in microbiology, genetics, and chemistry from Osmania University, India.

Priti lives in Switzerland with her husband and son.

Milton Keynes UK
Ingram Content Group UK Ltd.
UKHW011113280823
427620UK00004B/388

9 782970 162704